FIFTY YEARS

AMONG THE BAPTISTS.

DAVID BENEDICT
1779-1874

FIFTY YEARS

AMONG THE BAPTISTS.

BY

DAVID BENEDICT, D.D.

AUTHOR OF "BAPTIST HISTORY," "ALL RELIGIONS," ETC., ETC., MEMBER OF THE
RHODE ISLAND HISTORICAL SOCIETY, AND OTHER KINDRED INSTITUTIONS.

NEW YORK:
SHELDON & COMPANY
115 NASSAU STREET
1860.

The Baptist Standard Bearer, Inc.

NUMBER ONE IRON OAKS DRIVE • PARIS, ARKANSAS 72855

Thou hast given a *standard* to them that fear thee;
that it may be displayed because of the truth.
-- *Psalm 60:4*

Reprinted
by

THE BAPTIST STANDARD BEARER, INC.

No. 1 Iron Oaks Drive
Paris, Arkansas 72855
(501) 963-3831

THE WALDENSIAN EMBLEM
lux lucet in tenebris
"The Light Shineth in the Darkness"

ISBN #1-57978-361-9

FOREWORD

DAVID BENEDICT was born on October 10, 1779, in Norwalk, Conn., the eldest child of Thomas and Martha Benedict. He became a member of the Baptist Church at Stanford, Conn., in 1799. Supporting himself as a shoemaker's apprentice and as a private tutor, he was able to graduate from Brown University in 1806, having early expressed a profound interest in Baptist history. For twenty-five years, he served as the pastor of the First Baptist Church in Pawtucket, R.I.

His major publications include: **The Watery War, or a Poetical Description of the Controversy on the Subjects and Mode of Baptism, by John of Enon**, published anonymously when he was in college; **A General History of the Baptist Denomination in America and Other Parts of the World**, published in 1813 and revised in 1848; **Fifty Years Among the Baptists**, published in 1860; and **History of the Donatists**, published after his death, which occurred on December 5, 1874.

Dr. Benedict was the first American historian to write of the Baptists on a national scale. His research took him into all sections of the United States of the early 19th Century, one of our nation's most dramatic eras. A careful study of his **General History. . .** is essential to a study of the history of Baptists in America.

The value of **Fifty Years. . .** lies in its intimate and frank view of one of the most important half centuries in the development of our people in this country. This was a time when Baptists were searching for their true identity. The age of persuasion was past. A great unlimited field of expansion lay ahead on the frontier. Would Baptists maintain their age-old devotion to New Testament distinctives, or would they merge into the ever growing American Protestant movement? Dr. Benedict's work gives to us of today a unique glimpse at the dangers of such an assimilation.

Sicut lilium inter spinas sic amica mea inter filias

On The Cover: We use the symbol of the "lily among the thorns" from Song of Solomon 2:2 to represent the Baptist History Series. The Latin, *Sicut lilium inter spinas sic amica mea inter filias*, translates, "As the lily among thorns, so is my love among the daughters."

David Benedict

PREFACE.

MY main object in preparing this small volume has been to collect and preserve such portions of Baptist history as could not be conveniently inserted in my former writings on this subject. Although most of the incidents here recorded are of a very common character, yet they may be interesting to some of our people, who would like to review the doings of their brethren for the period they embrace; they may also afford aid to our future historians.

In the second part of this work, called the *Appendix*, I have given my comments on the model of the early Christians, in the construction of their churches, on the deaconship, on preaching, preachers and pulpits, and on church discipline generally, embraces the substance of my notes and comments on these matters for many years past.

As I have outlived most of my cotemporaries, and having from my youthful days cultivated a somewhat familiar acquaintance with all Baptist people, in all parts of the country, now in the evening of life, I leave for their perusal a few sketches of my experience and observations among them, for the last *fifty years*.

The form of *Decades*, or periods of ten years each, is a plan of my own, as I thought it would be more convenient, both for myself, and my readers.

PAWTUCKET, Rhode Island, *November* 12, 1859.

CONTENTS.

CHAPTER VI.

CHAPTER VII.

SECOND DECADE.

ON THE RISE OF THE FOREIGN MISSION CAUSE AMONG THE
AMERICAN BAPTISTS.

CHAPTER VIII.

CHAPTER IX.

CHAPTER X.

CHAPTER XI.

THIRD DECADE.

ON THE AGE OF EXCITEMENTS.

FOURTH DECADE.

CHAPTER XVI.

CHAPTER XVII.

CHAPTER XVIII.

CHAPTER XIX.

CHAPTER XX.

CHAPTER XXI.

CHAPTER XXVI.

CHAPTER XXVII.

CHAPTER XXVIII.

CHAPTER XXIX.

CHAPTER XXX.

CHAPTER XXXI

FIRST DECADE

CHAPTER I.

PREFATORY REMARKS.

Five Decades, or Periods of Ten Years Each.—My Travels and Extensive Acquaintance with Baptist Ministers in Early Times.—Summary View of the Baptists about 1800.—No Periodicals.—Old Baptist Magazine.—Mite Societies.—But Few Educated Ministers.—Rise of Benevolent Institutions.

This work is arranged in five decades, and is the result of my own observations from the early part of this century to the present time.

The following reminiscences were undertaken as an episode in the severe historical studies in which I had then (1856) been steadily and closely engaged about eight years, and while I was waiting for some works to come out, and come over, which were needful for the completion of my *Compendium of Ecclesiastical History*.

As I have outlived most of my cotemporaries, and have had considerable knowledge of Baptist affairs for the last half century, and having a desire, moreover, of recording whatever facts, with which I have been familiar, which were not found in my historical work, and which may be useful to our future historians—all these considerations have induced me to prepare the subsequent sketches.

My Own Times was the title which at first occurred to me as suitable to affix to this work, but as I did not design to enter into the details of events which have come under my observation so fully as the publications thus named have generally done, nor say so much of my own doings as has been said by the authors of the works here referred to, but merely to carry on my narratives by the use of the first person, I finally, on mature deliberation, decided on the above appellation for my diffusive memoirs.

There was a time when I claimed to be personally acquainted with more ministers of our order, to have traveled more extensively among the Baptists in this country, to have enjoyed the hospitality of more Baptist families, and to be more familiar with all the concerns of all classes of Baptists, than any man then living. But when Mr. Rice, and after him other agents, engaged in their extensive explorations in favor of missions and other objects of Christian benevolence, I stood in the background for a long course of years. Subsequently, however, when I reëngaged in collecting materials for Baptist history, with post office facilities for extending my information, together with more expeditious modes of traveling, and an increased number of correspondents, I in part regained my former position in the knowledge of our denominational affairs.

But for a number of years past, my old system of traveling and corresponding has been mostly laid aside, and I have been losing in the acquisition of that kind of knowledge which was formerly my main pursuit. Books of different kinds, ancient and modern, Catholic and Protestant, in number not a few, on the affairs of the whole of Christendom, in all ages and countries, of all churches, sects and parties, great or small, of all creeds and opinions, have been my principal companions, and the objects of my research, in a number of the best libraries of this region, both public and private.

As the work in which I am about to engage, embraces about fifty years, I propose to arrange my notes and discussions, which will have respect principally to my own experience and observations, under five divisions of about ten years each, and thus to speak of the events which happened, or the state of things which existed during each succeeding decade. As my narratives and comments will be summary and diffusive, I shall endeavor to pass on in my details by easy transitions, without referring to dates, only in general terms.

My main object in these memoirs being to record such minor matters as could not well be incorporated

in my late historical publication consistently with
the brevity of my plan for that work, I shall say but
little respecting the doings of the Baptists previous to
the commencement of the present century, when I
went over to them from the Church of England,
which, at that time, hung in colonial dependence on
the ordaining power at home.

But for the sake of exhibiting comparative views
hereafter of the growth of the Baptists in this country, I will give at this point a few of the statistics of
the denomination toward the close of the last century.

According to Asphund's Register, the whole membership of Baptists of all sects, in 1790, including all
the unassociated churches, was about sixty-five thousand, a much less number at that time, in all North
America, than is now found in each of the States of
New York, Virginia, Georgia and Kentucky.

From Backus and others we learn that in those
times there was an unusual declension in religion
throughout the country, which continued for a number of years. Among my epistolary documents I
find a letter from Morgan J. Rhees, a Baptist minister from Wales, addressed to Dr. Furman of Charleston, South Carolina, in which reference is had to the
low state of religion in all the northern States, in
1795. "The only revival I know of this year, has
been in New Hampshire," was his summary and

gloomy account. This Mr. Rhees was then on an exploring expedition in the middle States, in favor of a colony of his countrymen, who finally settled at a place they named Beulah, in the mountainous parts of Pennsylvania.

Under these circumstances, the progress of the Baptists was so slow that in the opening of the nineteenth century their whole number was but about eighty thousand, and as yet there were no seceding parties in the country. Then, about one fourth of all the Baptists in America were in Virginia; Massachusetts and North Carolina had about eight thousand each, while the State of New York, which now reports almost ninety thousand members, had then, but a little over five thousand. In all the other States the number was still less. At the time here had in view, no churches of our order were reported in any part of the Canadas, but a few in Nova Scotia, and none west of the Mississippi river; and in the vast region west of the Ohio river, then called the North-western Territory, in which have since arisen the States of Ohio, Indiana, Illinois, and other States and Territories, the whole membership of our order was less than two thousand. Now, counting only the associated class, the number amounts to over a hundred thousand.

In a little more than ten years from the last-mentioned date, our communicants amounted to about two hundred thousand, and at present, including the British provinces in America and the West India islands, the number may be set down at about a million, reckoning all who bear the Baptist name. And if we add to the sum those who are Baptists in fact, although not so in name, the grand total foots up over one million and a quarter.

The reader must bear in mind that, in all Baptist statistics, only actual church members are counted, while some other societies reckon their whole population.

Fifty years ago, or about that period, when I was taking a survey of the state of our denomination, with a view to the historical researches which I have since pursued, I found the society in what was then considered a very prosperous condition, and their number was rapidly increasing. For a few years then past, the very extensive revivals of religion, which had prevailed in most of the United States, then seventeen in number, had caused changes in the tone and efforts of our people, and in the enlargement of their boundaries very grateful to the whole community. The general aspect of its affairs was the subject of common remark and devout congratulation. The *wonderful accounts* of these revivals, which had been communicated from one region to another by letters of private correspondence, by the minutes of associations, and by the aid of a few pamphlets which had been issued for the purpose, led the long-despised and persecuted Baptists to thank God and take courage. Indeed, in the language of commercial men, the state of things among them on the whole was satisfactory, and probably at no period since have they been favored with such a rapid increase in their churches; seen in their members more fully developed the genuine spirit of the gospel; been so well united in faith and practice throughout the whole country, north and south, east and west; and been so free from jars and schisms, ites and isms, the apples of discord and the bones of contention.

The severe conflict of our brethren in Virginia, with the whole Church establishment, had long since subsided, and they were no longer subjected to legal restraint and disabilities; and the "according-to-law" system of New England, with which the obnoxious Baptists had, in many cases and places, been exceedingly annoyed from early times, was nearly extinct, and all were left at liberty to attend what meetings and hear and support what ministers they chose.

Fifty years ago, the number of educated ministers of the Baptist faith was very small, and the means of education, so far as our people were concerned, were on a very limited scale. Brown University, then called Rhode Island College, with only one building, was the only collegiate establishment under the Baptist name, in the whole country. A few private academies were, or had been, in operation, where classical studies were pursued; and among these institutions, that established by Elder Williams at Wrentham, Massachusetts, at an early day, was the most important in New England. Here, a large number of our young men, who were candidates for the ministry, were fitted for college, as were also a considerable number who engaged in other pursuits. As this then famous school was but a few miles from Pawtucket, I often visited it while the aged teacher was engaged in his classical teachings.

A few education societies had been formed in those early times for the purpose of affording pecuniary aid to theological students who here and there appeared among us, and it is not a little interesting to trace the progress of some of these feeble beginnings to a seminary growth, and, in the end, to collegiate maturity.

Should any one inquire of the missionary cause among the American Baptists, *fifty years ago*, the account is soon rendered, and the total amount of their doings up to that time may be thus stated: a few small societies for domestic missions had been established in Boston, New York, Philadelphia, Charleston, and a few other places, by the aid of which, missionaries were sent out, under temporary appointments, to destitute regions. The society in Boston was the oldest and most efficient of these bodies; and there, and I think elsewhere, female mite societies were among the principal contributors to these small organizations. In a few cases these efforts were directed toward the moral and spiritual benefit of the aborigines of our country. Elder Rooker, who was the first missionary of the Charleston society, was sent to labor among the remnant of the Catawba Indians in South Carolina. About the same time, the New York society sent Elder Elkanah Holmes on a mission among the Six Nations, so called, on the northern frontier of the State. This confederacy of Mohawks, Oneidas, and other Indian tribes, has ever since received missionary aid from the brethren of this State.

The Boston society went on a broad scale, and sent out missionaries to destitute regions in a number of the northern States, and also over the line into the Canadas and Nova Scotia. Stillman, Smith, Baldwin, Gano, Grafton, and other active ministers of that age, were among the principal founders and promoters of this northern institution for missions.

As yet, at no point did the leaders of our missionary enterprise appear to entertain the idea of having their missionaries, who were generally engaged only for a few weeks or months at a time, stop long in any one place. But to travel and preach, to search out the scattered sheep in the wilderness, to afford them tran- sient opportunities of the means of grace, and of min- isterial visitations, were the objects chiefly aimed at in all these early and benevolent undertakings. All the missionary societies above referred to, expended not far from thirty thousand dollars in the course of about ten years. This was then considered a noble effort, for the whole denomination, in the cause of missions. And beside this, a number of associations made an- nual collections for missionary purposes, which were expended under their own direction.

A number of our oldest State conventions grew out of the early societies for domestic missions.

The tract cause was still more in its infancy than that of missions, if its existence had now commenced, although our Boston brethren made early movements in this line, as some of the old untrimmed and rough- looking documents of this sort published by them, give evidence. "Give me the little book," I well re- member was the familiar language of Dr. Baldwin in an association, at an early day, while recommending these minor publications, which were then beginning to circulate among our people.

The Bible cause, in the modern sense of the term, was not engaged in by any religious community in this country at the period now under review. The

British and Foreign Bible Society was formed in 1804, and it was twelve years later before the old American institution arose, with which a portion of our people became identified.

Sunday Schools and Bible classes, and all the other institutions of modern times, for objects of Christian benevolence and moral reform, which are now in such successful operation with us, and other communities in the land, were wholly unknown in my early day. And as to the Baptist periodicals, nothing of the kind then existed, but the old Missionary Magazine, and the minutes of associations. These were the only means of circulating information on Baptist affairs in a printed form, from one end of the country to the other. The idea of a religious newspaper was then nowhere entertained, nor did any one think of going to the secular press with articles of a religious cast. The old magazine, which I have always nourished with great affection from its origin, and have gathered up all the old numbers I could find, for future use, was begun in Boston in 1803, and became the organ of the old domestic missionary society, lately named. It was published quarterly for twelve years; after that it was issued monthly. The first four volumes, called the *old series,* are now very scarce, and difficult to be obtained. I had nearly completed a second set of this work, which I designed to present

2

to some literary institution, when I gave my old friend
and coadjutor, Peck of Illinois, the offer to select from
it all that was needful to repair his loss by fire, a few
years since, with the mutual understanding that the
work should finally be deposited in the library of
Shurtliff College, Illinois, a favorite institution of this
its early patron and friend.   But still a large portion
of the set is left, with an abundant supply of almost
all numbers of the work, which I would be glad to
put into the hands of any one who will carry out my
original design, and he may select the place of de-
posit.

Dr. Baldwin, the projector of this now venerable
pioneer in the periodical line, among the American
Baptists, was for many years the life and soul of the
concern, and I well remember the pigeon hole in his
study, as he called it, from which once in three
months he drew out the communications and selections which had been accumulating for his next number.

As our brethren of that age had never known any
greater facilities for spreading information among the
people, or for promoting evangelical and benevolent
designs, and had but faint hopes of any great im-
provements for the future, they seemed well satisfied
with what now seems an intolerable state of privation.

The modes of traveling, also, in those days, how

slow, laborious and costly compared with the present time.

When I look back I can hardly realize the changes which have taken place in our denomination, in my day, in the means of intelligence and benevolence. It seems almost incredible that a society which so lately was so slow to engage in any new enterprise, and was so jealous of any collegiate training for its ministers, should at this early period have so many colleges and kindred institutions spread over the land; that such a flood of periodicals of different kinds should so soon be added to the old magazine; that so much should have been done by this people in the home and foreign mission departments, in the Bible cause, in the publication of Baptist literature, in Sunday Schools and Bible classes, and in kindred labors of various kinds; and all since I first began to collect the scanty and scattered materials for their history.

But, in the absence of the facilities of more modern times, at the period now had in view, our brethren performed a great amount of labor, under all their disadvantages, and amidst all the hindrances with which they were surrounded. Then each man did his own work, and the whole body depended less on agents and substitutes than at the present time.

CHAPTER II.

In 1802, as near as I can recollect, while I was engaged in classical studies, I first entertained the idea of becoming a Baptist historian ; but my youth, inexperience and want of pecuniary means, for some time, stood in the way of all my desires in the business. While meditating on this new project, I examined the histories of Crosby and Ivimey, four volumes each, Rippon's Register, Robinson's Ecclesiastical Researches and History of Baptism, with some minor publications from the pens of our British brethren. On the American side, I found Backus stood almost alone, as a standard author in Baptist history, of any considerable magnitude. Beside his work, we had, indeed, Callender's Century Sermon, which was confined to the early history of Rhode Island, and a few other productions of a local character. The writings of Morgan Edwards being in MSS., were then but little known. I have now enumerated the historical works which constituted the main dependence of our people, in both the mother country and at home, for information concerning their denominational concerns in all ages and conditions. But most of these works were hard to be obtained at any price, and beside, they abound in matter in which common readers of this age will take but little interest.

All these researches convinced me more and more of the need of a work which should be wholly Baptistical in its character, which would embrace the substance of all those above referred to, and most of all, bring down our history to the present time, and in such a condensed form, that all classes of readers might be able to procure it. And as the Baptist churches in America, in which were found more members of the denomination than all other parts of the world, were generally of a comparatively late formation, and as our people in all times had been exceedingly neglectful in preserving the records of their doings, whether ancestral or modern, I soon became convinced that if I pursued my undertaking to any considerable extent, I must travel. for it, and at the firesides of aged people, and all from whom I could obtain oral testimony, gather up the facts which were needful for the accomplishment of my plan. Accordingly, in the autumn of 1809, I commenced my historical explorations, in which, in the end, I traveled about seven thousand miles, in seventeen

States, the number then of the American Union.
With very few exceptions, the journeys now had in
view were performed on horseback, and alone. So
new were many of the regions which I visited, and
so circuitous were many of the routes which I had to
pursue to visit the persons and places needful for my
designs, that this was the only mode of traveling for
me then. Indeed, I thought of no other, and never
complained of this part of my labor. It was the way
in which nearly all our ministers traveled in that age,
in all parts of the country, except some few of the
abler class in a few locations in the old States.

I do not pretend to be much of a backwoodsman,
nor to have been much of a pioneer in frontier regions, nor yet to have been exposed to many perils in
the wilderness; but still I obtained some glimpses of
what is meant by these terms, in the limited travels
and the scanty explorations, which, in my early historical researches, I was compelled to perform.

In the journeyings thus referred to, I crossed the
whole range of the Alleghany mountains, first in
Pennsylvania, and in the next place in North Carolina, on my way from Tennessee to the southern
Atlantic States. On some parts of my route large
tracts of country were then in their native condition,
where wild animals were often to be seen. In one
large tract through which I passed, in the mountain-

ous regions of Tennessee, the Indian title had but
lately been extinguished, and a few of the natives, in
their peculiar dress, still lingered on the soil. For
the most part the roads, even in the wildest regions
through which my lonely travels were performed,
were so far designated, according to the custom of
new countries, that I had but little trouble in finding
them. The custom here alluded to, is to mark a sufficient number of the trees on the route which is ultimately designed for a highway, to guide the traveler
in his course. In this state of nature, the marks are
generally a *blaze* and a *notch*, to use the language of
the forest. A *blaze* is made by a stroke of the ax, by
which a slice is taken from the tree. The nature of
a *notch* all will understand. Two or more notches
I sometimes found answered the same purpose as
guide boards in older regions. These mere bridle-
paths, in time, became the thoroughfares of the country. When there was danger of embarrassments, by
the aid of friends, I would make a rough drawing of
my road for the day, in regions where settlements
were not often met with, to guard against mistakes in
turn-outs where no dwellings were near.

I generally found some of the black people near
the roads, both able and willing to give me the needful information, for greater or less distances ahead.
"Me go wid you, massa," was their common reply, if

the turn-out was not far off, and a little change never
came amiss to them.   This part of the business I was
careful not to forget, as a matter of encouragement
for their useful officiousness.   Log cabins of rude
construction and appearance, in almost all cases, are
the first edition of human abodes in new countries.
Buildings, of the same materials, but more capacious
and better made, or small frame houses, at length take
the place of the first hastily-formed shanties; and
finally, more spacious and well-formed mansions arise
as permanent fixtures of the premises.   But to log
houses, of the real primitive model, was I indebted for
shelter and comfort in many of my early journeyings
in newly-settled regions, and soon I became so accustomed to their scanty accommodations, and was so
well pleased with the hospitality of the people, as to
feel quite at home among them.

Pleased or not, however, the traveler had no alter-
native in the case; since for long distances no other
houses could be found.

As to public houses, there were none, in the common sense of the term.   The wagoners camped out
at night, near some spring or dwelling, and with their
camp-fires and their bustle about their teams, they
made quite a social appearance.

Amidst all these inconveniences, I found the people
generally happy and contented, and enjoying them-

selves, probably, as well as at any subsequent period
of their lives.

*Baptist Ministers of Distinction in their Various Lo-
cations in the Early Part of this Century.*

Then we had but few men of eminence for their
literary acquirements or learned labors.   We had no
literary works of our own in progress, to be supplied
with the productions of Baptist pens, and other societies did not look to our ranks for aid.   The number of our able pastors was considerably large, while
that of our zealous evangelists and gospel pioneers
was larger still.

About this period, but more especially at a somewhat earlier age, the Baptists had a running fight in
many locations with almost all the sects in the land,
for their life, on gospel ground, and for their claims
to belong to the brotherhood of respectable Christians.
A few of their ministers, in the principal cities and
towns, were admitted to be men of some decency, but
the sect as a whole was denounced as the dregs of
Christendom, and was reproached with a wild and fanatical pedigree, or, in other words, as being descendants of the *madmen of Munster*, and as being in their
terms of communion the most rigid and uncharitable
sect in the land.   And so incessant were the publica-

tions against our people, that most of the writings of those who wrote at all were in self-defense.

Fifty years ago, or about that time, amongst the ministers of our order, who were more or less distinguished for their talents, their locations, or their various services in the denomination, the following names may be recorded :

In Boston and vicinity, were Stillman, Baldwin, Blood, Paul, Collier, Grafton, Peckens, Bolles, Chaplin, E. Nelson, E. Williams, Peak, Batchelder.

To the north and west of Boston, were Robinson, Andrews, Leonard, Rand, Hartwell, Werden, J. Leland.

In a southerly direction, in the same State, were W. Williams, Read, Backus, Rathbun, Abbot, Coombs, Lovel, S. Nelson, the Briggses, Kendal, Glover, Bates, Lewis.

In New Hampshire and Maine, were Robinson, Hooper, Shepherd, Seamans, Crocket, Boardman, Wilmarth, Haines, Green, Tripp, Titcomb, Stearns, Case, Snow, Macomber, Pillsbury, Merrill, Roundy, Allen, Baker, Fuller.

In Nova Scotia and New Brunswick, were Burton, Ainsley, the Mannings, the Chipmans, the Dimocks, the Hardings, the Crandalls.

In Providence and other parts of Rhode Island, were Gano, Messer, Pitman, Cornell, Baker, Bradley,

Eddy, Curtis, Northup, Allen, Babcock, the Palmers, Steadman, the Manchesters, and the author.

In Connecticut, were Babcock, Hastings, Cushman, Bulkley, Miller, S. Higbee, Wilcox, Phippen, Goodwin, Grow, Dodge, Crosby, Wells, Morse, Ferris, Miner, Brown, Cheesbro, the Bollses, the Wightmans, the Darrows, the Palmers, the Reeds, the Randalls.

In Vermont, were the Kendricks, the Sawyers, A. Leland, Howard, Butler, Going, Green, Mattison, J. Higbee, Haynes, Rowley, Hurlburt, Huntington.

In New York city and Long Island, were Parkinson, Williams, Stanford, Maclay, Hall, M. Earle.

On each side of the Hudson river, and at no great distance from it, to the northern boundary of the State, was a long space of country where Baptist churches were few and feeble at the date of these recollections. In traveling up this extended region, often remotely situated from each other, might then be found S. S. Nelson, Fountain, Cole, Lathrop, Montanye, E. Ferris, Perkins, Davis, J. M. Peck, before he went to the West, Jenks, Henrick, Hull, Olmstead, Warren, Webb, Covel, Lahat, Sommers, A. Peck, Lee, Langworthy, Fox.

In the new and extended settlements of the State in a western direction, was found a large number of active ministers of our order, among whom we may name Douglass, Hosmer, Lawton, J. Peck, Bennett,

Furman, Bostick, Hurlburt, Vining, Brown, Lake, Robinson, Osgood, Card, Parsons, Eastman, Baker, the Butlers, Taylor, the Holcombs, Roots, Bacon, Spencer, Eddy, Handy, Holmes, Camp, Lamb.

These ministers all belonged to the Otsego Association, so called from a lake of that name, in 1806, and onward, for a few years, or until some of the number were embraced in kindred institutions, which were formed from the mother body, whose boundaries soon became widely extended.

Still further into the interior of this State, in different directions, about this period, were to be found Robertson, Cooley, Morton, Upfold, Freeman, Farman, Irish, Irons, Comstock, Rathbun, Lamb, Finch, Starr.

A. Bennett, above named, and who for a long time before he died was called *Father Bennett*, was licensed to preach in 1806.

All the men whose names are here recorded as active ministers in this State, I believe are now, 1856, dead, except Sommers, Perkins, and J. M. Peck, the pioneer of the West.

Dr. Peck has deceased since the above was written.

In New Jersey, belonging to the New York Association, were Brown, Edwards, Randolph, Vanhorn, Ellis, D. Sharp, then in Newark. Belonging to the Philadelphia Association, but in this State, were Allison, Smalley, McLaughlin, Wilson.

In Philadelphia, were Staughton, Rogers, Peckworth; near the city were S. Jones, D. Jones, H. G. Jones, Montanye, Mathias, Hough, Fleeson, Vaughn, Bennet, Carlile, Patten, Boswell, Sheppard, McGowan.

In the Redstone country, Pennsylvania, were Estep, Stone, Skinner, Phillips, Spears, Luce, Martin, Frey, Patterson, Smith, Brownfield.

In Delaware, were Dodge, Ferrell, Johnson, Jones.

In Baltimore, were Richards and Healey. In other parts of Maryland were Welch, Wilson, Green, Grice, Woolford.

In Washington city, was O. B. Brown.

In Richmond, Virginia, was J. Courtney. In other parts of the State were Semple, Broaddus, Ford, Clopton, Brame, Brice, Toler, Noel, Fitchet, Strauhgn, B. Watkins, Clay, Flourney, Richards, Dossey, Creath, Shelburne, Browne, Ritter, Mitchell, Shearwood, Chambless, Layfield, the Wallers, Pendleton, Purrington, Poindexter, Burghes, Dabbs, A. Watkins, Flowers, Jenkins, Kerr, Lovelace, Atkinson, King, Howard, the Fristoes, the Moores, Gilmore, Dawson, Munroe, Alderson, Osbourne, Lee, Wells, Patterson, Pritchard, Martin.

In North Carolina, were Burkett, Read, Bennett, Lawrence, Spivey, the Biggses, Lancaster, Biddle, Goodman, Thigpen, Cooper, Poindexter, Dossey, Wall, Ross, Daniel, Dobbins, Fuller, Purifoy, Gardner, Graves, Roberts, Brown, Moore, Pope, Slaughter, Culpepper, member of Congress, Brantley, father of the late Dr. B. Murphy, Posey, the Morgans.

In Charleston, South Carolina, was Furman ; and in other parts of the State were Maxey, Botsford, Johnson, White, Ellis, McKellar, Reaves, Roberts, Cook, Collins, Woods, Coleman, Moseley, Scott, Thigpen, Simmons, Boyd, Youmans, Sweat, Landrum, Head, Marsh, Whatley, Greer, McCreary, Rooker, Golightly, Ball, Davis, Grace, Barnett, Lancaster.

In Savannah, Georgia, were Holcombe and A. Marshall, lately deceased at a very advanced age, and H. Cunningham. The two last were colored men, and pastors of large churches of their own nation.

In the lower parts of this State were then Scriven, Clay, Polhil, Goldwire, Wilson, Williams.

In the upper country, were A. Marshall, near Augusta, and in that city W. T. Brantley, then a young man ; and at different distances from the older settlements, in southern and western directions, were Mercer, Sanders, Davis, Matthews, Reeves, Shackelford, Thompson, Rhodes, Franklin, Robertson, Hilman, Thornton, Goss, Baker, Williams.

Georgia was then a frontier State in a southern and western direction, and as yet there were but two States in what is usually denominated the valley of the Mississippi, namely, Kentucky and Tennessee.

In Kentucky, were Dudley, Verdeman, Suggett, Hickman, Barrow, Creath, Price, Redding, Graves, the Craigs, Waller, Taylor, Scott, Noel, Tribble, Pierson, Stockton, Hodgen.

In Tennessee, near Nashville, were Whitsett, Wiseman and Rucks; in other parts of the State, were McConico, Mulky, Ross, Ford, Adams.

In the Mississippi Territory, were E. Courtney and T. Mercer.

In Ohio, were J. Clark, Stites, and T. G. Jones.

In the Indiana Territory, were Ferris and McCoy.

We have now arrived at the outskirts of the Baptists, West and South-west, *fifty years ago.*

These last accounts are not so full as they might have been, had the late J. M. Peck been able to answer my last letter to him, in which I sought information wherein I was deficient.

In the foregoing selections of names, I have had respect, in part, to men with whom I became acquainted in my travels, and who afforded me assistance in my historical pursuits. A large number of the letters of these friends and helpers are preserved among my epistolary documents.

CHAPTER III.

BIOGRAPHICAL SKETCHES OF A FEW OF THE MINISTERS MENTIONED IN
THE PRECEDING CHAPTER. — STILLMAN, BALDWIN, GANO, SHARP,
CORNELL, STANFORD, PARKINSON, WILLIAMS, STAUGHTON, ROGERS,
JONES, J. RICHARDS, J. HEALEY, FURMAN, BOTTSFORD, FULLER,
MARSHALL, MERCER.

DOUBTLESS I have failed to mention many men in
the above list, whose names ought to be recorded
among our very worthy and useful ministers, who
were actively engaged in the various affairs of the
denomination about fifty years ago. Then the men
I have named were in the locations I have assigned
them. A few of them were quite young, and had not
been ordained; but as they arose to distinction afterwards in the ranks of our ministerial brotherhood, I
have thought it a matter of justice to enroll their
names as I have done. In a few cases the men were
near the end of their career, and were soon after
called from their posts; but as they were in active
service at the period now had in view, so I have reported them. Backus and Stillman of Massachusetts
died about the same time that Bennett and Leonard
of New York and Massachusetts were coming forward in the ministry. In 1806, A. Bennett was li-

censed as a preacher by the church in Homer, New
York, and soon after that date I find the name of L.
Leonard in the minutes of the old Warren Associa-
tion, with the designation of an *unordained* minister, in
Backus' old church, in Middleborough, Massachusetts.

Any thing like biographical sketches on the most
limited scale, of these Baptist laborers, would be in-
compatible with the brevity of these reminiscences;
but still I will venture to say a few things respecting
a limited number of them, and their locations at this
time.

Dr. H. Smith of Haverhill, Massachusetts, was one
of the most eminent ministers of our order in his day;
but he, with Manning and many others of a former
age, had ceased from their labors before I entered the
stage of action, and of course, according to my plan,
their names and characters must be omitted in these
sketches.

In Boston and Providence, Drs. Stillman, Baldwin
and Gano, in addition to their other laborious services, were often appealed to as counselors, by ministers and churches in a wide circuit around them.
They were also very frequently called upon to assist
in the ordination of ministers, in the formation of
new churches, and in the adjustment of the difficulties which were very common in those times. The
same may be said of our ministers generally in met-

ropolitan positions, who from their talents and large
experience in these matters, might have acquired the
confidence of their brethren.   But these ministers had
larger fields of operations, in labors of this kind, re-
spectively, for most of their lives, than any other
three men in all the New England States.   Their
bishoprics were quite extensive, not only in Massachusetts and Rhode Island, but also in a number of
the neighboring States.   Smith, and also Backus of
the older class, had in their day performed a great
amount of labor of this kind.

Mr. Blood, the first pastor of the church which
was so long and ably served by the late Dr. Sharp,
was a man of strong powers of mind, and of much
experience in church matters ; but his pastorship in
Boston was of short duration.

Mr. Paul was a famous man among the people of
his color—indeed, he was highly esteemed for his
pulpit talents wherever he went.

Elder Cornell, the only Baptist pastor then in
Providence, excepting Dr. Gano, although of an inferior education, was distinguished for his keen discern-
ment of men and things, and for that sort of sayings
which many were pleased to repeat.   He had been
a farmer preacher, or a missionary in new settlements,
until he was somewhat advanced in years ; and he
came to Providence to officiate in a dilapidated con-

cern, of New Light pedigree, where the former Pedobaptist pastor was so tolerant toward immersion that
it was difficult to tell under what head the body
should be classed. Under Elder Cornell's labors an
ingathering soon commenced; and as Baptist principles were fast gaining ground, it so happened that
while he was away on a journey to his former home
in Galway, New York, where he had a good farm,
the Pedobaptist portion of the reviving interest rallied
and put a minister of their own order in his place.
"Yes," said the patient old man, "when I went out,
I put on my boots, and when I came home I found
another man in my shoes." The effect of all this was
that the Baptist party went off by themselves, built
a new house, and thus organized the Pine street, now
Central, church, in Providence, which has lately entered a fine church edifice in a central part of the city.

Illiterate as Elder Cornell was, yet many of the
students in college, of the religious class, were pleased
to visit him to hear his sage advice and profit by his
apt and shrewd remarks. One of these students was
a good deal troubled with the blues, and had much to
say against himself, of the badness of his feelings, etc.

"You are wrong, my brother," said the elder to
the complaining young man; "you have got your
sink spout in front of your house; put it at the back
side, my brother, where it will be out of sight."

"Sister A., I wish you would ask me a question," said Elder Cornell to a friend at the close of a meeting, when away from home; "no one has tried me yet." "Well, elder, what is it?" said the friend. "If *I* will go home with you." "La me! why did n't I think of that before?" The point was now gained, and accommodations for the night were at once secured.

In the city of New York, to which I will now pass on, the churches and ministers of our order were very few, compared with the present time. Elder, afterwards Dr. Stanford, was somewhat advanced in years when I first knew him. The church of which he was then pastor, a long time since became extinct. To Dr. S. the old church in Providence, Rhode Island, is indebted for the brief account of its ancient pastors and general affairs, in early times. It was compiled in 1775, while he resided in the town, and officiated as the pastor of the church, as its temporary supply.

Elder J. Williams, father of the present Dr. Williams, a native of Wales, at the date of these recollections was laying the foundation of the large body now called the Oliver street church, under the pastoral care of Dr. Magoon. Mr. W. was a very plain but interesting preacher. Pathos and piety were distinguished traits of the character of his ministry, which I often attended in the early part of it, and well remember some of his shrewd and forcible expressions. On one occasion, while going over in detail the afflictions of Job, he wound up by saying, with his then peculiar pronunciation, "and to add to all his troubles his wife began to scold because he was too religious."

Elder W. Parkinson came to this city in the beginning of this century, and settled with the first church, then in Gold street. As I then resided in the city, and was a somewhat attentive observer of all passing events in the then small circle of our people, the zeal and eloquence of this new minister, his out-door preaching in the Park and elsewhere, his adroit management, so as to preach like a New Light under the restraints of the strong Calvinistic creed, which was the test of orthodoxy among our old divines of that locality, at that time, are among the reminiscences of my youthful days, while looking forward to the ministerial employment.

The now aged Dr. Maclay, the only survivor of the small company of Baptist ministers then in this city, commenced his labors in it about half a century since. Although he was a Baptist through and through, from the time he renounced the Pedobaptist creed, yet on account of his continued practice of weekly communion, to which he had formerly been accustomed, there was a little delay in his coming fully into our ranks.

In Philadelphia, Drs. Staughton and Rogers, and Elder William White, were the principal ministers among the Baptists, and near by were three of the Joneses, of whom Dr. Samuel, of Lower Dublin, the original seat of Baptist influence in this region, had long been distinguished for talents and usefulness. He was an old man when I first saw him in his own hospitable mansion.

Dr. Staughton, the pastor of the first church, was then in the zenith of his fame, as a popular preacher of our order in America; and from my own experience I can confirm all that has been reported of Dr. S. relative to his hospitality and kindness towards his brethren of all grades, and especially ministers of the younger class. Indeed, this may be said of our ministers generally of that age, however elevated their positions. Their houses were then the schools of the prophets, and they cheerfully became their gratuitous teachers and models.

At that time there was a harmony among our ministers in the city of brotherly love, which was sadly disturbed a few years later, when it was painful, instead of pleasant, to go from one house to another, of men who were full of complainings against each other.

Philadelphia, a half a century since, and for a long time before that date, and also many years later, both by the North and South, was regarded as the emporium of Baptist influence. In its vicinity originated the project of founding a literary institution for Baptist use, which in the end was located in Providence, R. I., and now bears the name of Brown University; and here, also, was founded the convention for foreign missions in 1814, then the most important institution of the kind which existed among the American Baptists, and here for a long time after was the center of its operations. In the outset of this body, there was but one secretary for correspondence, both for home and foreign affairs; and this office was sustained by Dr. Staughton for many years, or until he became the President of the Baptist College in Washington, D. C.

The Baptist Philadelphia Confession of Faith, so called, because it went out from this city, was a document of high authority among all the old Baptist churches in this part of the country, and generally throughout the South and West, when I first traveled in those regions. This document was published here, and was printed by Dr. Franklin.

In Wilmington, Delaware, Elder D. Dodge was then located. He was the same plain, common-sense man that he always was through his long and useful life.

In Baltimore, were Elders S. Richards and J. Healey, both of British pedigree, and very useful men in their day. Mr. Richards was supported by his people,

while Mr. Healey supported himself by means of a
dyeing establishment, in which, like Paul in tent
making, his own hands were employed, as their com-
plexion gave ample proof.

Mr. Richards was originally of the Lady. Huntington connection in England.

In Washington city, Elder O. B. Brown stood
alone, as to his own order of ministers. He went to
the capital about the time the United States Government was removed there from Philadelphia, and during the early part of his life he had governmental
employments, mostly in the post office line. He also
officiated as chaplain to Congress many years. By his
invitation I sometimes. accompanied him, when he
went to the old Hall, before the Capitol was finished,
for the performance of his *pro forma* service. When
he entered the Hall, all was bustle and talk here and
there, but as soon as the chaplain ascended the stand
down went the Speaker's hammer, and at once all
were still, till the *amen* was pronounced, when the
usual business of the body went on.

Dr. Furman, of Charleston, South Carolina, was
then the principal minister of our order, not only
in his own State, but in all the surrounding region;
indeed, I do not know of any one in the Baptist
ranks, at that time, who had a higher reputation
among the American Baptists for wisdom in counsel,

and a skill in management, in all the affairs of the
denomination.   When I first visited him, in 1810, he
was somewhat advanced in years, but actively engaged in his usual pursuits.   Four years after, he became president of the Baptist convention for foreign
missions, and as such, and by the appointment of that
body, which, from the beginning, was deeply interested in Bible operations, Dr. Furman wrote a letter
to Lord Teignmouth, then president of the British and
Foreign Bible Society.   A copy of this letter, in the
handwriting of the author, with many others of his
letters, is in my possession.   By the courtesy of Dr.
Furman's family, after his death I was permitted to
take from the house many valuable letters, which
were addressed to him by men of distinction from
different parts.   Among them were some from Dr.
Rippon of London; others from Drs. Maxey, Backus,
etc.

During my first visit to Charleston, I fell in with a
custom which I think would be well for our churches
if it more generally prevailed.   When a visiting minister was invited to tea among the members, it was
expected that he and all company would spend the
evening at the house, and that a short off-hand discourse would be delivered.   After I had gone on a
number of nights in this way, the good Doctor, one
morning, said to me, " My young brother, I fear our

people will tire you out. You must remember you
have to preach for me next Sabbath ; and beside this,
you, as a visitor of the city, will be expected to address the Orphan Asylum early in the morning of that
day."

"Perhaps the Doctor is afraid your pond will run
out," said a friend slyly, to whom I gave the account.

This custom of family preaching, I believe, came
from England; but wherever it came from, it pleased
me much, although I abstained from it for the rest of
the week, at the suggestion of my kind and much
esteemed counselor and friend.

Beaufort, a handsome little island town, midway
from Charleston to Savannah, Georgia, was then in-
habited chiefly by people of wealth, whose landed
estates were at different distances from their homes.
Among them was Mr. Thomas Fuller, the father of
Dr. R. Fuller of Baltimore, who was an unordained
Baptist preacher of the local class. His splendid and
hospitable mansion was my home while I was in the
place. Mr. Fuller had property on some of the neighboring islands, and among his overseers was a Baptist
preacher of his own grade. One day, after fitting off
the man with a boat load of articles for the scene of
his labors, and after his departure, brother F. said to
me, "There goes a good man, and a good preacher,
too. I am sure I know a great deal more than he

does, and yet in preaching he can far outdo me, so easy is his delivery, and so apt are his representations."

Dr. Johnson was then a sprightly young man, who had but lately left the profession of the law for the ministry among the Baptists.

Elder E. Botsford, of Georgetown, was somewhat advanced in years when I first saw him at his own home. He came from England in early life, and lived and labored in Georgia and South Carolina, but mostly in the latter State, to a good old age. This kind old minister was very helpful to me in mv historical pursuits.

In Georgia, in early life, I became acquainted with a number of our ministers, who then were, or who afterwards became, quite distinguished in the denomination. Of only two of them shall I give my brief biographical accounts.

Elder, afterwards Dr. J. Mercer, and A. Marshall, were then conspicuous men among the Georgia Baptists, especially in the upper regions of the State, in which the denomination was rapidly increasing at this time, and where its numerical strength has now become very great. Mercer had not attained the meridian of life. His circumstances, as to property, were very moderate, and the wife of his youth was still living. Both of them afterwards made me an agree-

able visit at my own home, and not long after their
return, the good woman was called to her rest. By a
second marriage, Dr. M. became quite wealthy, and
after this, people seemed to think he was made of
money, as he wrote me, while alluding to the numerous calls he received for pecuniary aid. Mercer University, an important Baptist institution in this State,
was so named in consequence of the liberal donations
made to it by this eminent man. This efficient coadjutor in my historical pursuits did more than any
other minister in the country, in disposing of my old
history of the Baptists, and until the close of his life
a regular correspondence between us was maintained.

Abraham Marshall was considerably older than
Mercer when I first visited his comfortable home,
not far from Augusta, in 1810. This man, being
descended from the *New Lights* of New England,
through all his active life exhibited much of the
zeal, the energy and independence of that peculiar
people. In his earlier years he was much distinguished as a pioneer in a wide extent of country,
both in the old settlements in the low country, and
in the higher regions south and west of his residence, in what were then the new settlements of the
State. The names of Abraham Marshall, moderator,
and Jesse Mercer, clerk, appear in the minutes of the
Georgia Association, the oldest body of the kind in

the State, for a long course of years. In one of his excursions down the country, in the suburbs of Savannah, not far from where once stood Whitfield's famous orphan house, Mr. M., in one day, baptized forty-five persons of color, formed them, with others previously baptized, into a church, and ordained Andrew Bryan as their pastor. This was in 1788. Thus arose the first African Baptist church in Savannah, which soon became a distinguished community of this people. Bryan lived to the age of ninety in this pastoral station. He was succeeded by his nephew, Andrew Marshall, who held this pastorship with good reputation to old age. He died lately at Richmond, Virginia, while on a visit to that city. Both these men were highly honored in their death, by large concourses of people, not only of their own race, but also of citizens of all grades and distinctions.

From the labors of these plain, colored preachers arose an important Baptist dynasty among the African race, in this region; and I have been thus particular in these details for the purpose of coming at a question of Baptist discipline which may appear of no little importance to some of our people. Abraham Marshall, in forming this now old church, a large account of which was published by Dr. Rippon, of London, in his Annual Register, in 1791, acted alone, as no ordained minister could be had to assist him. " I acted the part of a bishop, in this case, from necessity," said he to me, in relating this story. His brethren, however, sanctioned the measure at the time. Whether the leaders of our church affairs would do so now is a question which I shall not attempt to decide, as I do not recollect having seen it discussed in any of our treatises on church discipline. It is the usual custom of our churches to convoke a council or presbytery, or eldership, in the language of our southern brethren, on such occasions, but in a case of necessity, why may not our ministers, as well as Titus, ordain elders alone?

When I was about to leave Mr. Marshall, among his various messages to his New England relations, "Tell them," said the aged man, "that I am yet in the land of the *dying*, but am bound to the land of the *living*."

"Then," said I, "you reverse the common form of expression on this subject." "There is no death there," was his reply, "while all things are dying here;" and as I started my horse he waved his hand and retired towards the old family mansion.* Before I visited this region again, this venerable man, as we may confidently believe, had gone to the land of the living.

* This was the home of his father, the famous Daniel Marshall, the Baptist pioneer of this part of Georgia. Some vestiges of the old log cabin, in which he first resided here, were still to be seen when I first visited the place.

CHAPTER IV.

FIFTY YEARS AGO it was as unconstitutional and unusual for ministers of our order to preach by note as it was for the old Scotch Seceders and many others; but extempore speaking was the almost universal practice. There was no established rule on the subject, but so decided and strong were the prejudices of the people against written discourses, that very few of our ministers ever presumed to use them. If at any time they saw fit to prepare written sermons, to relieve themselves and the people from embarrassment, they would announce the fact beforehand, as the following account will show: In 1807, one hundred years from the forming of the Philadelphia Association, the late Dr. Samuel Jones, by appointment, preached a century sermon before that body. This performance, the venerable preacher introduced by saying, "I have had it on my mind that it would be proper for me, before I proceed, to confess openly, that I am not going to preach, but to read. * * * I must, however, observe that I think reading is admissible on particular occasions, especially such as the present, when the chief of what is to be said, is to be historical. * * * After saying this much, I need not be at any pains to conceal my notes. I had some thoughts of committing the whole to memory, but I did not like it very well, * * * by pretending to do what I did not. * * * I will now enter on the subject before us—'*Enlarge the place of thy tent,*' etc."

Dr. Jones, in his remarks thus quoted, probably had more respect to popular prejudices than his own feelings; but from these remarks, especially those which have respect to concealing his notes, we may see the embarrassments under which ministers then labored, in this region, who wished to make use of any written preparations in their pulpit services. Many amusing accounts in the concealing operation might be given.

The notions of our people in Boston and vicinity were not so rigid in this business; still but few of our preachers, in all this part of our country, made any display of papers in the pulpit. If they employed any it was done with such care and dexterity as not to be generally observed.

Dr. Stillman had the reputation of preaching by note, but of doing it with such facility as to appear to speak in an extempore manner. A number of the

pulpit preparations of this eminent divine are before
me, which are rather ample skeletons than full discourses of common length.

With very few exceptions, in my early day, our
most distinguished preachers pursued the extempore
mode. After hearing Dr. Furman of Charleston,
South Carolina, in his own pulpit, I find it entered
in my journal, " he is a very correct extempore
speaker."

A large majority of Baptist preachers in early
times had no inclination to offend the people with
written sermons, had they been capable of producing
them, but as a new generation came up, with more
education, a change gradually took place, not always
for the better, however, in the view of many of the
old members, in whose minds a broad distinction was
still kept up between *reading* and *preaching.*

The Scotch system of writing and committing to
memory, as Dr. Jones was inclined to do, was never
practiced to any great extent among our ministers.
When the new race, with permission, or without it,
had surmounted the old extemporaneous barriers
which had stood in the way of their predecessors,
they found it more convenient to trust to their eyes
than their memories, and as Baptists are more tolerant in this business than the Covenanters, the reading of sermons has become about as common with

Baptists as Pedobaptists in many parts of the country. And what is a little singular, while many of our ministers are going into the practice with increasing expedition, many in old dynasties are going out of it as fast as possible.

On the Habits of our Ministers.—Their Support— Circumstances—Trials—Faithfulness.

Fifty years ago, the ministers of our order were generally a hardy and active set of men. Then we never heard of a very prevalent disease of modern times, nor was it common to go on distant voyages for the restoration of health. Instead of this, they often sallied out on horseback into remote and destitute regions, as evangelical pioneers. This was done in many cases by ministers under pastoral engagements, who, after spending a few weeks or months in such services, would return to their pastoral stations.

How it happened that the ministers of that age, who were exposed to so many hardships and privations, who so often preached in log cabins and in other pent-up places, or in the open air, should have so much better organs of speaking, stronger lungs and firmer constitutions, than their successors, whose labors are so much less severe, and who are so much better cared for, I could never fully understand.

In my early experience among the Baptists, the

spirit of preaching was very prevalent; and licensed
or local preachers, who did not look forward to any
pastoral charge, were so numerous in some of our old
associations, that they out-numbered the ordained
class.

It was very common with our old-fashioned preachers to open a door, as they called it, for others to
speak; and the local preachers, and even the lay
brotherhood, were included in invitations of this
kind. This practice is still continued in many places.

At the period now alluded to, it was a very uncommon thing for any of our ministers to give up
preaching or relinquish pastoral stations for the want
of support. Instead of that, they would devise some
way to support themselves and keep on their work;
and what may seem a little singular, I have always
found our ministers of property among the self-supporting class, rather than with those who have been
well cared for by their people.

*On the Ways in which Ministers Sustained Themselves
and Families.*

A considerable number of our preachers in this
age were physicians, some kept school, others followed trades, or were engaged in mercantile pursuits
of different kinds; but by far the greatest part of
them, throughout the whole range of our country,

were literally farmer preachers; and in my extensive travels among them, I was somewhat disappointed in finding such a large portion of these laborious men, in their spiritual vocations, in such comfortable circumstances as to their worldly concerns. And not a few of them were wealthy compared with the citizens around them. Lands were cheap and were easily obtained, in a new and uncultivated state, and were paid for by degrees; and when a minister had commenced a settlement, his brethren and friends would join in log-rolling, and soon a farm would be secured for the family, by whom, for the most part, it was cultivated and cared for, while the head of it was engaged in evangelical labors in a wide circuit in his new location.

The early settlers in the western country went principally from the southern Atlantic States, in search of a more productive soil, and the advantages which new countries afford to the primitive occupants. Many Baptist ministers were found, among the swarm of emigrants who thus sallied over the mountains in pursuit of western homes, who had no certain places in view. In some cases, churches were formed by emigrating parties before they set out on their western tour, and ministers and people would travel and locate together. Such a body on the road, might be styled the church in the wilderness.

To illustrate the vagueness of pastoral relations in the new settlements, I will mention that I found instances of ministers locating in desirable places, without any respect to a church, although they intended to continue their ministerial labors. As preachers then and there made no dependence on the people for support, their first object was to provide a home for their families, like other men; and when this was accomplished, their next business was to collect together the scattered sheep in the wilderness, organize them into churches, get up log meeting houses, and set in motion religious operations with as much regularity as a new country life would afford. Although the western regions, which were settled principally by emigrants from Virginia and the Carolinas, are here referred to, yet it is a well-known fact that half a century since most of our ministers, everywhere, were under the necessity of laboring and planning for their own support, and that the Baptists generally were more parsimonious in their doings in this line, than almost any other party in the country.

"The Lord keep thee humble, and we'll keep thee poor," was then the doctrine of the South, according to Dr. Furman. "They loved the gospel, and they loved its ministers, but the sound of money drove all the good feelings from their heart," according to J. Leland.

But still these same people were generous at their homes, so far as hospitality was concerned. In this business there was no stint nor reluctance.

The great mass of our ministers then had no settled income for their services, and where moderate sums were pledged, in too many cases they were slowly paid, if paid at all. Under these circumstances, the zeal and assiduity of so many laborious men is the wonder of the present age. Their perseverance in their ministerial work, in the midst of so much ingratitude and neglect on the part of the numerous churches which they planted, and the poverty and privations which they endured through the whole of their ministry, are matters of high commendation and grateful remembrance.

In that early age we seldom heard of any one retiring from a pastorship into ministerial inactivity, on account of the parsimony of the people; and very few non-preaching elders were then to be found.

In all the new countries in which our churches were planted, before the rise of any societies of sufficient means to support stationary ministers, the scarcity of ministers was so great that it was necessary for each one to divide his time among a number of churches. The support of the men was not the main thing, as in this business but little was attempted by the people, or expected by the hardy, self-denying gospel pioneers. The grand difficulty was, the men were not to be found, and out of this state of things arose the *monthly system*, so called, which began from necessity, but which has been thus far continued from choice, from neglect, or from some other cause, in most of our churches in the South and West. The attendance of a pastor once a month is all that is expected, and for a minister to have four churches under his care is a sure indication of his popularity. His name appears in the minutes of the association against the churches which claim him as their pastor. Where this system prevails, *one of my churches*, instead of *my church*, is the common language of ministers.

Thirty-day Baptists is a term which some have applied to those who thus manage their pastoral concerns.

In the cities and larger towns, through all the regions where the monthly system is still kept up, our churches generally have pastors in the usual manner, who have but one pulpit, and one congregation to care for ; but in all the country parts of these regions, it was, and probably now is a thing of rare occurrence to find a minister every Sabbath in the same pulpit. If there has been a change from the monthly to the weekly system, it must have been made since I ceased traveling in the South and West. When I was last in Kentucky I found the late Dr. Noel the only Baptist minister in the whole State, where the

denomination was very numerous, as it has been
for half a century past, who had a support from the
people he served, and this came from two churches,
one in the city of Frankfort, the capital, the other at
the Great Crossings, a few miles distant. To these
two bodies he preached every alternate Sabbath.

A Brief Account of a Monthly Pastor.

On my first visit to Georgia, I found the late Jesse
Mercer the pastor of four substantial Baptist churches, each of which were able to give him a comfortable
support. At this time, and during a subsequent visit
to this efficient coadjutor in my historical pursuits, I
went the rounds of his quadruple engagements in the
pastoral line. As the churches had the communion
monthly, the pastor, of course, administered the service weekly, and consequently was, himself, a weekly
communicanist.

Saturday, with all monthly meeting churches, is
the day for church meetings for all kinds of business,
secular and devotional; and Mr. Mercer delivered discourses at the houses of the members who were remote
from the central point, while going to and returning
from it; and as these four churches were for the most
part contiguous to each other, a portion of the members would be found at the second station on the succeeding Sabbath, and so on for the whole of the circuit.

One small item in this fourfold pastorship yet remains to be named: as there are fifty-two Sabbaths in the year, and Mr. Mercer's four churches claimed but forty-eight, the four days' overplus, once in three months, he gave to a feeble body, outside of the circle of his usual labors.

And after all the close figuring of this combination of able churches, for the pastoral care of a very worthy and laborious man, so limited were their contributions for his support, that he found it needful to have the care of a farm and other secular concerns at home.

The above account affords a sample of the manner in which monthly pastorships were conducted at the time here referred to. In many cases, however, able ministers had a less number of churches under their care.

The reader may infer from the foregoing account that the churches in the regions of this monthly system are without ministers or meetings three fourths of the time. But this is not always, and, perhaps we may say, not generally the case. Other ministers of less notoriety on the ground, or those of the itinerating class from other parts, often preach in the places left vacant by the stationed pastors.

Voting supplies for the churches which were destitute of all pastoral aid, was an important item in the

doings of our old associations. This method was pursued, before any arose, for the promotion of missionary labors of the most limited and temporary kind.
This practice prevailed mostly in the northern States.

Fifty years ago there were but little more than thirty Baptist ministers in all the country who had been through a course of collegiate training, and but eight on whom the title of D. D. had been conferred. Manning, Foster and Smith had died before that time.

On the Permanency of Pastoral Relations.

In all times our ministers of a certain class have often changed their locations, or, as the phrase is, have been on wheels; but, on the whole, there has unquestionably been a great increase in the frequency of ministerial removals, during the last half century.

In the cities and principal towns, in my early day, the pastors of our churches, generally, were retained in office till old age; and in many other locations, in all the States, there was a large class of pastors who lived and died in the places of their early settlement. If they were not eminent, or attractive as preachers, and if a portion, or even a majority of their congregations, would have preferred other men, a change could not then be so easily effected as now.
Many of these men lived on their own foundations; they had always supported themselves, and on the

score of living were wholly independent of their people, who, from their neglectful and parsimonious habits, would have found it very difficult to raise a support for a new man.

This difficulty often occurred when the old incumbent ceased from his labors, or voluntarily resigned his charge.

The causes of ministerial removals and changes, a half a century since, were not so numerous or pressing as they have been for many years past. Then the vehement spirit of numerical gain in the churches, and the restless desire for available ministers for the augmentation of congregations, had hardly begun to show itself. The old staid churches had more respect to the sound and certain teachings of their ministers than to any thing merely captivating in their discourses. Again, the numerous excitements of modern times, about matters foreign to the work of ministers of the gospel, in which not a few of our more modern pastors have been involved, and by means of which many have been run off the track, were unknown in my early intercourse with the Baptists. Once more: the influence of restless deacons to effect pastoral changes was then but feeble compared with later years. It was, indeed, felt more or less in some few churches, but it was afterwards greatly increased, and many an embarrassed pastor has been obliged to succumb to its controlling sway. Finally, a scanty income was not always a sufficient reason for a ministerial change, in the public mind, or in that of the minister himself, but often he would hold on, year after year, under the most embarrassing circumstances, rather than leave his flock in a pastorless condition.

In those days, while church members were generally quite poor, and as many of them had come from the Pedobaptists of different parties, they were exposed to opposition and reproach of a painful nature; and on these accounts there was a very strong sympathy and affection on the part of the pastor towards these poor and despised people, and a reluctance to leave them without an under shepherd, stronger than is now felt by many ministers in their sudden changes.

CHAPTER V.

FIFTY YEARS AGO, not an agent for collecting funds for any object of benvolence or literature was to be seen in the whole Baptist field. Some pastor of an embarrassed church would occasionally sally out in different directions in search of aid for finishing his house of worship, or for clearing off its incumbrance of debts.

Long before this time, agencies and efforts, somewhat vigorous and extensive, in this country and England, had been employed in favor of Rhode Island College, then struggling for existence amidst poverty and embarrassments. In these undertakings, Dr. Smith, in this country, and Morgan Edwards, in the mother realm, acted conspicuous parts. Smith went as far south as Georgia; Edwards traversed England, Ireland, etc., and met with very good success, considering, to use his own words, "how angry the mother country was with the colonies for opposing the stamp act."

No one then dreamed of so soon seeing such an army of agents in the field, for so many different ob-

jects, and that the business would become a distinct
vocation, of indispensable necessity, for carrying forward our benevolent plans, and for performing our
denominational work.

The principal agents, in my early day, were found
in our sisterhood, for collecting *mites*, in aid of a few
small societies for the support of domestic missions,
and for the promotion of ministerial education. These
agents were self-supporting and unobtrusive.

*A General View of Houses of Worship among the
American Baptists in the Commencement of this Century.*

In my brief description of our church edifices, in
my early acquaintance with them, I shall refer, in the
first place, to those in the principal towns and cities
on the Atlantic coast; next, to those of the better
sort, in interior regions; and finally, to shanties and
log cabins in the new settlements.

In Boston, the houses occupied by Drs. Stillman
and Baldwin, when I first saw them, were commodious and in good repair, but they were barn-fashioned
buildings, destitute of any architectural style or attraction.

The house in which the late Dr. Sharp officiated
more than forty years, was dedicated in 1807. This
building was then considered number one, of the kind,
among the Massachusetts Baptists.

The old church in Providence, Rhode Island, now an octogenarian among church buildings, was, I think, the only one then existing in this country, and perhaps in any other, for Baptists, which was planned by scientific rules. A Baptist meeting house, of such broad dimensions, with a steeple two hundred feet high, and all in so much architectural taste, was a wonder to our people far and near. I myself was not a little surprised, when I first saw this stately temple, at being informed that it was the place of meeting for our plain, old-fashioned sort of people, as I had resided mostly in a region of country where our people would not suppose there could be found any Holy Ghost in such a house as that, and where, moreover, they had been accustomed to associate steeple houses with formalism, bigotry and intolerance. The American Baptists then had no zeal for steeples—the cost of them was a hindrance, if nothing else; and our British brethren could not have them if they would, as the law of the country did not allow of them among dissenters. To this prohibition, some have thought, the Providence people meant to refer in the inscription on their first great bell, which read thus:

> "For freedom of conscience the town was first planted,
> Persuasion, not force, was used by the people;
> This church is the oldest, and has not recanted,
> Enjoying, and granting bell, temple and steeple."

A drawing of this then superior building for Baptist worship to any in America, was sent to Dr. Rippon of London, who published it in his Annual Register more than sixty years ago.

In the whole of Connecticut, my native State, our people had no good houses of worship, anywhere. In Hartford was one of small dimensions, in New Haven none at all.

A similar account may be given of the entire State of New York, except one building in the city, belonging to the first church, then located in Gold street. This was a substantial stone edifice, then but lately erected. It bid fair to last for ages, and might have done so, but for the uptown fever among the people, who, under the ministry of the late Dr. Cone, reared their costly temple in that direction.

In Philadelphia, the famous rotunda, or round house, commonly called Dr. Staughton's church, in Sansom street, was an object of much attention in its early day, for its size, being ninety feet in diameter, for the singularity of its form, and for the large assemblies which the eloquence of its famous pastor collected there. Besides this, there were three good buildings of an ordinary form, for Baptist use, in this Quaker city, where, if I remember right, there were but two steeples on the church houses of any denomination. In one of these churches, Bishop White officiated, and the other was also of the Episcopal order.

In Baltimore, was one church for Baptists, of the first class, for that age.

In Washington city there was then but one small house for Baptist use, which was of an unattractive appearance.

The same may be said of Richmond, Virginia. This edifice, after a number of additions, has fallen into the hands of the colored people, and is the resort of a very large church of our order.

Dr. Furman's church, the only one in Charleston, South Carolina, for the Baptists, was a good, commodious building. The same may be said of those in Beaufort and Savannah.

In this hasty sketch I have included all our church edifices of the first class in this country, at the date of these reminiscences, and but few of the best of them would be considered very splendid or costly in these times. In my early day, twenty-five thousand dollars was considered a very large sum to expend on a house for religious worship. But a small portion of those referred to in the foregoing summary statements cost so much, independent of their sites, which in some cases had been occupied by former buildings.

In the second class of meeting houses, almost every grade could then be seen, from plain, well-finished

4

buildings to those of a very inferior character; and man*y* of all classes were in a state of dilapidation and neglect. The further back we go, the less we see of the credit system among the Baptists in this business, and also of seeking aid far from home. They then went according to their own means, and made the best of their humble sanctuaries.

Compound motions in meeting-house operations were considerably in vogue in former times, which did not always work well. The way this was done, different societies would unite in getting up a place of worship, to be owned in common, and to be used in turn. Such houses were of course of the *omnium gatherum* kind, and were very common in their use. So limited were the means of our people in those times, and so closely were they obliged to calculate in planning their meeting houses, that school rooms were sometimes fitted up in them. In other cases, you might see stores and warehouses underneath them. In the basement of one of these buildings a grocery store was in full operation, in which, according to former custom, the ardent article constituted no small part of the trade. This gave occasion for some wag to place on the building the following lines :

> " There's a spirit above and a spirit below,
> A spirit of joy and a spirit of woe ;
> The spirit above is the spirit divine,
> The spirit below is the spirit of wine."

We will now make a few remarks on the lowest
grade of Baptist meeting houses, half a century since.

In all new settlements in this country, log cabins
are generally the first edition of dwellings for families, and also of sanctuaries for religious assemblies ;
and how many thousands of the best of meetings
have been held, by multitudes of our people, in rude
and unsightly structures of this kind, from the Canadas to the remotest parts of the South and West. In
my early travels I saw enough of them to form some
opinion of the inconveniences of new country life,
and my complaint of the people in these countries,
and in the older regions, too, has often been, that they
were too remiss in providing more comfortable and
commodious houses for religious worship, and that
they kept in old and desolate buildings in some cases,
and in log cabins in others, long after their early
family mansions had been exchanged for those of a
far superior style.   In view of this neglect of our
people in former times, how often have the words of
the prophet, respecting the ceiled houses of the people, and the desolation of the house of God, occurred
to my mind.

But after suffering greatly in their own comfort and
conveniences, and by their parsimony and neglect
hindered the growth of many societies and of the denomination at large, Baptist communities, in encour-

aging numbers, have aroused to new and vigorous efforts in this business; so that for a few years past the spirit of erecting new edifices for Baptist use, and repairing old ones, has much increased. Very often now, in different quarters, we hear of new undertakings in this line, and the danger at present is, that at some points they may go to the other extreme, and go as much too far in future, in splendor and profuseness, as they did of old in parsimony and plainness.

In my youthful days, the old Baptists never paid any bills for stained glass and inside adornments of their most finished religious temples.

In the times here referred to, our people were well satisfied if they could get the outside of their meeting houses well painted; this, with a good white-washing within, was all that they asked for.

The custom of painting and papering the inside walls is of recent date, and is rapidly gaining ground, in imitation of their more stylish neighbors of other creeds.

But after all, a pure white wall, in my judgment, is the most befitting for a religious sanctuary. In the language of the poet, we may say it is,

"When unadorned, adorned the most."

CHAPTER VI.

ON THE CHANGES IN BAPTIST CUSTOMS IN THE COURSE OF FIFTY
YEARS.—IN CHURCH AFFAIRS.—ASSOCIATIONS.

UNDER this head I shall have respect principally
to the moral habits of church members and the regulation of their church affairs.

1. *In their strictness of church discipline.*

Fifty years ago it was contrary to Baptist rules for
their members to frequent such places of amusement
as multitudes of them now resort to without any official censure or complaint. Our people then made a
broad distinction between the church and the world,
and if any of their members went over the line to the
world's side, they were at once put under church
discipline. Then the Baptists sternly prohibited the
practice of brother going to law with brother, under
any circumstances whatever. All matters of offense,
or complaints of wrong doing, must be laid before the
body according to gospel rule. And if rash or inexperienced members hurried their complaints there,
without taking gospel steps, as the phrase was, they
were required to retrace their course and go first to
the offending member. Achans in the camp were

then much dreaded, and church members were assiduously taught not to suffer sin upon a brother.

In our well regulated communities all the members
of all grades, and of both sexes, felt bound to watch
over each other, and become helpers in all matters of
discipline; and all were held to a strict account in
their moral conduct generally, and especially in their
business transactions.   Then we had no standing
committees in our churches, either to prepare cases
beforehand for their being brought into them, or to
assist in keeping them out of them.   Neither the aids
nor the hindrances which may result from these essentially Presbyterian bodies, in the expedition of
business on the one hand, or in the suppression of investigation on the other, with which a portion of our
people now seem so well pleased, had anywhere been
introduced among them.

2. *In the manner of conducting church meetings.*

In some few cases this was done with closed doors,
but by far the greater part of our churches throughout the land did not adhere to this rule.   Any
neighbors or friends might sit and witness the transaction of church business; and in times of revivals,
when many were coming into the churches, large
congregations of outside people would assemble.
There is a tradition that the famous Thomas Jefferson caught the idea of some things in the Constitution

of this republic while witnessing the doings of a small Baptist church in his neighborhood. As the story goes, some of the primordial principles of the great document which he afterwards penned were conceived from observing the successful movements of a little self-operating body which acknowledged no allegiance to any other power. This story has been currently reported, and on good authority, as I am inclined to believe.

3. *In the mode of singing in public worship.*

In a few places at the North they had singing choirs as at the present time, but congregational singing was then the prevailing mode in a great majority of Baptist congregations, and this is probably so now, taking into view the whole denomination in this country, notwithstanding all the changes which have been made in church music in the older churches, in favor of organs, and in having select companies of performers in this line, where these instruments have not been introduced. The most systematic way of conducting this service, where all the people felt free to participate in it, was, for the leader to stand down in front of the pulpit, in view of the whole congregation, who followed him according to their ability and disposition. Through the South and West ministers very often took the lead in the singing service. This was considered a matter of course, for such as had a

gift for it, in the absence of a leader among the members, and this practice, I presume, still prevails very
extensively. In some parts of England, in olden
times, keen disputes were maintained at one period,
whether there should be singing at all, and by some
congregations it was omitted altogether. In some of
my early travels I found a remnant of this non-sing-
ing policy in this country, mostly in the interior of
Rhode Island; and "are you a singing Baptist?"
was a question proposed to me now and then, by
those who had been educated in it. This strange
omission began in persecuting times, when dissenters
from the dominant church were obliged to meet in
retired places, and conduct their religious services in
as still a manner as possible for fear of discovery
and disturbance; and, in many other cases, a practice which was at first adopted from necessity was afterwards continued from choice, and became a law
among the people.

4. *In the posture of prayer in public worship.*

This was always standing or kneeling. Then, for
any one to remain seated during this service, would
have been considered extremely irreverent and the
height of impropriety in men, women or children,
unless they were sick or lame. Thus to do, would
have been regarded as evidence of imbecility or indolence. The kneeling posture was about as common

among the Baptists as the Methodists, especially in
the South and West. It was often adopted by ministers in their pulpits, or on their preaching stands;
and such was their humility and sense of duty, that
they were not deterred by any inconveniences to
which they might be subjected. Many, and perhaps
most places of worship, where now the kneeling practice prevails are in a neglected and slovenly condition.
Thus while Baptist worshipers in one section of country, in prayer time, remain seated on soft cushions,
in a much larger portion of it they kneel on hard
floors, unswept for an indefinite length of time, and
illy fitted for their use.

5. *In their familiarity with the Scriptures, and in the
readiness of all classes of members, male and female, to
defend their peculiar sentiments.*

Fifty years ago there was a very vigorous renewal
of the baptismal controversy in this country, and
all the old arguments of the Pedobaptists, and the
whole catalogue of bad stories against the Baptists,
were circulated by their opponents with uncommon
zeal and activity. This unusual excitement followed
the conversion of Rev. Daniel Merrill of Maine, with
most of his large church, of the Congregationalist
creed, to the Baptist faith. Dr. Baldwin, of Boston,
with other ministers of the order, assisted in the
re-baptizing of this large Pedobaptist community,

4*

and forming them into a Baptist church. And from this followed a watery war, in which multitudes on both sides engaged for a long course of years. The various writers on the Baptist side, as usual, took pains to show how fully their sentiments were established by the original terms in the Scriptures which pertain to this subject. Those writings were so thoroughly studied by the common people, and were so often quoted by them, that one of the ministers, in his defense of Pedobaptism, sarcastically said, " Even the Baptist women talk Greek, in disputing with me on the subject of baptism."

Although I would not undervalue the ability of multitudes of our members of this age to discuss and defend their peculiar opinions, yet it is doubtful whether the number of this class is so great now, in proportion to our population, as in former times.

6. *In their modes of supporting their ministers, and in their superior doings now in that line.*

In my earliest examinations into Baptist affairs, I did not find one society in the whole connection which made much dependence on pew rents for ministerial support, except in Boston. In a few cases, the remnants of pews which remained unsold were rented, and the funds thus obtained formed an item of the minister's income. Free pews, or benches, were then the general rule. The idea of paying any thing for seats in a Baptist meeting house, much less of having the annual rent of them defray the expense of the establishment, ministers and all, had not entered the minds of our people, and, as their meeting houses were, nothing of the kind could have been done, if they had attempted it.

In some instances, the pews in houses of the better sort had been sold and became the private property of the buyers, but subject to no tax, not even for the repairs of the building. In Boston, the Baptists, following the custom of the place from its early settlement, have from time immemorial, depended on pew rents for the support of their ministers and the payment of current expenses. This being the policy of the old dynasty, in this ancient capital, the Baptists here were exempt from the taxation, law suits, vexation and spoliations to which their brethren in many parts of this commonwealth were so often, for a long time, exposed.

Farms and funds I sometimes met with in the hands of our old societies, for the support of their ministers; but as a general thing, annual subscriptions, too often poorly paid, were the main dependence of those ministers, who looked to their people for any part of their support. Many received considerable in donations of such things as they needed for themselves and families, from their more liberal members; and the itinerating class generally carried home more or less in funds, from collections which were made for them in their preaching excursions. But on the whole, all ministers of our order, out of the cities and principal towns, who were not on farms, or in some kind of secular employment, had but scanty fare.

At the period now alluded to, the best of livings, so to speak, among the Baptists, would but little more than supply tenements to the present incumbents. Five hundred dollars per annum, with a parsonage, sounded quite loud then for ministers of the first class who had the care of our best located and most able churches; very few of them received over that amount, except in extra donations; and I am inclined to think that not twenty such livings could be found among the American Baptists. This was the amount of Rev. William Collier's salary, during the short time he was pastor of the first church in the city of New York, as he informed me at the time, a little more than half a century since. The old parsonage where John Gano so long resided was demolished when the new stone church in Gold street, in which Mr. Collier officiated, was erected. Whether Mr. C. had a house found for him or paid his own rent is a question I can not decide.

Mr. J. Williams had no fixed salary when I attended his ministry in that city, but depended on the col-

lections which were made at the close of his discourses,
a thing not uncommon in those days. In all churches
then, in New York and in many other places, whatever might be their financial arrangements in other
respects, boxes, plates, or some such contrivances
went round to receive the oblations of the people at
the close of each meeting.

In Providence, for about ten years from his settlement in the place, Dr. Gano's stipend was the sum
lately named; but when his father's old flock in New
York sought to transfer him to their then new house,
the dedication sermon of which he preached, his salary was made three fourths of a thousand, and so remained to the end of his ministry, in 1828.

Drs. Stillman and Baldwin, of Boston, were well
cared for by their respective flocks, according to the
custom of the times, but with any details on this subject I am not familiar; I remember, however, to have
heard Dr. B. observe late in his life that he never
had occasion to say any thing to his people respecting
his support, but that they, from time to time, increased
it of their own accord, which but few of our ministers
could say then, or since.

As to the company of our ministers of old, compared with the present time, what shall we say on
this point? If they have more *callers* now, then they
had more *stayers*, bag and baggage too, with more or

less of their families and friends. Baptist people, and
those who sympathized with them, in olden times were
very gregarious and loved to flock together; and what
places were more suitable than the houses of their
ministers? These were often and very appropriately
called *Baptist taverns*, where the guests frequently out-
numbered those of the neighboring inns. In the days
here referred to, in Baptist parsonages, as at the old
vicarage of Wakefield, might be seen denominational
kindred of all classes and affinities to the eighteenth
cousins. But hospitality was the order of the day,
and the good old pastors kept open doors for guests
of all descriptions. And although at times persons
were quartered upon them, who had very slender
claims on their hospitality, if any at all, yet there was
very little complaining in such cases.

7. *In the manner of conducting the business of associations.*

These were the only great meetings we had in my
early day, as the age of our present anniversaries was
far ahead. The whole number of associations then in
all America was about seventy-five, where there are
now upwards of six hundred. The manner of conducting those which I attended while young was more
devotional and less formal than now, in many places:
and there was more preaching and exhortation, more
freedom for men of less brilliant powers of speaking

to take a part in devotional exercises, and an entire
absence of agents to bespeak the good will of the people in favor of their different objects. And at that
early period there were none of the distracting *ites*
and *isms* of later times, nor of the conflicts which they
always engender, which have so often marred the enjoyment of associational meetings. Then we had no
periodicals except the old Missionary Magazine once
in three months. The way in which our people at all
distances communicated with each other as to the state
of their churches and their general affairs, was by
means of corresponding letters for this purpose, from
one association to another. In process of time, these
letters were printed in the minutes of the associations;
but when I first began to attend some of the oldest
bodies of this kind they appointed men on the spot
to write to all with which they had agreed to correspond; the letters thus formed were sent to them in
manuscript; this was a slow way, but it was the best
they knew then. The next step was to prepare one
letter of a general character for all corresponding associations, some of which were in distant States, and
to print it in the minutes. By this method a good
deal of labor was saved to the few men who were
generally selected to write corresponding letters.
But when periodicals began to circulate, and new
and more expeditious modes of communication were

opened, this old item of associational doings was laid
aside.

With the old Warren Association I became connected in the early part of this century, when its annual gatherings were so attractive to the people that
large companies of males and females encountered
long and laborious journeys to attend them. This
body, at one time, extended from Rhode Island,
where it originated, eighty years since, over all Massachusetts, except the western part, and into New
Hampshire; and the places of its annual meetings
were at times about one hundred miles distant from
each other; but the zeal of the people led them to
undertake these long journeys with cheerfulness, with
their own slow conveyances, so confident were they
of being repaid for all their labor. And this was
done not only by delegates, but by many others. Revivals then were very frequent; the reports of these,
and the revival spirit with which the body was often
so deeply imbued, made its anniversaries much more
attractive than they have generally been in later
times. In the absence of the facilities of this age for
traveling, all the attendants of these interesting convocations went with their own teams, and by a law
of custom, the whole company was to be provided for
by the people in the places of their meeting; and the
keeping generally of from one to two hundred horses,

in time was felt as a burden in some locations, but mostly in the cities and towns, where the population was of the non-farming class. At one time, the late Oliver Starkweather, of Pawtucket, took one hundred and fifty horses to his own premises, while many were otherwise provided for. This was the golden age of Baptist associations, and whereunto the old Warren would grow, and how many churches would be able to receive it, became, at length, a serious question with many. In point of attraction there was no religious assembly like it among our people, or any other, on the ground over which it was spread, where now a large number of similar institutions exist. Among the various plans of relief from this popular pressure, which some close calculators devised, one was, to limit the number of delegates which each church should send, and that the people should not be bound to provide for any others. But wiser men decided against all restraining measures of this kind, as being not only very unsocial and ungracious, but in opposition to the true interests of the denomination ; and soon all schemes of this sort were abandoned. " Let them come," was the general saying of the people. " House room for twenty-five, and heart room for a hundred," was the language of an old pastor, in a central location.

All efforts to diminish the number of attendants of

associations soon became needless, after the old plan
of conducting them was exchanged for one of a less
edifying character.

The first time I saw Backus, the historian, was at
the thirty-seventh anniversary of the Warren Association, in 1805, in the town from which it took its
name, only ten miles from my residence. I well remember the grave and venerable appearance of the
man so famous in Baptist history, and the conversation we had on historical affairs. But little aid, however, did I receive from him while living, as his home
was upwards of twenty miles from me, and he died
the next year. But after his death, by the courtesy
of his family, a large amount of historical papers, of
great value in my then new undertaking, was I permitted to take from the places in which they had been
left, carefully arranged, by this old and industrious
collector of historical facts and documents.

Thus far, the old manner of conducting associations
seems to have been better than that of later years, so
far as the free flow of religious feeling and the ardor
of piety were concerned; but in one point of view
the old times were much worse than the present—and
for the change for the better, all may be thankful for
the beneficial influence of the temperance reform.
Then, in all places and among all people, the ardent
article was freely used, and no one seemed conscious

of any thing amiss in the practice, and to have failed to have had an ample supply of the popular beverage at gatherings of all kinds, and especially at associations, would have been considered an indication of parsimony or neglect. And on the other hand, some sort of apology was deemed necessary for a non-compliance with invitations to partake of it. Great were the hazards then, of all whose proclivities were in the wrong direction in the temperance line, which the teetotal doctrine happily relieved.

As to the doings of Baptist associations, I would merely observe, that while they keep to the original design of their organization, namely, the spiritual welfare of the churches which have voluntarily united to compose them, they are always found to be harmless, interesting and useful; and no encroachment on the independence of the churches need be feared in their operations. But when they become arenas of debate, especially on matters of an extraneous character, their sessions are scenes of trial rather than enjoyment; and when, moreover, they assume a tone of dictation and control on any subjects whatever, they are rather to be dreaded than desired, and the churches composing them may well prefer an unassociated and strictly independent condition.

CHAPTER VII.

THE further back we go into antiquity, the more fully we see the prejudices against our people developed by their opponents, and the less willing they were to allow them a place in the brotherhood of Christians. Pedobaptists of all classes were down upon them for their criminal neglect of their duty towards their offspring, according to the popular sentiments of their adversaries; and the supporters of the church and state policy were equally severe against them for opposing any dictation or compulsion in the concerns of the gospel. So generally, in my early life, did the idea prevail that children should be christened, as the phrase was, especially among the Episcopalians, among whom I belonged, for their spiritual benefit, that the neglect of the rite ought not to be tolerated among Christian people. And to leave all men free to adopt their own religious creed, to hear what ministers they preferred, to attend what churches they chose, or none at all, and to act in all things concerning religion, and in the business of ministerial support, according to their own wills—all these principles and practices were then regarded as having a tendency to undermine the foundation of the Christian religion. "Poor heathen" was a term of reproach often applied to the children of Baptist parents, while "levelers of the gospel system" was the designation of all the advocates of the Baptist creed.

In the time of the severe persecutions of the old Waldenses the Catholic priests got up a story that their children were born with black throats, that they were hairy and had four rows of teeth, with one eye, and that placed in the middle of their foreheads.

In this country I never heard of any location where prejudices against this people were carried so far, but in the early part of my ministry a very honest and candid old lady, who had never been far from her retired home, said to me in a very sober tone, " Your society are much more like other folks now than they were when I was young. Then there was a company of them in the back part of our town, and an outlandish set of people they certainly were. You yourself would say so, if you had seen them. As it was told to me, you could hardly find one among them but what was deformed in some way or other. Some of them were hair-lipped, others were blear-eyed, or hump-backed, or bow-legged, or clump-footed ; hardly any of them looked like other people. But they were all strong for plunging, and let their poor ignorant children run wild, and never had the seal of the covenant put on them."

In the age here alluded to, *close communion*, so called, was the most available argument with the opponents of our denomination, not only with the ministers but with the whole of their lay membership. This was a theme so continually harped upon, that many members of Baptist families had a hard struggle to surmount a stumbling block so continually thrown in their way ; and in some cases persons of this description were actually taken from the society of their relatives and carried over to the Pedobaptist side.

The Munster affair never failed of being held up to the public by all writers of the Pedobaptist class and many of their preachers also.

On the whole, such was the strength of public opinion against our obnoxious sect, that had its existence depended on the good will of a large class, of leading men on the other side, all their churches no doubt would have been scattered and dissolved. At that time the exchange of pulpits between the advocates and the opponents of infant baptism was a thing of very rare occurrence, except in a few of the more distinguished churches in the northern States. Indeed, the doctrine of non-intercourse, so far as minis-

terial services were concerned, almost universally prevailed between Baptists and Pedobaptists.

I will here recount a few of the examples of unwise policy and objectionable customs of our brethren
in times of old.

1. *In the location of their houses of worship.*

Then for Baptists to plant their churches in market
streets, or in central and conspicuous locations, was a
circumstance of rare occurrence. Instead of this, their
more common practice was to fix on some remote and
obscure situation. In country places, as a matter of
courtesy, they would often go near to some influential family; and as their church buildings, for the
most part, were neither costly nor durable, when new
ones were called for, a stronger influence would be ex-
erted in another direction; and then would come up
the perplexing question about the burying ground,
whether a new one should be opened, or the old one
should continue in use. About a matter of this kind
two old deacons had a discussion of a rather singular
nature, which may be thus reported:

Deacon A.—I stick to the old burying ground as
my final resting place.

Deacon B.—I shall go to the new ground.

Deacon A.—Well, you may all go there that want
to, but I'll never be buried there as long as *I live.*

Deacon B.—Nor I neither, was the quick reply; as

long as *I live* I don't want to be buried anywhere.
But when I am dead I am willing my friends should
place me in the new ground.

In towns and villages Baptist meeting houses, for
the most part, were located on their outskirts, because
some brother· or friend would give the society a lot
there, either as an act of benevolence or to increase
the value of other land.

And not a few of our old preachers, conscious of
their deficiencies as public speakers, would encourage rather than dissuade the people from fixing on
such remote and obscure locations where the towns-
men would not be very likely to come.

2. *In licensing to preach, some who could talk very
well on their own ground and within their own bounds,
but were not suitable to be sent out as ministers at large.*

"Liberty to improve their gifts wherever Providence shall open a door," was the usual form of li-
censes in times when lay and local preachers were
much more numerous than now, especially in old
churches, particularly in the South and West. Many
of these men, while operating in domestic circles,
were very useful. There their deficiencies in education and talents were easily overlooked, which was
not always the case when they went out into the
world.

A portion of the men under consideration, possessed in a high degree the powers of imagination and invention, to which many modern preachers of literary training can make but small pretensions. They valued themselves on their skill in managing knotty texts. Figures and metaphors were their favorite themes, and, by some means or other, they would make all things about them plain. As for parables, they would never leave one till they made it go on all fours; and so fond were they of allegories, that you would think they had been taught in the school of Origen, that everlasting allegorizer.

These curious preachers would often astonish many of their hearers with the ingenuity of their expositions, which, for the most part, however, were as good as many which are found in the writings of some of the Fathers.

3. *In their extreme caution in avoiding the faults, real or supposed, of other denominations.*

Our old Baptists were so much disgusted with many things around them, that in some cases they would be too cautious in their doings, particularly in the business of ministerial support, the evils of which still remain among us. They had suffered so much in some parts of New England, and in Virginia, from taxation and legal coercion from the dominant parties, for the support of ministers, whom they had disowned, that they stood aloof from all systematic

measures in favor of their own preachers. Many of
them went so far as to refuse to lend their names for
the support of ministers, or for any other object. "If
I have any thing to give, I will give it, and be done
with it," was the laconic reply of these men to all
who sought their aid.

"Let not thy left hand know what thy right hand
doeth," was a favorite passage with this kind of people.

"Yes," said one, "some members have no trouble
in following that rule, for neither hand does any
thing for the support of ministers."

The clergy of the standing order, so called, were
generally men of collegiate training, and as the Baptists had often been grievously oppressed for their support, ministerial education itself, by many, was lightly
esteemed. This came from the incorrect reasoning of
our people. But there were other things which caused
a strong dislike, on their part, of the ministers of the
old order, among which we may mention their sacerdotal airs—the dullness of their performances—their
cold, and in some cases, their contemptuous treatment
of all without their pale, whether Baptists or others
—all these things combined to produce in the minds
of our old-fashioned members a settled aversion of the
whole Pedobaptist concern, its priesthood, lay membership and all. And the urgent need of college

learning for ministers they decidedly denied; and this
sentiment was strengthened by observing the less
formal, more animated, and, to them, more edifying
preaching of their own uneducated ministers.

4. *In the want of a progressive spirit in forming new
churches, by sending out colonies from old ones.*

One church in a place was enough, according to
the old Baptist policy, and seldom did a second one
arise, in an entirely peaceable manner.   The idea of
colonizing for the general good of the denomination
and the cause of religion, was but little thought
of among our people in my younger years.   Our
old pastors were, indeed, always pleased with large
churches; yet they could never afford to part with
enough of their members to form a new and strong
interest near them.   And strong men, who were well
satisfied with their spiritual homes, never thought of
leaving them for the public good.   Disaffection was
generally at the bottom of all the new movements
now under consideration.   The first examples of getting up new churches in large and growing places by
colonizing, if I am not. mistaken, were set by our
Boston brethren, many years since.

The old fogyism, above alluded to, among our ministers and people, in former times, has often hindered
the growth of the denomination in this expanding
country, in which our sentiments are viewed with so

much favor now ; and well would it be for us, if less
of its paralyzing influences were felt in some locations
at the present time.*

5. *In having their churches too large, or too small.*

We had a few ministers, in former years, who were
famous evangelists in large districts around them.
They were men of ardent piety and zeal, and many
flocked to their standards ; and wherever they collected converts sufficient for the purpose, they would
unite them into an informal church, under the name
of a *branch*. It was the settled policy of these successful preachers to retain all their converts under
their pastoral care, however widely they were scattered around them ; and the converts themselves felt
in duty bound to continue their membership where
they first joined, whatever changes might take place
in their locations.

Dr. Shepard, of Brentwood, New Hampshire, was
a famous pastor of one of the great churches now
under consideration.

This good old Baptist elder, whom I visited in
one of my early journeys for historical purposes, was
both a preacher and a physician, and was highly es-

---

* I once said to a pastor of a large church, from which, against his
wishes, a new interest was about to be formed, that if they had *five
acres* of members, in the language of politicians at their mass meetings, they would not be willing to spare enough for a new body, which
could go alone at first.

teemed in both capacities in a wide circuit around his residence, which he owned, and which had the appearance of the premises of a good thriving farmer. His pastoral relation was a fixed fact, as was the case with many of our farmer ministers of that age. His church might with propriety be called a bishopric, over which he presided with a mild episcopal sway, having under him a number of able preachers, who, in his absence, officiated in his room, in the different branches of his wide-spread charge. One of these preachers became a governor of the State.

Another church of this description arose near New Lebanon Springs, New York, in the latter part of the last century, under the ministry of Elder Jacob Drake. Others of a similar character might be named. These extensive churches were so unwieldy and so difficult to manage, that but a few of our ministers were disposed to encourage their formation or continuance.

For small churches the Baptists in this country have at all times been peculiarly distinguished, and it is probable that now, no large denomination in the land has such a large proportion of feeble and pastorless communities under the name of church organizations as are found on our lists.

Baptist Publishers and the Baptist Press.

These terms, now so familiar with our people, were

but little known among them in my early acquaintance with their affairs.

Fifty years ago the publishing houses of Manning & Loring, and Lincoln & Edmonds, of Boston, were the only ones of much extent in their operations among the American Baptists. Teibout, of New York, and Dobson, of Philadelphia, were both Baptists, but their doings had not much respect to the concerns of the denomination.*

The newspaper press, half a century since, was almost wholly in the hands of men of different creeds from our own, and was altogether secular in its character. A few papers admitted notices of religious meetings and brief details of religious concerns, which, however, were not unfrequently accompanied with some sneering remarks, especially if there was any thing in the articles pertaining to the foreign mission cause, which was then exceedingly unpopular with many men of the type. The plan of sending men and money out of the country for the purpose of attempting the conversion of the heathen in foreign lands, in the view of these men was a most preposterous one, a project, as they said, not only visionary in its design, but impracticable in its nature.

* " I am of the Baptist persuasion, but not of the Baptist connection," said the then aged Dobson to me while conversing on our affairs. He was, through a long life, the pastor of a small church of Scotch people, in Philadelphia.

With a flippant editor of this class I had a newspaper war of long continuance; the proprietors of the paper being my personal friends decided that I should not be denied the use of its columns, according to the wishes of the editor. My opponent gave out that he felt in duty bound to oppose the foreign mission scheme as a waste of money, which would be much more useful at home, and that he should continue his opposition till he put it down. To this argument of my opponent I replied, that if he fully believed it was his duty to put down the cause of foreign missions, I as fully believed that he would die without performing it.

In the course of my defense of this then obnoxious undertaking, I predicted that the time would come, when the missionaries to foreign lands, who were then so lightly esteemed by many, and especially those of literary pretensions, would become literary pioneers in distant regions, in matters pertaining to the geography, the history, the languages, laws, customs, etc., of the distant countries to which they were sent; and that literary men, instead of treating them with disrespect, would honor them as the friends of science and the promoters of useful knowledge. In my arguments in favor of my position, I observed that missionaries, as a general thing, were then, and must always be, men of intelligence, industry and enterprise; and that by residing in remote regions hitherto wholly or but partially explored, and mingling freely with the inhabitants, would be enabled to be much more accurate in all that pertains to them than passing travelers can possibly be.

It is now about forty years since these predictions were made, and how often have I since been highly gratified in seeing them so literally fulfilled by our own men and those of other communities, and yet I am inclined to think that the contributions to general knowledge, by the aid of missionaries, in connection with their professional labors in the future, will greatly increase.

Baptist Councils in Former Times.

As far back as the time of the active life of Backus, as I find from some of his old papers, he had much to do in assisting churches to adjust difficulties among their members. "Call a council," seems to have been the first idea in the minds of many church members in early times when troubles arose among them, which they could not easily settle; and very small affairs at times were the occasion of these meetings, which in more modern times are seldom known, the churches having learned how to manage their own affairs without troubling their neighbors with them.*

---

* In the course of one of my early journeys for historical purposes, in a new region in a northern State, I fell in with one of the kind of coun-

Councils or presbyteries, as they are termed by our brethren South and West, in former times invariably met in the morning for the examination of the candidates, and in the afternoon for the public services. In the interval a sumptuous dinner was partaken of, either at a public house or at the residence of a wealthy member. This was a wide departure from the custom of primitive times, when they *fasted* and prayed before they engaged in the work of ordination.

The extra efforts for style and abundance at ordination dinners, I suppose, came down to the Baptists from their Puritan ancestors, who in some cases encountered heavy expenses in the settlement of their ministers.* The evenings after ordination, by the young people were devoted to amusement.†

cils above described, which was called simply to adjust a difficulty which had arisen between two church members; and singularly enough these members were a husband and his wife, and more singular still, the difficulty originated in a disagreement about the management of the dairy of the farm. The woman would *skim the milk* too much for the good of the *cheese*, and this dispute ran off into other matters. Although they made me the clerk of the council, yet at this distance of time I can not report its doings; but as near as I can recollect, the meeting leaned to the husband's view, as more correct in theory and as promising a better article for market.

* Something over a century ago, in a country town not far from Boston, Massachusetts, the cost of an ordination of a Pedobaptist minister was between two and three hundred dollars. The bill for the ardent article was not small.

† Ordination balls were among these amusements. On consulting a minister of that order as to the truth of these reports, he observed, that although such balls were sometimes had, yet he did not think they

A very good practice has latterly been adopted by
our people, in some places, namely, of having a meeting of the ordainers beforehand, to examine candidates
and see if matters are all right, so as to guard against
the unpleasant delays which sometimes occur on such
occasions.

The *installation* of ministers, by which term is
meant the settling again those who have been ordained, is seldom heard of among the Baptists, at the
present time. Formerly, the thing was quite common among the Pedobaptists, and, in rare cases, it
was practiced by our people.

If this harmless custom would help to keep ministers longer in their stations, it might be well for us
to revive it.

Old-Fashioned Pulpits among the Baptists.

In their construction, no uniformity was apparent,
but, as a general thing, they were of small dimensions,
a good deal elevated in their positions ; and a sound-
ing-board overhead, and a pulpit window, were regarded as indispensable fixtures.

Dr. Stillman's pulpit in Boston looked strange to
me when I first saw it, as it had no window in com-

had been common.   I never heard of any thing of the kind amongst
the Baptists, and my impression is that they have seldom occurred
among the old order, of late years.

mon style. On inquiry, I learned it had been closed
by the Doctor's request, to avoid a current of air on
his back, from a large tide-water millpond in the rear
of the house. This pond was long since filled up and
built over.

The pulpit in which Calvin preached, is said to
have been thirty feet high. From his time, preaching stands have gradually declined in height, till
they are nearly on a level with the people.

I will here repeat a few remarks on the proper
form of a pulpit, made to me lately by a young
preacher, who had left the law for the ministry.
"When," said he, "I used to address a jury, I
wanted a clear space between us, that I might watch
their eyes and their countenances, to see what effect
my arguments had on their minds ; and now, when
I address the people, I want but a simple platform,
and nothing in front of it ; then, with brief in hand,
or with none at all, I feel at home, as I can move
about, and talk to my hearers, as lawyers do to
juries."

Fifty years ago, and at a somewhat later period, I
was generally sorry to hear of the conversion of
ministers of distinction of other creeds, to our side ;
and the reason was, that they might become disappointed and discontented, and go back with evil reports of our land, and especially of the parsimony

of our people, in most cases, in the support of ministers, and in their doings generally in aid of benevolent undertakings. About that time we had some unpleasant cases of the kind to which I now allude.

SECOND DECADE.

ON THE RISE OF THE FOREIGN MISSION CAUSE
AMONG THE AMERICAN BAPTISTS.

CHAPTER VIII.

JUDSON AND RICE BECOME BAPTISTS.—THE TRIENNIAL CONVENTION.
—THE MISSIONARY UNION.—RICE BECOMES AN AGENT.—THE CO-
LUMBIAN COLLEGE DIFFICULTIES ABOUT MISSIONARY MONEY.—
DEATH OF RICE.

ABOUT FORTY YEARS AGO the dormant energies
of our denomination in this country began to be
aroused in favor of some systematic efforts in favor
of sending the gospel to the heathen. The cause of
this movement may be traced to the conversion of
Adoniram Judson and Luther Rice to the sentiments
of the Baptists, while on their way to India as missionaries, under the patronage of the Pedobaptists.
This unexpected change in these two young men, as
a matter of course, made no small stir in the Pedobaptist ranks, as might be naturally expected. Mr. Judson at the time of his baptism, in Calcutta, preached a
sermon on the baptismal controversy, which was re-
published and widely circulated in this country. This
became the subject of much comment among his former associates, and laid the foundation of an extended
controversy between the advocates and the opponents
of the Baptist cause. A copy of the original Calcutta
edition of this discourse is among my documents of
this kind.

Mr. Rice soon returned to America to solicit pecuniary aid for assisting in establishing a Baptist mission in the East, and to select suitable persons for an
undertaking to which the attention of the American
Baptists was now directed in a sudden and unexpected manner.

Up to this time, this large and increasing body
seemed to have had no idea that they had either the
call or the ability to send out missionaries to foreign
lands. The maximum of their doings thus far in the
enterprise in which they have since so largely engaged at home and abroad, consisted in the support
of a few feeble societies for the promotion of domestic
missions.

It ought here to be mentioned, however, that
amidst the general apathy and neglect of our people
thus referred to, something had been done in a few
locations in the early part of the foreign mission enterprise, in the following manner: the reports which
frequently came to this country of the successful operations of our British brethren in India, under Carey, Marshman, Ward, and others, and particularly of
their wonderful progress in the translating department, had excited a generous sympathy among a portion of our brethren in Boston, Salem, Philadelphia,
and a few other places, which led them to make liberal collections for that age, in favor of their distant de-

nominational friends. But still neither this portion of
our community, nor any other, then contemplated the
undertaking of sending out missionaries on their own
account to the East, the West, or in any other direction. Nor as yet was it considered possible to adopt
any feasible plan for commencing missionary operations amongst the numerous tribes of the American
Indians. Dr. Carey, then in India, wrote to Dr. Baldwin, of Boston, on the subject, at an early period, and
inquired why the American Baptists did not direct
their attention towards the bringing of the aborigines
of our western wilds under the influence of civiliza-
tion and Christianity.   Dr. Baldwin, in reply to his
distant friend, named, among other things, the want
of a written language among the red men, as one of
the greatest impediments in the way of all attempts
in their favor, and little did he, or any of his cowork-
ers in the cause of benevolence, expect that in so short
a time after this correspondence, this then insurmountable difficulty would be surmounted. Very remote, in
their view, was the period when the untamed and
wandering red men of our distant and uncultivated
forests would advance to the positions which they
now occupy as an enlightened and Christian people.

Mr. Rice becomes a successful Agent in the Foreign Mission Cause.

Soon after his arrival from India, this zealous and laborious young man commenced the most successful agency, the circumstances under which he commenced it being considered, that was ever performed among the American Baptists. His native eloquence, his unusual affability of manners, and his untiring assiduity, made him at once a distinguished favorite with his new denominational friends, and secured for him unusual attention and respect from many who were out of the pale of the Baptist communion. Young people, old people, and all people hailed his approach to their firesides and the pulpits of their churches, as a young apostle in the foreign mission cause, which was always on his lips, not only in his public addresses, but in public houses, in public conveyances, in the family circle, and wherever he traveled or sojourned. Being a man of a robust frame and of vigorous powers, both of body and mind, he was enabled to perform an unusual amount of labor in his new vocation. At that time, railroads were unknown, steamboats were comparatively few, and stage-coaches were costly and uncomfortable ; and as his business led him in all directions through the country, to be present at associations and public gatherings of all kinds, where he could tell his story and make known his wants, he generally traveled in his own one-horse light conveyance, and he often astonished his brethren with the rapidity of his movements and the suddenness of his transitions from one place to another.

Mr. Rice, in his public performances, dwelt but little on sectarian matters, but the deplorable condition of the perishing heathen was his principal theme; and although he had resided but a short time in a heathen land, yet he had seen and heard enough while there, to impart a vividness to his descriptions of the darkness, wretchedness and cruelty of that land, far superior to those which are made from mere reports. It was expected at first, by himself and friends, that he would return to India after he had made arrangements for a regular and adequate support of a mission there, under the patronage of the Baptists in this country. This plan was always uppermost in all his public addresses and private conversations, and added greatly to their interest among the people wherever he went. He soon traversed the whole of the United States, and formed an acquaintance of great extent, and at an early day, by means of printed circulars, which were scattered broadcast over the land, and letters of his own writing, this industrious man opened a correspondence with all who had shown any sympathy for the cause in which he

was engaged. Soon societies of various kinds arose
in all directions, for the promotion of this new undertaking, and thus a foundation was laid for the formation of

The Old Baptist Triennial Convention.

This body was organized in Philadelphia, in May,
1814, and under its direction all Baptist affairs pertaining to foreign missions, for about thirty years,
were managed, when the name of the body was exchanged for that of the

American Baptist Missionary Union.

This change was made in New York, in May, 1845.
This was a time of great trial and difficulty with the
old Convention, which was seriously threatened with
dissolution, on account of questions which for a number of years had been agitated in a very unpleasant
manner. The perplexing discrepancies which arose
between the northern and southern wings, of a body
which was spread over all the States, was the principal cause of the troubles here alluded to.

The Missionary Union came into being in a very
amicable manner at first, but soon objections, from
some quarters, were started against some parts of its
constitution, as not conformable to Baptist principles
and usages, and these objections still exist in the

minds of many ; and added to these, complaints from
various quarters against the management of the men
at the missionary rooms have become loud and wide-
spread, and now, March, 1857, very serious difficulties are apprehended at the approaching anniversary
of this important Baptist institution.

*Mr. Rice connected other Objects with his Missionary
Agency.*

These were two periodicals, and a college at Washington for Baptist use, with reference, in the first place,
I believe, to fitting men for the missionary service.

In this place it may be proper to give a brief account of these three undertakings of Mr. Rice.

The Latter Day Luminary was in pamphlet form,
and was continued six years. It was under the patronage of the General Convention, as the organ of that
body, and for the first two years of its existence it
was published in Philadelphia, when it was removed
to Washington. Staughton, Allison, H. G. Jones
and Rice constituted its publishing committee at first,
but Rice was the life and soul of the concern. He
calculated, when he undertook the work, that it would
require about one fourth of his time.

The Columbian Star was in the newspaper form,
and it is still alive in Georgia, under the name of the
Christian Index. It was transferred to this State

many years since by the late Dr. J. Mercer, the liberal and untiring helper of the foreign mission cause.
While this paper was published in Washington, the
place of its origin, among its editors in succession
were J. D. Knowles, late of Newton, and Dr. Stow,
now of Boston.

But the *Columbian College*, now in a flourishing condition at Washington, D. C., was the greatest labor
of Mr. Rice's life, and one which for many years involved him and his friends in much embarrassment
and perplexity. " This institution," says Mr. Taylor
in his memoir of its founder, "was never completed
according to its original plan. All the buildings, in
the language of the superintending committee, were
intended to range with the cardinal points of the com-
pass, and to exhibit the best possible view from every
direction, combining economy, utility, convenience
and magnificence."

Thus we see that Mr. Rice in a few years after he
commenced his agency for the foreign cause, had his
hands full of appendages to his main employment.
All admitted that his projects were praiseworthy and
promising, but many complained that they absorbed
too large an amount of the funds which had been contributed for mission purposes only. As pecuniary
embarrassments came on, much of the attention of the
managers of one wing of the Convention was engaged

in examining and setting right the alleged stretches of power in the diversion of funds by the other. Every new project had its advocates and opponents, and in some of the meetings, which I attended, it was about as much as those who had no cause, or other interests at stake could do, to calm the troubled waters, in which they found themselves most disagreeably involved. A number of the meetings now had in view were scenes of trial rather than enjoyment. The sacredness of missionary funds was always most strenuously insisted on by men on one side; and this doctrine was fully conceded by those on the other; and if at any time the treasury had been drawn upon for secondary objects, the explanation was, that it was in loans from the main department, in aid of those of minor importance, which were soon to be repaid by the commanding eloquence and herculean efforts of a hitherto most successful solicitor, in favor of his various undertakings, all of which promised well for the missionary cause and the Baptist community at large. New periodicals might be useful in their way, if they would support themselves, which was the doctrine of their friends; and a new institution for literary and theological training was greatly needed for a vast range of our country; and its being located at the capital of the nation was considered a most auspicious arrangement, and all parts of Mr. Rice's complicated machinery seemed to work well and to general satisfaction, until an empty treasury and unsatisfied demands upon it to an alarming amount stared the whole denomination in the face. Most of these demands were for the collegiate institution, and poor Rice, on account of his position and agency, had to bear the blame of his coadjutors and confederates. "It can not be concealed," says Taylor in his memoir, "that others who had the management of the institution greatly erred in allowing him to sustain so much of the burden incident to the erection of the buildings, the support of the faculty, and the payment of the debts. And at the time when a system of retrenchment had just been commenced; when vigorous efforts were about to be made by him especially to raise funds in the South for the entire extinguishment of the debt, such was the strong feeling against him that he was called home and detained there for a series of months in the investigation of his accounts."

As the result of these investigations, which were made by a committee appointed for the purpose, a long report was drawn up, which is among my historical documents, which exhibits a heavy balance against Mr. Rice.

To this report is appended a certificate that it was unanimously accepted.   Signed,

B. S., *Secretary.*

Directly under this is the following:

I certify that the foregoing report was not *unanimously* accepted.   O. B. B., *President.*

Too much of the feeling and cross firing here indicated, had at an early period unhappily become somewhat common among some of the managers of this then embarrassed concern.

Mr. Rice's heavy indebtedness to the Convention resulted from his assuming personal responsibility in all his doings in behalf of that body. No one to my knowledge suspected him of appropriating any of the moneys he collected to his own use.

The following extracts from a letter of Dr. Baldwin, of Boston, to Mr. Rice, exhibit his views relative to the diversion of missionary funds from their original design:

"BOSTON, November 22, 1819.

"* * * You mention the unfavorable impression which the result of the late meeting of the Board in New York had on the minds of our friends, at the South and West. I do not perceive in what way it should affect them. I have been apprised of Dr. Furman's dissatisfaction with the proceedings relative to the institution generally. * * * It must be evident to Dr. F. and to every other person, upon the slightest observation, that the institution was not set in motion in conformity to the *principle* established by the Convention, viz., 'when competent and distinct funds shall have been raised for that purpose, the Board shall proceed to institute a classical and theological seminary, etc.' It will not be pretended that *competent* funds distinctly assigned for that object have been raised, either before, at the time, or even since the establishment of the seminary. This hasty, unauthorized procedure is probably the ground of Dr. Furman's objections. For my own part, though I would not adopt the principle that the end sanctifies the means, yet if the institution can be supported without resorting at all to the funds of the society, I shall wish it success with all my heart. But there is an extreme tenderness with respect to these funds manifested from all parts of the country. Indeed, they ought and must be held sacred for the object for which they were given.

"I suggested to Dr. Staughton, some little time since, and I will now take the liberty to mention the same thing to you respecting the Luminary. The blending of this with the missionary concern, you probably know, has given much uneasiness to many of the friends of the mission. It was so different from what we had reason to expect that we hardly knew how to account for it. * * *

"I am, dear sir, very respectfully your fellow laborer in the kingdom and patience of Jesus Christ,   THOMAS BALDWIN."

About this time a long letter was addressed to Mr. Rice by the late Judge Tallmadge, of New York, then in Charleston, S. C., relative to the grounds of Dr. Furman's dissatisfaction, etc., which were much the same as those expressed by Dr. Baldwin and others.

But notwithstanding the objections alluded to above, such was the demand for the institution in question, that its prosperity was earnestly desired by the denomination at large, and very liberal contributions were made for its support, and for the liquidation of its debts, which was finally accomplished.*

---

* Among these debts was a loan of $10,000 from the late J. Q. Adams. For the payment of this sum, at my instance, while I was a

In process of time the college was entirely separated from the Convention, both as to its government
and its pecuniary concerns, and a large number of
agents entered the field, which was then the whole
United States, to collect funds for the one, while Mr.
Rice devoted all his time and energies in favor of his
favorite literary institution. And as he was never mar-
ried, to this object of his kindest affections, in his own
familiar language, he was wedded for life; for it he
lived, and labored mostly in the southern States, and
in its service he finished his laborious, peculiar, and
earthly career, in South Carolina, in 1836, at the age
of fifty-three.

member of the Board, a mortgage was given on the college premises.
My argument was, that as Mr. Adams loaned this large sum in good
faith, to a denomination with which he had no connection, in the crippled state of the institution, he ought to have as good security as could
be given him. This fact I had the pleasure of stating to the President
in his own house in Washington. This business was finally settled to
the satisfaction of this distinguished benefactor.

CHAPTER IX.

As Mr. Rice acted so conspicuous a part in the
early movements of our society in their foreign mission enterprise, and as I was familiar with all his doings in this business, it seems suitable that in this
place I should record a few facts respecting him. My
familiar intercourse with this laborious man commenced soon after his return from India, and my
friendship for him remained firm to the last, notwithstanding all the complaints of his bad financiering,
etc. " As a financier," says his biographer, " he certainly did not excel, and the formation of contracts,
the disbursement of funds, and even the duties of
treasurer should have been committed to other hands.
His own were full of other matters." But this was
the way things were managed in those times, not only
by our society, but by some others, at the hazard of
troublesome embarrassments of long continuance.

With the go-ahead disposition of Mr. Rice I was pleased from the first of my acquaintance with him, and as we were about equal in age, as I heartily entered into his views of attempting to call the attention of the American Baptists to the plan of a mission in India, and as from my then recent experience in the traveling line, I could give him needful information, as to men, places, etc., an intimacy commenced between us, which continued through all the varieties of his eventful life.

My epistolary correspondence with this assiduous agent in the foreign mission cause was long, frequent, and familiar; and copies of almost all the circulars, and other printed papers, which he frequently sent abroad, for the promotion of his various undertakings, are among my historical documents. And, in addition to these, I have a volume of more than two hundred letters addressed to this very popular agent, from 1813, and onward, in answer to his inquiries respecting his benevolent designs. In these letters are found the autographs of nearly every prominent minister then on the stage of action among the American Baptists; also of a considerable number of those of laymen, in distinguished positions, both mercantile and official. A small portion of the letters here referred to were written by missionaries in the East, English as well as American. In looking over this file I have

often been agreeably struck with the tone of cordial
approbation of the mission then on foot, and of the
encouragement held out to this new agent and solicitor.   Here, and there, and everywhere, he was invited
to spread the cause before the people, and ask for contributions for its support.   Probably never was an important undertaking set in motion among our people
with so much unanimity, or under circumstances so
auspicious.   All the active friends of this new enterprise were pleased with the sudden and surprising
change in the denomination in this matter.

A few of these early correspondents of Mr. Rice,
of this friendly cast, whose kind epistles are before
me, did, indeed, soon turn against both him and his
work, and became zealous supporters of the anti-
mission cause.   These men were generally, if not
altogether, found in the southern and western regions.
As the efforts in favor of the missionary cause extended, its opponents increased in their number and
zeal, until in the churches and associations of our order, in this country, which oppose all organized efforts
for the support of missions at home and abroad, are
about sixty thousand members; a number nearly
equal to all the Baptists in America, in John As-
plund's time, a little more than sixty years ago.   But
as these opposing members, whose mistakes we all de-
plore, have, from the first, generally been of the do-

nothing class at home, the work might have still gone on without any serious impediment, and without so many agents in the field, as there have been from the time that Mr. Rice left it, had not too many of the denomination left their first love for this work, and settled down into a state of apathy and neglect respecting it. To this too numerous class of our members, the term, not ANTI-, but OMISSION, or NON-MISSION Baptists, has been very properly applied, by some of our writers on this subject.

CORRESPONDENCE OF MR. RICE WITH MISSIONARIES IN INDIA.

MR. RICE TO DR. MARSHMAN OF SERAMPORE, IN 1813.

* * * "Notwithstanding the war, it will be very practicable for me to return to India by way of Brazil—perhaps by the way of the Cape of Good Hope. And I am exceedingly rejoiced to find that the Lord is putting it into the hearts of our brethren in this country to come up to the help of the Lord against the mighty. The effort, I have no doubt, will be beneficial to the Baptist interest in this country—will advance the cause of piety and truth here—besides the good to the heathen which will, with a divine blessing, result from it."

MR. RICE TO MR. JUDSON IN 1814.

* * * "The Baptist Board for Foreign Missions, instituted by the Convention, readily undertook your support and mine, but thought it necessary for me to continue my labors in this country, for a time. I hope, however, in the course of five or six months, to get the Baptists so well rallied, that the necessity of my remaining will no longer exist. And I certainly wish not to remain here a moment longer than my stay will more advance the mission than my departure for the field again."

Mr. Judson to Mr. Rice, from Rangoon, in 1816.

* * * " You remember that the furlough which we gave you at the Isle of France, extended to two years only. Little did we then think that three or four years would elapse before we met again. I rejoice, however, that you are able to give so good an account of your time. I congratulate you on the success which. has crowned your labors in America. It really surpasses my highest expectations." * * *

Mr. Judson to Mr. Rice, Rangoon, 1818.

* * * " Your mention of ten years has cut off the little hope remaining of uniting with you as an assistant in missionary labors It seems that our paths are diverging from the Isle of France, until they have terminated in scenes of labor the most remote and dissimilar possible. * * * Brother Hough and I have done pretty well together. He is just going to Bengal. * * * We should, however, be very sorry to lose him, especially as he is a printer."

Mrs. Judson to Mr. Rice, from Rangoon, in 1819.

* * * " At the end of six years' residence in this country Mr. Judson finds himself *still alone* in missionary work. * * * You, by dear brother, are the person we need just in this stage of the mission. Your age, judgment, and experience, qualify you in a peculiar manner to be of most essential service in these cases of difficulty and trial to which we are so frequently subject in this country. Your correct ear, and aptness for acquiring languages, together with the means and helps which Mr. J. has prepared, would enable you in *one year* from the time of your arrival, to begin to communicate religious truths to the perishing people."

MR. JUDSON TO MR. RICE, RANGOON, 1822–23.

* * * "I little thought when the boat rowed away from the ship in the harbor of Port Royal (in the Isle of France,) and I left you standing on the deck, that I should see your face no more. Poor Nancy has gone on a pilgrimage for health and life to the shrine of old England. * * * Her absence is universally regretted by our Burman acquaintance. * * *

"You are evidently absorbed in the college. But it is a great and worthy object; and there is no truer maxim than that a man never does any thing to purpose, unless his whole soul is in it."

The Isle of France, or Mauritius, so often named in the foregoing extracts, is the place to which our American missionaries fled when they were ordered away from Calcutta by the British authorities of India, soon after they landed there.

Rev. G. H. Hough, whose name occurs above, was one of the earliest selections of Mr. Rice for the Baptist mission in the East. He still lives in Maulmein, but he has for a long time been disconnected with the missionary service, and has been a teacher under the patronage of the government of the country. Previous to his going to the East, he with his small family had resided with me about two years, and by him was transcribed for the press most of my old History of the Baptists. This scene carries us back almost fifty years. Very few of the men who were identified with the incipient movements in our foreign mission cause are still alive, and *our* connection with the board of managers ceased about the same time.   I

went out by rotation; he in consequence of some dislike of the board, or at least of some of its influential
members. In anticipation of Mr. Hough's dismission,
as his personal friend, and as a matter of justice to a
man for whose repudiation I saw no adequate cause,
I asked for and secured the passage of a vote for the
payment of the passage home, for himself and family,
should he choose to return. But as he had become familiar with the country, its language, customs, etc.,
he chose to remain and support himself.

From the letters and journals of Mr. Hough, and
by means of my correspondence with other missionaries in India, who were early on the ground, English
as well as American, I became somewhat familiar with
the management of missionary affairs, both at home
and abroad; and was often sorry to find that serious
complaints were made, both by the home managers
and the foreign laborers; on the part of the managers
the principal complaints were of too independent action in the foreign field, of disobedience, insubordi-
nation, and of thinking too much for themselves. On
the other side, the terms partiality, favoritism, prejudice, neglect, dictation, etc., were not unfrequently employed by the missionaries. I learned more in detail
in these matters than was ever published in missionary documents, or than I am now disposed to repeat.
Let oblivion rest upon them all.

In these early operations there was a want of system in their doings, and especially in reporting them at home. " We want to hear oftener from the missionaries," was often said by their friends and supporters. "Well," said Dr. Going on one occasion, " we hear from them often enough about *sicca rupees*, if not of other matters." *Sicca* was generally appended to the name of this coin in those times.

I was always anxious to hear about the manners and customs of the heathen in their every-day transactions, and how their educated and thinking men could swallow the monstrous dogmas of the heathen mythology. When Mr. Ward was in this country, whose two large quarto volumes on the History, Literature, and Mythology, of the Hindoos, I had previously carefully perused, I had a number of interesting conversations with him on these matters, and in answer to a number of my inquiries he made the following replies:

" We have men of great literary attainments, in some departments, and of strong mental powers, but their minds are so beclouded with the superstitions with which they have always been surrounded that they do not stop to reason on the characters of their innumerable deities, of whom they often speak with great disrespect, and whom they are taught to *fear*, but not to *love*. Nothing like the Christian doctrine

of the love of God, is inculcated in the religion of the
Hindoos.

"And as to the most important trait of character of
this people, in their every-day transactions, it is this:
A Hindoo will follow you from morning till night,
and his constant cry is, money, money, money."

As to the languages of the East, which our missionaries must acquire before they can enter on their work,
I never studied them but in an historical manner, so as
to gain information respecting their general construction, their pedigrees, and their elemental characters.

At an early period Dr. Marshman sent to Dr. Gano
and myself a copy of his Chinese Grammar, and his
translation of a portion of the Old Testament into that
language. The grammar is a quarto volume of upwards of six hundred pages. From a partial study
of this work I learned something of the general character of this singular language, but for the want of a
living teacher I made but little progress in acquiring
a knowledge of this ancient and multiform tongue.

At this time the exclusive policy of the Chinese
government, which has since been materially modified, rendered it difficult to do any thing with this
singular people, or to acquire a knowledge of their
language, except among those who were settled outside of the empire.

The *Sanscrit*, the sacred language of India, and

which, like the Latin, is the foundation of many others, I never studied at all; but from what I learned of its history I became well satisfied that from this ancient oriental tongue, some portions of the English language were derived. The reasoning for the support of this theory is as follows: in unknown ages past, portions of the Sanscrit language traveled westward, through Persia and other countries, and finally settled down among the Celts, in Europe; and from them they found their way into the vocabulary of our Anglo-Saxon progenitors.

Strange relationships of this kind are sometimes discovered by comparing languages of very remote origin together. A long time since I somewhere read from the writings of Martin, or some other English missionary, that he often found old acquaintances in the Persian language. A similar idea, if I remember right, was advanced by Dr. Mason, one of our missionaries in India, in one of the able and scientific communications, which came from his pen, during his late visit to this country.

I do not want all our missionaries in foreign fields to spend much time on matters not absolutely needful for their main employment; but I am pleased to see some exhibit much depth of research in literary pursuits, and the more so as it fulfills my predictions to which I lately referred.

With the apostles at first no study of other tongues was needful, but now without this study nothing can be done for the heathen; and how much have I regretted that so many of our men in the East, who by severe labor have become able to preach to the natives, should on any account be diverted from this important work.

CHAPTER X.

NEW PHASES IN THE DOCTRINAL CREED OF THE BAPTISTS.—THE FULLER SYSTEM COMES INTO VOGUE.—ON THE CHANGES WHICH FOLLOWED.

FORTY YEARS AGO large bodies of our people were in a state of ferment and agitation, in consequence of some modifications of their old Calvinistic creed, as displayed in the writings of the late Andrew Fuller, of Kettering, England. This famous man maintained that the atonement of Christ was general in its nature, but particular in its application, in opposition to our old divines, who held that Christ died for the elect only. He also made a distinction between the natural and moral inability of men.

Dr. John Gill, of London, was, in his day, one of the most distinguished divines among the English Baptists, and as he was a noted advocate for the old system of a limited atonement, the terms "Gillites" and "Fullerites" were often applied to the parties in this discussion. Those who espoused the views of Mr. Fuller were denominated Arminians by the Gillite men, while they, in their turn, styled their opponents Hyper-Calvinists. Both parties claimed to be orthodox and evangelical, and differed but little on any other points except those which have been named. On Election, the Trinity, etc., they all agreed.

In the age when this discussion arose among the American Baptists, as none of the modern subjects of agitation had been introduced into their churches, the speculative opinions thus briefly described, for a number of years were the occasion of unhappy debates and contentions in many locations.

Our old Baptist divines, especially those of British descent, were generally strong Calvinists as to their doctrinal creed, and but few of them felt at liberty to call upon sinners in plain terms to repent and believe the gospel, on account of their inability to do so without divine assistance. They could preach the gospel before the unconverted, but rousing appeals to their consciences on the subject of their conversion did not constitute a part of their public addresses.

In expatiating on the strong points of their orthodox faith they sometimes ran Calvinism up to seed, and were accused by their opponents of Antinomian tendencies. In that age it was customary for many of our ministers to dwell much on the decrees and purposes of God, to dive deep, in their way, into the plans of Jehovah in eternity, and to bring to light, as they supposed, the hidden treasures of the gospel, which they, in an especial manner, were set to defend. In doing this they discoursed with as much confidence as if they were certain that they were not wise above what is written, but had given a true report of the secrets of the skies.

This extreme of orthodoxy has been followed by laxity and indifference.

The Philadelphia Confession of Faith, published in that city, in 1742, was the standard of most of the oldest Baptist churches in this country, especially in the middle and southern States. This Confession was copied mostly from one published by the Baptists in London, in 1689, and this again agreed in its doctrinal sentiments with the Westminster Confession.

The old Baptists in New England, although, for the most part, they held with their brethren elsewhere the doctrines of Depravity, Election, Divine Sovereignty, Final Perseverance, etc., yet they were not in the habit of enforcing them so strongly as were those in New York, Philadelphia, and further South.

That class of Baptists which arose out of the *New-light* stir in New England, which, as I have before stated, sent colonies into all the southern States, and in the second generation, over the mountains into the West, were Calvinists of a still milder type. Indeed, their orthodoxy was often called in question by the old school party in Virginia, the Carolinas and Kentucky. These zealous reformers, in their public performances dwelt mostly on the subjects of Christian experience and practical religion, while the strait Calvinists labored much to explain and defend the strong points of their system.

The kind of preaching now much in vogue, at the period and among the people here had in view, would have been considered the quintessence of Arminianism, mere milk and water, instead of the strong meat of the gospel. Then, and with our orthodox Baptists, a sermon would have been accounted altogether defective which did not touch upon Election, Total Depravity, Final Perseverance, etc.

"Total depravity," said a good sister to her minister, "must be as true as the Bible. So I read and so I feel. But your new-fangled way of preaching goes to undermine it, and to make people much better than they are, and also to make them think they can do something for themselves. I know that I am totally depraved. I tell you, Elder ———, this kind of preaching will never do. You take away my depravity and you take away my all." "O, no, my good sister," said the elder, "I hope not; I think better of you than that; I think there would be something left still." With a hearty laugh on both sides the discussion closed.

In my early day the Associated Baptists were all professedly Calvinistic in their doctrinal sentiments. The term, however, was not agreeable to many, as they did not subscribe to all the sentiments of John Calvin, but they submitted to it for distinction sake, and in contradistinction from those whose views were less orthodox on Predestination, etc. Beside the people of our order in the associations, the Freewill and Seventh Day Baptists were then coming into notice, and they, with but few exceptions among the Sabbatarians, were decidedly opposed to some of the distinguishing doctrines of the Calvinistic creed. The Methodists, too, who often came in contact with the Baptists, and with whom I frequently associated in my early travels, were extremely severe in their feelings and comments on the orthodox faith, so far as Election, etc., were concerned. Some of their circuit riders of that age conducted as if they considered themselves predestinated to preach against Predestination. And some of our illiterate elders were about a match for them against the Wesleyan creed. And the cry of fatalism on the one hand, and of salvation by works on the other, was continually sounded by the parties.

I was often not a little surprised at the bitterness of feeling which, in many cases, was displayed by the anti-Calvinists against the doctrine of Election, and of their readiness, in season and out of season, to assail it by reason and ridicule. Many could hardly be civil towards their opponents, who were silent all the while.

I well remember, to me, at the time, a very striking instance of this kind. A minister of another class of Baptists, but who had rendered me essential service in my historical pursuits, amused a large company in a public house, in which we happened to be at the time, and which company, also, happened to be of his own way of thinking, by repeating, evidently for my special benefit, some doggerel verses, the chorus of which was,

> "Then fill up the glass, and count him an ass
> Who preaches up predestination."

But for many years past the asperity of feeling above described has been a good deal mollified, so that the differing men can meet together without taunting each other with their offensive creeds. On this subject I lately remarked to a Freewill Baptist minister, "Your side has been coming up, and ours has been going down, till the chasm between the two parties is by no means so great as formerly."

On the introduction of the Fuller system a very important change followed on the part of many of our ministers in their mode of addressing their unconverted hearers on the subjects of repentance and believing the gospel. Hitherto they would use circumlocution in their discourses on these matters, instead of direct appeals and exhortations to those whose conversion they desired. They would describe the lost condition of

sinners and point out the duty of all men to repent
and believe the gospel ; but beyond this, their views
of consistency with the doctrine which ascribes the
whole work of salvation to God alone, would not permit them to go. As a general thing, the discourses
of that age were very dull and monotonous, and were
greatly deficient in the pathos and fervor of that class
of evangelical preachers who were not trammeled by
such rigid rules in their theological creed. Church
members then received much more attention from our
public speakers, than those who stood without its pale.
At times men of more than ordinary zeal would over-
leap the bounds of their restricted rules, but with
studied caution in their use of terms; and I well remember with what ingenuity and dexterity this class
of preachers would so manage their addresses to their
unconverted hearers, as to discourse to them much in
the style of reputed Arminians, and yet retain the
substance of the stereotyped phraseology of their orthodox creed.

The Fuller system, which makes it consistent for
all the heralds of the gospel to call upon men everywhere to repent, was well received by one class of
our ministers, but not by the staunch defenders of the
old theory of a limited atonement. According to their
views, all for whom Christ suffered and died would
certainly be effectually called and saved. These con-

flicting opinions caused altercations of considerable
severity for a time, among the Baptists, who had
hitherto been all united on the orthodox side. The
Gillites maintained that the expositions of Fuller were
unsound, and would subvert the genuine gospel faith.
If, said they, the atonement of Christ is general in its
nature it must be so in its effects, as none of his sufferings will be in vain; and the doctrine of universal salvation will inevitably follow this dangerous
creed. While the dispute went on, it was somewhat
difficult for the Fullerites to pass muster, on the score
of orthodoxy, with the old school party, or be on
terms of entire cordiality with them. But so greatly has the standard of orthodoxy been lowered, even
among those who are reputed orthodox, from former
times, and so little attention do most of our church
members of the present day pay to the doctrines which
are advanced by their ministers, that this whole story
will probably be new to most of them, except of the
older class.

A few persons may now be found in most of our
congregations, who are so well informed, and who pay
so much attention to the preaching they hear, that
they are able to detect any unsoundness in the doctrines advanced; but this is not so generally the case
with the great mass of our members as it was in a
former age. At present, the modes and manners, and

the eloquence of their ministers, engage more of the
attention of our people, than their doctrinal expositions; and most of all, they look for those attractions
which are pleasing to young people, and which will
collect large assemblies, and enable them to compete
with their neighbors in numbers and style.   With this
end in view, nothing that will sound harsh or unpleasant to very sensitive ears must come from the preachers; the old-fashioned doctrines of Predestination, Total Depravity, Divine Sovereignty, etc., if referred to
at all, must be by way of circumlocution and impli-
cation.   "Ever since he was settled with us," said one,
"our minister has preached up election, and still never mentions it openly."

As a general thing, now, our people hear so little,
in common conversation, in their every-day intercourse with each other, on doctrinal subjects, before,
at the time, and after they become church members,
and are so much accustomed to vague and indefinite
references to them, that, different from former years,
they have but little desire to hear them discussed.
Indeed, many of them would sit very uneasy under
discourses in which the primordial principles of the
orthdox Baptist faith should be presented in the style
of our sound old preachers of bygone years.   As
for themselves, some of them might bear this tolerably well, but they would be thinking of others and

of the adverse remarks of outside hearers, and weaker members.

In the business of ordinations, how little scrutiny is made of candidates as to their belief in the strong points of our system, compared with ages past.

While our creed, like the thirty-nine Articles, remains the same, this moderating still goes on, in theological training, in ministerial functions, and in public sentiment, and to what point of moderation we shall in time descend, it is difficult to foretell.

John Leland, although a Calvinist, was not one of the straitest class. Two grains of Arminianism, with three of Calvinism, he thought, would make a tolerably good compound.

An English statesman once said of his own church, "We have a Calvinistic creed, a Roman ritual, and an Arminian clergy." This in time may apply to us, minus the ritual, in some cases.

CHAPTER XI.

FORTY YEARS AGO, a small company of our strong
men, mostly ministers, began to falter in their course,
and eventually went over to the Unitarian side. Most
of them, up to that period, had stood firmly on the orthodox platform.

The head-quarters of this defection was at Providence, R. I., although a few of the men who were involved in it resided at no great distance, in the same
State, and in the adjoining regions.

As is usual in such cases, the men in question were
very zealous in propagating their new opinions. And
as my acquaintance with them had been of long duration, and very familiar, I was at once placed in a
position to hear much of their reasoning in favor of
their new system of doctrine, and against the orthodox creed. Works of different kinds were handed
me to read, and an abundance of others were recommended for my perusal.

7

Thus situated, I resolved to set about a thorough examination of the whole Unitarian controversy, from first to last; and for this purpose I went over the most approved authors for and against the Trinitarian doctrine, with a determination to follow my convictions of truth on this subject, wherever they should lead me. Hitherto my mind had been at ease on the divinity of Christ, and on all that pertains to the Trinitarian creed. Like the Christians of the early ages, or before the rise of Arianism, I received this creed as a part of the Christian religion, with all the mysteries connected with it, which I did not feel bound to explain, nor at liberty to reject.

I had been accustomed to rank the anti-Trinitarian party under two heads, namely, Socinians and Arians, but I soon found my views on this point were very imperfect, and that their subdivisions were much more numerous. Wardlaw, on the Socinian controversy, has pointed out ten shades of difference among this people, varying from Humanitarianism to high Arianism. The first class make Jesus Christ a mere man, the son of Joseph and Mary, who was born, lived and died, like other men. This class, of course, reject the idea of his atoning sacrifice for sin.

The high Arians, on the other hand, make the Son of God a super-angelic being; they speak of him in the most exalted terms, and ascribe to him the highest character that a finite being can possess. But still his eternity and proper divinity they refuse to admit.

By this time I felt prepared to canvass matters with more freedom and confidence with my non-juring brethren, between one of whom and myself, in the early stage of my discussions of this kind, the follow-ing brief dialogue ensued:

A.—Good morning, brother, B.; I want to convince you that I am not such a heretic as you suppose, after all my objections to my old creed, which I, with oth-ers, have believed without due investigation.

B.—You have always been a strong advocate for the doctrines of the Trinity, and of the Divinity of Christ; none of us have defended these doctrines with more confidence and decision than yourself.

A.—This I confess with regret, and can only say with the apostle, when I was a child, I spake as a child, but when I became a man I put away childish things.

B.—All children must have time to grow; if you have got ahead of your minor brethren, be patient with them in their childhood; in due time they may become men. But tell me, my brother, what latitude you are in, and whether you find yourself in the tor-rid, the temperate, or the frigid zone of Christianity.

A.—I am in the temperate zone, to be sure; and your unkind insinuation about the frigid tendencies

of the liberal system are founded in mistake. I find
no less disposition than formerly to advocate with
fervor the vital principles of the gospel. and if they
will let me and my people alone, we shall pursue
the even tenor of our way, as we have thus far done
since I renounced the absurdities of my old orthodox
creed.

(A., as yet, held his position as pastor of an orthodox Baptist church. This connection, however, was
soon afterward dissolved.)

B.—As far as my experience in these matters has
gone, there is a natural coldness in what you call the
liberal system ; and if I am not mistaken in my observations, those who embrace it in preference to the
orthodox faith, soon entertain different views of human nature, and of all that pertains to sin and redemption ; they also make but little account of that
vital experimental religion, which you have heretofore so strenuously enforced.

A.—I have no idea of going thus far in the doctrinal speculations in which I am now engaged.

B.—Permit me again to enquire, what advances
you have made in these speculations, and what sort of
a theological skeleton you have got up, by your new
anatomizing process ? John Huss, in his day, published a piece entitled, *The Anatomy of Antichrist*, in
which he exhibited all the different parts of the body

of the Man of Sin, and their operations. Show me some of the bones of your skeleton, and I will give you my opinion respecting them. Some anatomists, we are informed, are so skillful in their art, that when you show them a bone, they will inform you to what animal it belonged, and from what part of the animal it came. I do not pretend to be thus expert in theological anatomy, but still I have some general idea of the different parts of the broad Unitarian platform.

A.—I begin with the great first principle of true religion, the *divine unity ;* and my main object, in all I say and do, is to assert and maintain this unity, in a consistent and intelligible manner; and my investigations thus far have led me most decidedly to reject the old Trinitarian notion of three persons in the godhead of equal dignity and power. The downright tritheism of this creed I can no longer endure.

B.—Please to give me your present opinion of the character of Jesus Christ, in distinction from your former belief.

A.—Well, I have no fellowship with the Humanitarians, who make Christ a mere man; they go as far in one extreme as the Trinitarians do in the other. The real Son of God, in my estimation, is exalted far above prophets and apostles, angels and archangels, and all the most glorious beings in the universe; indeed, I ascribe to him the highest titles of honor and perfection, except those which imply underived and essential divinity.

B.—Well, my good brother, you have now come to the point, and have shown me some of the bones of your skeleton, which certainly belong to the Arian system; and at present I shall set you down as an Arian of the strongest kind. Indeed, the term " high Arianism" would not be improperly applied to the doctrines you have now advanced. And yet your most lofty conceptions, and most labored expressions in my opinion fall infinitely below the Scripture account of the genuine character of the Son of God.

At this point, with mutual expressions of fraternal respect, we parted from each other.

In the course of my investigation and inquiries concerning the new theory of my dissenting brethren, I observed, on their part, a growing disposition to lower the standard of piety and to tolerate almost all sorts of opinions except those of the orthodox class; but on these I found them exceedingly severe. I also noticed that the old-fashioned ideas among the Baptists, respecting human depravity, conviction and conversion, and what they call the religion of the heart, were but lightly esteemed among the smooth theologists of the liberal school; and, furthermore, that by many of these men, as they advanced in their course, all such fanatical notions were treated with ridicule and contempt. And still more, I ascertained that Unitarians of the highest culture and of the greatest influence were Universalists at heart. This information I obtained in the following manner: when I was collecting materials for my work on *All Religions*, in which I exhibit the sentiments of all sects and parties in their own language, I called on prominent men of all creeds, in the principal cities, from Boston and vicinity, to the city of Washington; and among the rest I had free conversations with Dr. Kirkland, then President of Harvard University, and with Dr. Freeman, then pastor of the King's Chapel, so called, in Boston. I spent an evening with Dr. Kirkland, but our conversation was of a general character. He referred me to Dr. Freeman, who, at the time, was regarded as the corypheus ef the party in this country, with whom I spent a much longer time. This was at a time when Unitarianism was rapidly gaining ground in Massachusetts, especially in Boston, often at the expense of the old orthodox party. I found this amiable old gentleman very free and communicative, and apparently entirely willing to open to me the depths of the Unitarian system. While we were discussing the probabilities of the future theology of Harvard College, I well remember his remarks, and the emphasis with which they were made. To the question, " whether Unitarianism was sure to continue the pre-

dominant theology in that institution?" he answered,
" No, there is no certainty that our doctrine will continue in the ascendant there for a great length of time.
You may live," continued he, "to see great changes
at Cambridge, and so you may at Andover."

The main design of this episode I will now bring
out: after the venerable old man had made some free
disclosures of the primordial principles of the Unitarian faith, I said, " Why, you must then be Universalists at bottom." " So we are," was his quick reply,
" as we have no idea of the endless punishment of the
wicked."

A little before this interview there had been a very
sharp controversy between two strong men, the one
a Universalist, of Boston, the other a Unitarian, of
Charlestown, an adjoining town, on some denominational affairs, in which they combated each other with
all the acrimony of rival sects. Referring to this col-
lision, I inquired of my aged friend why it should so
happen, since both agreed as to the final destiny of
all mankind? " This," said the doctor, " I will explain in a few words, and I hope to your entire satisfaction:

" 1. The Universalists highly value their name;
they seek to make capital with the multitude out of
their favorite dogma from which their name is derived, and always hold it out in a prominent manner

before the people for its *ad captandum* effect, while
we suffer this dogma, to which our most thinking
men subscribe, to remain quietly at the bottom of our
system.

"2. The Unitarians are generally men of superior
intelligence, and many of the laity are in high positions, which can not be said of the mass of the Universalists, and the defenders of the liberal creed depend more upon the power of reasoning than on
popular declamation.

"3. There is nothing very strange or unusual in
the disagreement in question ; the advocates of the
endless punishment of the wicked, while they agree
on this point, have endless discords and jangles
among themselves on other matters."

My main object in all conversations of this kind
was to ascertain facts respecting all parties, but not to
debate on creeds or opinions.

At this point we slid off to other subjects.

The more I examined the system of the Unitarians,
the less I was inclined to embrace it, and at the same
time the more thoroughly I was persuaded that the
vitality of religion was less likely to remain and flour-
ish with the liberals than with the orthodox, notwithstanding all the arguments urged by the liberal party
to show that the orthodox creed tends to inactivity
and neglect of practical religion. By degrees I be-

7*

came convinced that the Unitarian system, besides
subverting my belief in the doctrines of the Trinity
and the Divinity of Christ, would naturally superin-
duce, in my mind, different views of human nature,
of human depravity, of the work of the Holy Spirit
on the minds of men, and of all that pertains to the
experience and life of a Christian. I early set about
examining all the objections which were urged by
my new teachers against the orthodox faith, particularly with regard to its mysteries, which, as they
maintained, no rational being ought to be called on
to believe. The doctrine of the mysterious union of
the divine and human nature of Jesus Christ, I observed, was exceedingly offensive to the men now in
view; and while pondering over the subject, and preparing for my next interview with them, I fell in
with some old writings which afforded me material
aid in combating their subtle arguments and expositions. The following brief extracts exhibits the spirit
of these writings:

"Divinity alone is too high to converse with man;
humanity alone is too low to converse with God; but
Jesus Christ, by uniting the divine and human nature
in his own person, was qualified to lay his hands
upon both, and bring them into a state of perfect rec-
onciliation."

"That three beings should be one being, is a proposition which contradicts reason, that is, our reasons but it does not from thence follow, that it can not be true; for there are many propositions which contradict our reason, and yet they are demonstrably true. One is, that the very first principle of all religion, the being of God. For, that any thing should exist without a cause, or that any thing should be the cause of its own existence, are propositions equally contradictory to our reason; yet one of them must be true, or nothing could have existed. All these difficulties arise from our imagining that the mode of existence of all beings must be similar to our own, that is, that they must exist in time and space, and hence proceed our embarrassments on the subject. We know that no two beings, with whose modes of existence we are acquainted, can exist on the same point and space, and that therefore they can not be one. But how far beings whose mode of existence bears no relation to time and space, may be united we can not comprehend. And, therefore, the possibility of such a union we can not positively deny.

"To attempt to explain a mystery is absurd. A mystery explained is a mystery destroyed; for, what is mystery but a thing not to be understood?

" Great is the mystery of godliness, God manifest in the flesh," etc.

As I looked around on the lives of the members
of the different parties in question, I found, as I supposed, among the orthodox, a superior activity in religious concerns of all kinds, notwithstanding all that
was said against them by the liberals of the fatalism
of their creed, and the obtuseness of mind, and indifference of feeling, which, as they affirmed, it was calculated to produce. Among this class of professors
of the Christian religion, according to my apprehen-
sion, there was much more of that godly sorrow for
sin, of that self-denial, and cross-bearing spirit which
the Saviour has enjoined on his disciples, and of that
charity, without which, according to the gospel, we are
nothing, than among those who professed to be far
their superiors in Christian knowledge and graces.
Among the adherents of the old obnoxious creed I
observed the active friends of missions, at home and
abroad, and of the various institutions of benevolence
which were then beginning to receive a large share
of the attention of evangelical Christians of different
denominations. In a word, among the believers and
advocates of the Trinity, and of the proper divinity
of Jesus Christ, and his vicarious atonement, I found
those whom I had always regarded as the best of
Christians, and whose ideas of man's ruin and remedy, of the conflicts between the flesh and the spirit,
of the worthlessness of human merit, and of salvation

by grace alone, were what I had always most cordially approved.

Some of those who went over to the Unitarians
afterwards fell back to the orthodox faith, and one
of our ministers of this class gave me an account of
his experience while under the influence of Unitarian
principles. This man had a more than ordinary share
of mental power, and was accustomed to close thinking on religious subjects.

According to his description, while on Unitarian
ground, he was often astonished at the easement of
mind which he generally felt as to all those heart-
searchings and compunctions of conscience, which he
experienced under his previous orthodox belief. Indeed, what he had before regarded of great importance
in the life of a living Christian, seemed on the new
theory to be of little account, provided the external
duties of religion were correctly performed.

I have thus related some of the leading facts of my
experience in the Unitarian school, and have presented some of the reasons which led me to give the parting hand to those of my Baptist brethren who continued in it.

During the long time which had elapsed since I
commenced the study and discussion above alluded to,
I had said nothing on the subject to the people of my
charge, either privately or in my public discourses,

but I knew that many of them well understood the
conflicts and embarrassments in which I had been involved, and from my silence respecting them, had become suspicious of my leaning towards the Unitarian creed, and with a view to set matters right, and to
allay any fears of my friends, I engaged in the preparation of a series of discourses, in which, according to
my ability, I embodied the principal arguments on
which the opposers and defenders of the orthodox system rely for the support of their respective opinions.
These discourses, seven in number, I delivered at intervals to my congregation; and as by this time I had
become somewhat familiar with all parts of the controversy, I was enabled, from a full conviction of its
truth, to take a firm stand on the orthodox side. All
the fearful forebodings of my friends, as to my theological opinions, were thenceforward dispelled.

It is now about two-score years since the process
above described was undergone, and all my observations since have disinclined me more and more from
entering the Unitarian pale. I do not say that good
men are not found in it, but their goodness is in spite
of their creed, which is too easily embraced by unre-
newed men. This system, as I understand the matter,
leans to formalism rather than to spirituality in the
concerns of religion; to a growing remissness to communion and baptism, whether of adults or infants; to

a contentment with mere pulpit eloquence, instead of heart-searching preaching; and to well-regulated forms of religious worship rather than to devotional exercises. And I have been led to suppose, that faithful church discipline, according to gospel rules, is rarely administered by churches of this class. And finally, in the early operations of the *liberal* party I found them excessively *illiberal* towards all men and all orders who dissented from their creed. But for some time past, as I am informed, a portion of them have shown a disposition to come back, in some degree, to old-fashioned practical piety, and to be dissatisfied with the system which, after all, has but little heart-felt piety in it, either in theory or practice.

As I understand the thing, there is a constant downward tendency in the Unitarian system, so far as its doctrinal creed is concerned, on the part of those who follow their speculations to their final end, till little is left of the gospel but its name; and I have often wondered that men who have gone this whole course should continue to adhere to the name and to the forms of the Christian religion.

CHAPTER XII.

The Laying On of Hands.

THIS was a practice of high antiquity in our denomination in other countries, and in this country it formerly prevailed much more extensively than at the present time. I find traces of it in the history of many of our oldest communities. In the old church in Providence, R. I., I conclude it was always in use until about the middle of the ministry of the late Dr. Gano, when it was gradually laid aside.

This practice, I infer, came to us with our ancestors from the old world, where, by some of our oldest churches, it was tenaciously adhered to as far back as their history is recorded.

The laying on of hands, as a religious rite, as far as I can learn, has always been practiced in the same manner. The candidates for church membership, after being baptized, as a final act of admission come forward to the minister, the same as those do who receive

the right hand of fellowship ; and the minister, instead of taking them by the hand, puts his hands on
their heads and prays, and then their initiation is completed.

This rite, by Episcopalians has been denominated,
familiarly, a Baptist confirmation.

Dr. Gano did not object to the thing itself, which he
admitted was a proper way of receiving church members, but he disliked the idea of its being considered a
church ordinance, which he found was the sense of a
portion of his members; and as its relinquishment all
at once would have been grievous to some of the aged
members, who were most attached to an order in this
primitive body, to all appearance from time immemorial, it was left optional for new members to come into
it under hands, or by the hand of fellowship, as they
might choose. After continuing the two forms of admission for a few years, the practice of laying on of
hands was wholly discontinued.

The church of Pawtucket, which was a branch of
the old Providence community, arose about the time
of the discontinuance of this ancient custom in the
mother body. In this new interest the practice in
question was not introduced, nor was there ever any
discussion on the subject, either at its origin, or at any
other time ; my own impressions, however, were rather favorable than otherwise towards a practice so sig-

nificant, and of such high antiquity, as the one under consideration.

The people called Six Principle Baptists, most of whom are in Rhode Island and vicinity, are the decided advocates for the practice of the laying on of hands. Their name is derived from Hebrews, vi. 1, 2, where, as they maintain, this number of Christian principles are laid down, and among them, the laying on of hands holds a conspicuous place.

The Washing of Feet.

From time immemorial this oriental custom, so often referred to in the history of the early Christians, has been observed by small groups of Baptists, in a religious manner, in different parts of this country. In early life, I was acquainted with such a company, who, being Bible Christians to the letter, felt themselves bound literally to comply with the following direction of Christ, namely: " *If I then, your Lord and Master, have washed your feet, ye also ought to wash one another's feet. For I have given you an example, that ye should do as I have done unto you.*"

The general exposition of this passage, or the sense in which most of our divines understand it, namely, that the Saviour here meant to teach his disciples humility and hospitality, did not satisfy the old-fashioned Baptists to whom I have alluded, and many others of their class. In their opinion, it was in some sense a divine institution.

Among the Mennonites, as I understand the matter, the practice of *feet washing* is still uniformly maintained, and is performed at the close of their communion service ; while with our people it has generally been discontinued. While this ancient custom was kept up, the observance of it was not confined to communion seasons, but it was performed at the close of conference meetings and social gatherings of Christian friends.

Devoting Children, or Dry Christening, Love Feasts, etc.

John Leland, in his Virginia Chronicle, in 1790, informs us that the *dry christening* ceremony prevailed to some extent in the Old Dominion at that time. This unusual rite among the Baptists, which long since went out of use, was founded on the incident of parents bringing little children to Christ to bless them, and was thus performed : as soon as circumstances would permit, after the birth of a child, the mother carried it to meeting, when the minister either took it in his arms, or laid his hands on it, thanked God for his mercy, and invoked a blessing on the little one, in a public manner. At the same time the child received its name. This rite, by those who practiced it, was called *devoting children to God,* while outsiders, as they saw no water connected with it, called it *a dry chris-tening.* It prevailed in early times in many parts of Virginia, but mostly within the bounds of the Sandy Creek Association in North Carolina, and in the wide-spread branches of that ancient and extensive com-munity. This association was founded by the *New Lights* from New England, to whom I have often al-luded, and the ceremony under consideration, I am inclined to think, originated with this people. Al-though they were thorough-going Baptists, so far as the baptismal service was concerned, yet in their early operations, they adopted a number of rules of disci-pline which were not common with the denomination then, nor before, nor since. Besides Baptism and the Lord's Supper, which usually constitute the whole of the Baptist ritual, these people held to a long list of religious rites, namely, *love feasts, laying on of hands, washing feet, anointing the sick, the right hand of fellow-ship, kiss of charity, and devoting children,* or the *dry christening.* They also held to *ruling elders, elderesses, deaconesses, and weekly communion.*

This portion of our brethren, it will be seen, la-bored to conform to all the suggestions of the Scrip-tures in their fullest extent, in the rites and rules above enumerated; but if any of their churches omit-ted any of them, this omission was freely tolerated by the more rigid party. By degrees, however, these

numerous observances of an unusual character, for
Baptists, fell into disuse, so that when I was on the
ground, more than forty years ago, the descendants
of the old New Lights in their *modus operandi* were
much like other Baptists.

*A Decline in the Use of the Terms "Brother" and
"Sister" among the Laity, and of "Elder" as applied
to Ministers.*

In my early day, among by far the largest portion
of the Baptists, the terms "*brother*" and "*sister*" were
in common use in the every-day conversation of this
people, when speaking to or of each other. This language was so familiar with them that they employed it
in all places and before all people, in the market places,
in public conveyances, on the highways, and wherever
they had occasion to speak to, or of each other. In this
respect the Baptists and Methodists were much alike
in their fraternal language with reference to each other. And what is said of former times may also be
affirmed of this time, among a very large portion
of the great Baptist family. A great change has, indeed, taken place in this business in some locations,
where much less of this old-fashioned familiarity of
speech is heard than formerly ; and this change is the
most apparent in the older and more populous parts
of the country, where forms and fashions have pro-

duced such a worldly conformity on the part of the
Baptists, that their language relative to church associates is as cold and formal as that of worldly people.
I once heard an aged minister of our order, of the popular class, whose notions were somewhat precise in
matters of this kind, complain of his country brethren, who came to the city on business affairs, for using the brotherly language too freely in the streets,
and everywhere, before all people, on all occasions,
and of calling loudly on "brother A., B.," etc., in
their worldly transactions. This language, he thought,
should only be employed in church meetings and religious doings, where it would not be desecrated by
being made too common. Of multitudes of Baptists,
of modern times, this venerable and very worthy doctor would have no occasion to complain of their being
too free and unguarded, too familiar and too method-
istical in their use of the old-fashioned terms, "brother" and "sister."

The term "elder," as a proper distinction for our
ministers of all grades, old or young, in my early day,
was, and indeed from time immemorial it has been, the
usual title for them. Office instead of age has always
been intended by it. But there has been a great
change in this respect among the more fashionable
class of Baptists in many parts of the country, where
the term *reverend* has taken the place of the old and

favorite cognomen above referred to. Still, in the country parts of the older States, and in nearly all the newer regions, the people *still* distinguish as formerly their spiritual guides. And not only so, but they often thus distinguish the ministers of other creeds. I have often been amused in our region of country, where the Baptists were the first settlers, and where they always have been numerous, to hear our old-fashioned people, especially among the sisterhood, apply the term "elder" to ministers of other denominations as freely as they do to their own order.

Ruling elders, in addition to deacons, in former times, in a few instances, were found among the Baptists; but at present I know of no church of our persuasion where this office is maintained. The people where they once were found, may have copied the rule from the Presbyterians, or else have taken it from the words, *the elders that rule well*, etc.

Ruling elders were almost everywhere met with among the Puritans of this country in early times, but we do not find them anywhere among the old Baptists, who came out from them, till we come down to those which arose in the New Light stir. The few churches in which these officers were found were mostly in the middle States.

In the chapter on the Deaconship, yet to come in, I shall advocate the primitive practice of having seven men of good report, full of the Holy Ghost and wisdom, for every full grown church of our order, to coöperate with the pastor in the management of church affairs, then there will be no need of ruling elders, nor of executive committees for this business. I shall also recommend that deacons be appointed for a limited time, instead of for life, as is now done; and this rule I would apply to the officers of all our benevolent institutions. Four years is the term I propose.

A full exhibition of my views of the present evils of our deaconship, and of the proper remedies for these evils, will be given in the chapter referred to.

THIRD DECADE.

ON THE AGE OF EXCITEMENTS.

CHAPTER XIII.

QUIET CONDITION OF THE BAPTISTS GENERALLY. — AGITATIONS
ABOUT FREEMASONRY AND SOUTHERN SLAVERY.—THE TROUBLES
WHICH FOLLOWED.—THE DIVISION OF CHURCHES. — THE REMOV-
ALS OF MINISTERS.—THE NAME OF STAYSHORT APPLIED TO MANY.

THIRTY YEARS AGO the Baptist denomination, as a
general thing, throughout the country, was free from
the numerous and disastrous excitements which soon
arose in many places, and which in in some extensive
regions, by the altercations and divisions they occasioned, essentially hindered the prosperity of the society, which was then, in numerical strength, ahead of
all the great communities in the land so far as church
membership was concerned. For a long course of
years prior to the period now under consideration,
extensive revivals of religion had prevailed amongst
our people in almost all parts of the country where
Baptists were found; the cause of missions was rapidly gaining ground among us; the same may be said
of the interests of education in all their departments;
and a disposition was very apparent among an increasing number of our influential men, both ministers and laymen, to arouse and concentrate the energies of our growing and wide-spread community in

favor of benevolent and evangelical efforts at home
and abroad. Such was the state of things among the
American Baptists about one third of a century since.
But a sad reverse of this pleasing picture was at hand,
and the painful scenes in which many of our ministers
became very deeply involved spread their baneful influence far and wide.

Freemasonry, and southern slavery, soon became the
subjects of the greatest interest among the contending parties, and, as a natural consequence, respecting
these new matters of excitement in their then present
shape, the most ardent altercations arose among the
combatants in this new warfare on Baptist ground,
which involved questions, about which, our churches
had never legislated, nor adopted any rules of discipline. New laws of course had to be made by these
churches before they could proceed in dealing with
their members under the complaints which were preferred against them by their accusing brethren. This
caused no little embarrassment at first, with the more
thinking class of men, but as the excitement became
more intense, law or no law, majorities ruled, and
proscription was fully inaugurated in many locations.

Up to this date, the members of Baptist churches
were not molested in their religious standing on account of their connection with the mystic order; and
multitudes of the most staunch defenders of the Bap-

tist faith found themselves all at once in an embarrassing dilemma in consequence of the new church laws, which they never subscribed, and against which they entered a solemn protest. In some cases, this kind of reasoning caused a stay of proceedings against the obnoxious members, but where the new reformers were determined on victory, and had majorities on their side, no arguments were of any avail. Wily statesmen, who had ambitious schemes ahead, not unfrequently stimulated our church reformers in their undertakings, and thus, by a combination of influences, political and religious, between outside agitators, and inside managers, many of our hitherto strong and harmonious churches, mostly in the northern States, were shaken to their center on mere matters of opinion, *pro* and *con.*, respecting the character of a professedly secret institution, and were crippled for long succeeding years in their harmony and prosperity.

In this new Baptist reform, many strong men, and not a few who could not properly be placed in this class, were engaged, with a zeal which they had never before manifested against any of the evils of the land, real or imaginary. The details of the strifes and commotions which followed this modern warfare against a fraternity of very high antiquity, I shall not attempt to repeat.

The disputes among our people about slavery, in an earnest manner, were nearly cotemporary with those just referred to. These disputes also, in the outset, were respecting a system, with the evils of which they had but little knowledge, only by report; and as in the business of masonry, new questions came up on the subject of church discipline. Heretofore, ministers and members of the great Baptist family, North and South, had freely exchanged pulpits, and united together in all their religious exercises at home and abroad. But now, strong efforts were made by many northern men to restrain the freedom which had thus far been exercised, and the operation of these efforts, in the end, led the southern brethren to go off by themselves. The details of the long struggle here referred to, at present I shall entirely omit. The formation of a new convention, which combines all the doings of the Baptists in the southern States, for benevolent objects generally, I shall briefly describe in its proper place, and under a separate head. It is not my intention, however, in any of my reminiscences of Baptist affairs, at the North or South, to identify myself with either of the parties, or to denounce or defend the men on either side, but to present the facts as they appeared to me at the time.

It so happened that about the time that the agitations above alluded to were at their height, I found it necessary to take a journey through all the southern States in pursuit of historical information for my late work on the history of the denomination, when I found a material change from former years in the feelings of our brethren in those regions towards the institution in question, and in their conversations respecting it. Formerly they were accustomed to use the language of apology for a system which they could neither regulate nor abolish, but which they would be very glad to be rid of, if this could be done in a legal and peaceable manner; while now, they defended it on scriptural grounds. And when I inquired of one of our prominent ministers in the city of R——, the reason of this change, he discoursed to me on the subject in the following manner: " Formerly, we viewed ourselves on a level with our brethren in the free States, but the language and resolutions which for a long time have been coming down to us from the North, place us in the background. Indeed, if we remain as we are, if these brethren mean all they say, we are not fit to be ranked among gospel ministers or real Christians. And as we were not disposed to renounce all our professions at once, we set about a new course of study, and made new and more thorough examinations of the Bible, to find where we stood; and soon we were surprised to discover from the sacred word how easily we can defend our cause, from

the practice of the early Christians, among whom we
believe slavery most certainly existed." This mode
of reasoning, I have found, is now pretty generally
adopted by the ministers and the people of all parties
in the slaveholding States; so that instead of pleading for toleration and forbearance from their opposing
brethren, they now stand on the defensive with much
decision; and some of the ministers of our own order,
as well as those of others, have become champions in
defense of a system which, by multitudes in the free
States, is most intensely opposed; and as the unpleasant feelings between the parties were daily increasing
in strength and severity, as was painfully apparent at
the great meetings in which they attempted to work together, and with a gloomy prospect for the future, I
was glad when the line of demarcation was peaceably
drawn between the North and South, for the sake of
peace on both sides, and for other reasons which I
shall assign in the chapter on the Southern Baptist
Convention.

Since the separation, thus briefly described, took
place, the two wings of the great Baptist community
in this country have each pursued their own way,
without any clashing with each other; and have done
much more in the support of missions at home and
abroad, and other objects of benevolence, than they
could have done had they continued in one body.

The southern Baptists never had much disputing about masonry, and none about slavery among themselves, but matters were very different at the North, where, in the exciting times now had in view, multitudes who stood aloof from all matters of controversy, were in continual fears for the safety of their hitherto quiet spiritual homes, on account of divisions, which they could neither hinder nor heal.

The disputes respecting Freemasonry and Slavery stood foremost in the order of time, as they did in point of importance, in the minds of the most active promoters of these agitations. With them, all other evils in the Baptist ranks were of minor importance, and in support of their opinions on these subjects all available arguments and measures were by them resorted to. Ministers in cases not a few became lecturers and agents, and leaving their pastoral stations, they traversed the country far and wide, in pursuit of their new vocations. These men were joined by many of the secular class, whose preferences were not very well settled on religious opinions of any kind; and soon Baptist pulpits, which had hitherto been devoted exclusively to the preaching of the gospel, were freely opened to a promiscuous company of declaimers of all castes and creeds, by whom the objects principally aimed at were of a politico-benevolent character. Such was the opinion of many outside observers.

8*

The Baptist lecturers, however, preferred to labor for the cause of religion and humanity only.

Out of these agitations, as an unavoidable consequence, arose confusion and division in many of our churches; and in others, where no rupture took place, coldness and deadness ensued, and an estrangement of feeling among most intimate friends.

At associations, conventions and other large gatherings within the range of these troublesome discussions, there were men always ready to introduce resolutions in favor of their *anti-isms* of various kinds, the agitation of which, in many cases, it was difficult to avoid, with the free principles of the Baptists, and with their notions of equal rights when met in public assemblies. The consumption of time on these extra matters, which was needful for legitimate objects, was an evil often complained of, but the bad blood which was engendered between contending parties was a greater evil still.

For a long time previous to the peculiar age now under review, the old-fashioned longevity of Baptist pastorships was getting more and more out of fashion, every year; and now these relations, in many cases, were so much narrowed down, that a multitude of our ministers could truly say on this subject,

> " A span is all that we can boast,
> A year or two of time."

And each of these migratory shepherds, on retiring from their transitory stations, could say, "Few and evil have been the days of my pilgrimage, with an uncomfortable, discordant, and inefficient people."

A writer in the Christian Watchman and Reflector, in Boston, not long since gave a good description of a minister, under the significant cognomen of Mr. *Stay-short*, who, in consequence of the ardor with which he entered into every agitation afloat, was constantly on the move. He would resolve, on his entrance into each new place, that he would avoid his former mistakes and let all agitations alone, but such was the constitution of his mind, and so large was his bump of combativeness, that none of his prudential resolves were of any avail. So strong in his mind were the convictions of duty, and so fully did he believe that without *his* aid, the truth would suffer, and the interests of justice and humanity would be trampled under foot, that he *must* speak out, *hit* or *miss*, and come what would, he *must* contend earnestly for the truth. And soon away he would go to some new location.

This meddling with all new excitements which arose in such quick succession about these times, while it unseated many who had heretofore devoted their whole attention to the gospel ministry with reputation and success, served to diffuse a spirit of discord and contention into many churches, who, up to this period, had been distinguished for concord and quietness.

The family of Stayshorts in the pastoral line has been greatly augmented in our denomination since the age of excitements commenced. Men who will plunge into controversies on any subjects ought to be making arrangements for a change of location without much delay, and especially if on the matters of dispute, the people of their charge are divided in their opinions and pursuits.

The *Staylong* preachers, as a general thing, are non-committal in the midst of all the contests here referred to. When it comes to the question of truth and duty, as gospel ministers, the case is very different, but even here the mild spirit of the gospel should be cultivated in preference to that of acrimony and contempt. A minister whose mind is deeply imbued with the Spirit, and who is wholly devoted to his divine calling, will easily avoid the evils in which his combative and inconsiderate brethren too often become involved.

In this free country, and with our free principles, all must be left to their own choice, and the minister who attempts to interpose and influence on any side, either in political or any other contests, which may agitate the minds of the people, will see his mistake often when it is too late.

In addition to the injurious influence on the Baptist cause, from the agitations which I have thus briefly described, its former tranquillity was much disturbed, and its prosperity was very seriously retarded by the continued hostility of the anti-mission party, which was spreading its paralyzing principles far and wide, and which erected barriers at every point against the progress of all the benevolent and reforming operations of modern times.

The Campbellites or Reformers, in the southern and western States, thirty years ago and onward, were in the full tide of success, and were making proselytes from the Baptists with great rapidity. Not unfrequently ministers and whole churches espoused the cause of the zealous Reformers, and churches not a few, which made strenuous efforts to maintain their ground, were in the end essentially enfeebled or wholly destroyed

The Campbellites are intensely Baptistical, so far as the baptismal service is concerned.

The Millerites, or Adventists, about this time, and at a still later period, made inroads on our ranks much more extensively than many have supposed. Mr. Miller, himself, was a plain Baptist minister in the earlier part of his life, and as immersion was the standing rule of his party, the Baptists could carry with them their old favorite practice when they rallied around their new and popular leader.

On the whole, the decade now under review may be properly denominated the iron age of the American Baptists. Revivals of religion, like angels' visits, in most parts of the country were few and far between, and it may be truly said the dearth was sore in the land.

Such is a brief account of the depopulating measures and influences which our extended community had to encounter during most of this decade, and of the inroads which by them, were made upon our ranks.

CHAPTER XIV.

THIRTY YEARS AGO the foreign mission cause
stood very high in the estimation of the American
Baptists as a body; for this object the choicest fields
for agents were assigned. The whole denomination,
North and South, acted in concert, so far as it was
aroused to any benevolent action in supporting this
then favorite undertaking. But with all these facilities for revenue, the annual income of the Convention was but about twenty-five thousand dollars, and
a considerable portion of this sum came from female
mite societies, on which much reliance in that day
was placed for the support of all our benevolent operations.

The Meeting of the Convention in New York, in 1826.

The number of delegates appointed to this meeting
was seventy-eight; six of them were absent. Their
names were thus recorded:

MAINE.—*Thomas B. Ripley.*

MASSACHUSETTS.—Lucius Bolles, Daniel Sharp, J.
D. Knowles, William Staughton,* Jonathan Going,
Heman Lincoln, G. F. Davis, Bela Jacobs, *Abiel
Fisher, Francis Wayland, Jr., Irah Chase*, James Lor-
ing, B. C. Grafton, *Henry Jackson, Jonathan Bachelder*,
Levi Farwell.

VERMONT.—Joseph W. Sawyer, Jonathan Merri-
am, John Conant.

RHODE ISLAND.—Stephen Gano, *D. Benedict*, William Gammell.

CONNECTICUT.—Asa Wilcox.

NEW YORK.—Spencer H. Cone, J. C. Murphy,
R. Thompson, William Colgate, *Archibald Maclay,
Aaron Perkins*, Thomas Stokes, *S. W. Lynd*, Daniel
Hascell, Elon Galusha, *Daniel Putnam, H. Malcom*,
John Stanford, Thomas Garniss, Thomas Purser,
Joshua Gilbert, C. G. Summers, William C. Hawley,
Rufus Babcock, Nathaniel Kendrick, Lewis Leonard,
Stephen Olmstead.

---

* Dr Staughton and a number of other members of this Convention
are reported from States in which they did not belong. This occurred
in this way: no one could be a delegate unless it could be shown that
there had been paid into the treasury of the body by himself or friends
one hundred dollars per annum. And as the contributions of some
States fell short of the amount necessary to send the number of delegates they desired should go, those in which there was a superabundance afforded them a helping hand. This practice was in conformity to
the constitution of the Convention.

NEW JERSEY.—Thomas Brown, *James E. Welch.*

MARYLAND.—Samuel Eastman. J. M. Peck.

PENNSYLVANIA. — *John L. Dagg*, David Jones, William E. Ashton, Joseph Maylin.

DISTRICT OF COLUMBIA.—O. B. Brown, *G. S. Webb*, Isaac Clark, Samuel Cornelius, Luther Rice, Joseph Thaw, *William Ruggles*, Enoch Reynolds, *Robert Ryland*.

VIRGINIA.—Robert B. Semple, John Kerr, *William Crane*, Eli Ball, H. C. Thompson, Noah Davis.

SOUTH CAROLINA.—Joseph B. Cook, *William B. Johnson*, Charles D. Mallory, James Graham.

GEORGIA. — Jesse Mercer, William T. Brantley, *Abdiel Sherwood*, Abner Davis.

Officers of the Convention.

Robert B. Semple, ... *President.*
Howard Malcom, ... *Secretary.*
Heman Lincoln, ... *Treasurer.*

Under the old dispensation a Board of Managers of thirty-eight was chosen once in three years. Former members might be reappointed.

This Board of Managers was much like the present Executive Committee.

Officers of the Board of Managers.

William Staughton, ... *President.*

Jesse Mercer, ... ⎫

Daniel Sharp, ... ⎬ *Vice Presidents.*

O. B. Brown, ... ⎪

Nathaniel Kendrick, ... ⎭

Lucius Bolles, ... *Cor. Secretary.*

Francis Wayland, Jr., ... *Rec. Secretary.*

Heman Lincoln, ... *Treasurer.*

The other members of the Board were, William T. Brantley, *J. L. Dagg*, S. H. Cone, Joseph B. Cook, *William Crane*, Enoch Reynolds, Bela Jacobs, Elon Galusha, *Samuel Cornelius, Thomas B. Ripley,* John Kerr, Jonathan Going, Stephen Gano, *Henry Jackson, D. Benedict*, J. D. Knowles, Thomas Stokes, Levi Farwell, Abner Davis, *Irah Chase,* Stephen Chapin, Lewis Leonard, Abner Forbs, Gustavus F. Davis, John Moriarty, Asa Wilcox, William Gammell, *Charles Train,* Nathaniel W. Williams, David Jones.

It will be seen that there were a number of men in the Board who were not members of the Convention. This was according to an article of the constitution which provided that the Managers might be chosen out of the societies, associations, churches, etc., which helped to sustain the general cause.

About three fourths of the men above named have

ceased from their labors.   The names of those who survive are put in *italics*.

Of the thirty-eight members of the Board of Managers all but ten have died.

At this time our institution for foreign missions had been in operation twelve years, and thus far all the services pertaining to its management had been gratuitously performed without an executive committee or missionary rooms.

Philadelphia at first, and for a number of years after, was the seat of the operations of this body, when it was removed to Washington, D. C., and finally to Boston, where it has remained to this time, a period of about thirty years.   (This was written in 1856.)

Additional Items respecting the Doings of the Convention in New York.

At this meeting the recent deaths of Drs. Baldwin of Boston, Furman of Charleston, and John Williams of New York, were duly reported, and suitable *resolutions* respecting them were passed and entered on the minutes.

Among the doings of this Convention, fourteen standing committees were appointed, besides a large number for special purposes, as the business went on. Three of these committees only had respect to foreign missions.   The affairs of the American Indians, the

Luminary, the Star, the Columbian College, the debts of these concerns, and Mr. Rice's financial transactions generally, engrossed most of the attention of the body at this session.   Respecting this laborious man, who had labored for many years in the Baptist cause, and who was now present, the following resolution was voted and recorded :

" From various developments, it appears that Mr. Rice is a very loose accountant, and that he has very imperfect talents for the disbursement of money."

Succeeding this vote, a committee of fourteen was appointed, of whom only Drs. Wayland, Chase and the writer survive, who, among other things, recommended that Mr. Rice should continue his agency for the college, for the collection of funds; that Rev. Elon Galusha assume the office of treasurer of the institution, and immediately remove to Washington for this purpose; and that an effort be made to raise fifty thousand dollars for the liquidation of its debts, and for sustaining its future operations.

The plan of locating the Board of Managers in Boston was unanimously adopted by the Convention, in 1826, which carries us back thirty-three years.

At this meeting, also, strong resolutions were adopted in favor of having the nomination of the trustees of the college made by some other body besides the Convention, on which this duty had thus far devolved.

This plan, however, was not fully matured until a number of years later.

On the whole, the doings at this time were of no small importance, as they did much toward disengaging the Convention from those entangling and embarrassing alliances with outside operations, in which the well-meant, but ill-advised plans of Mr. Rice and his coadjutors had involved the body, and which had for a long time been the occasion of protracted, and not always harmonious discussions, and especially at the session now under review.

The income of the Convention at the end of this decade had arisen to a little over sixty thousand dollars; but its expenses had so far gone ahead of its revenue, that the treasurer, in 1838, reported a debt of twenty-five thousand dollars. Such unwelcome reports have often gone out from the treasury of this institution for the last twenty years. But the Baptist public have stood by this favorite undertaking with a promptness and decision of a highly commendable character.

The compound motion of this old Convention, in its early movements, in which was embraced ministerial education, and much of the labor which is now performed by the institution soon to be named, seemed to be a matter of necessity in the early stage of benevolent operations. The system worked very well for a few years, but at length, from the painful experience of the disagreeable friction of this compound machinery, and the want of efficiency on this account, the expediency of having new organizations for other objects, and of having all the energies of the Convention directed to foreign missions alone, became most obviously apparent.

The Baptist Home Missionary Society.

The need of such an institution had long been felt by many of our brethren in different parts of the country, particularly in the western States and Territories, and in remote regions where the old domestic societies could do but little in the cause of missions. But few, however, cared to suggest the idea of getting up a second organization for missionary purposes among our people, so fearful were they that it would not be supported by the churches, and so careful also, were they of encroaching on the rights of the foreign department, whose revenues were obtained with great labor and cost, and, moreover, were often inadequate to the demand for sustaining the increasing labors in the foreign fields, where new enterprises were continually undertaken.

At the meeting of the General Convention, in 1826, to which I have so often referred, in the report of the Committee on Domestic Missions, of which J. M.

Peck was chairman, there was evidently a looking forward to our Home Mission and Bible Societies, and to augmented efforts in favor of ministerial education and Sunday Schools.

My observations at present will have respect only to the Home Mission organization, which was effected in the city of New York, in 1832. But the incipient movements, in which may be discovered the germ of the institution, were commenced in Boston two years before, by certain members of the old Baptist Missionary Society of Massachusetts. These movements were seconded by similar bodies in New York, Philadelphia and elsewhere, and in process of time most of the old domestic communities were merged in the new Home Society, or had grown into State conventions, which coöperated with it.

To the late Dr. Going may be ascribed much of the labor in getting up this very useful Baptist institution, and in setting it in successful operation; and in his explorations for the purpose of ascertaining the need and the practicability of the undertaking, he found a willing and efficient coadjutor in Dr. Peck, the laborious pioneer of the West. This assiduous promoter of all new and promising measures among our people, traveled extensively with Dr. Going, over an extensive field, with which he was entirely familiar, and united with his eastern friend in laying a good foun-

dation for an institution which has thus far operated
in a very beneficial manner for the interests of our denomination.

The machinery of this body is very simple, and
costs but little compared with our foreign department
—nor has there been any of those painful collisions
between the managers at home and the missionaries
under their appointment, which, in the foreign cause
for a long time past, has been so distressing to a large
portion of the American Baptists.

The most troublesome thing I have seen in the operations of the home concern, was the project for getting up a new building for its accommodation.   This
scheme, as I understand the matter, originated in the
unwillingness of Dr. Cone and others to occupy the
rooms which had been fitted up for the institution,
and were offered it free of rent.   A subscription was
opened in favor of this new mission house, but hitherto the plan has not been carried into effect.

In the early operations of the Home Society, efforts
were made for the Baptist State Conventions to become
auxiliary to it, and to turn in their spare funds to its
aid.   But, as each convention found enough to do at
home, this plan was never fully matured.

The reports of the doings of the Home Mission Society give but an imperfect view of this kind of labor in the whole country, since the State conventions

and single associations probably perform as much, if not more, in this line, than the general institution. The State conventions, especially in the older States, appropriate most of their funds in aid of feeble church es, which are not able to give a full support to their pastors, or else in efforts to organize new bodies in favorable locations, where the Baptist interest has hitherto been neglected. But many associations, mostly in the South and West, appoint one or more ministers for a part, or all the time, to labor with destitute churches, and in destitute regions, within their own bounds, and, in some cases, beyond them. This was the way of doing this business in the early operations of domestic missions, as they were then called, in the old States, where a different system is now pursued. How many miles traveled was, and still is, an important item in the reports of this kind of missionary service.

9

CHAPTER XV.

IN this business all sorts of methods have been
pursued by the Baptists, but, as a general thing, I am
sorry to say, they have been deficient in system, and
still more in the liberality of their doings in favor of
their spiritual guides. In a few of our churches the
pastors had an adequate support, and the pastoral
relation was more permanent than at the present time,
since it was more disreputable then, than now, for ministers of the first class to make removals, unless for
very obvious reasons, and especially if they listened
to a louder call, in the business of support, to use the
language then very often employed. But in old times,
and in all succeeding ones, a very large proportion of
our ministers in the whole country, and especially in
the more newly-settled and remote regions, have been
obliged to look out for themselves, having had but a
scanty assistance from the people they served; and as
to their settlement or induction into their pastoral stations, it has often been very informal and indefinite.

But wherever any regular agreement had been made, it was by the year. It was often customary then for people annually to hire ministers for their pulpits, as they did their laboring men on their farms. "Have you hired your minister for the coming year, and what is the price?" was the language which might often be heard among many of our economical brethren, especially in New England.

But there was a large class of our ministers, in my early day, who worked on from year to year without any agreement whatever, either as to time or compensation, and in some cases, they did more for their people in pecuniary matters than was done for them. The property which enabled these men to pursue this generous course, in some instances came to them by inheritance, but for the most part they acquired it by their own industry and energy while in the ministry, or before they entered it. It was no uncommon thing then for ministers to be engaged in farming and other secular pursuits, like other men. Pastors of this description were, of course, less liable to change their pastoral relations than those who depended on their congregations for support. They were men of but a moderate share of education; but demands on this score were less urgent than now; but few complained of them on this account, and after all their disadvantages, they gathered large and stable churches, were

respected by their own people, and not a few of other
communions, and were very useful men in their day
and generation.

Many men who had a partial support, under yearly
engagements, often retained their pastorship, many
years, notwithstanding the precarious tenure by which
they were held. The annual voting of the people
was rather a matter of form than otherwise, but there
were serious evils attending it, with pastors, whose
attachment to their flocks was strong and endearing. If any controlling deacons, or other disaffected
members, were seeking for means to stir up opposition to them, on any account, and to crowd them
off, by curtailing their support, they had very favorable opportunities in these annual doings. A minister of my acquaintance, towards the close of a long
pastorship, was accustomed to observe, he dreaded
the *May storms,* as that was the month in which his
settlement was made.

This yearly operation was a bad system at best, and
it was often made worse by the careless manner in
which it was conducted. Not unfrequently the year
would run out before any thing was said or done
about a new engagement, and all this time the minister was in suspense as to his future course, and to
add to his trouble, more or less of his scanty salary
was unpaid. In this dilemma, the credit system must

be resorted to, and after all, he might be compelled to change his location, or at least, be left without a re-appointment, in the midst of debts which he felt in duty bound to discharge, no one could tell how, as what was due him, if paid at all, came slowly, and often with a heavy discount.

In these times many of our churches, especially in country regions, were greatly deficient in their finan-cial arrangements, in all that pertained to their relig-ious concerns. They had men of fiscal talent, who calculated well in their own secular affairs, and met their engagements promptly; while they gave up the business of providing for the support of their spirit-ual guides to incompetent and neglectful hands, and threw off all responsibility in the matter, after making liberal contributions themselves. If subscriptions thus poorly attended to fell short at the end of the year, as it often happened, I have known instances of the men who held the papers counting up the amount of do-nations to the minister and his family, to help through with their tardy operations.

At the period now under review, the subscription system was generally adopted, wherever any systematic efforts were made in the business of ministerial support. Indeed, in all former years, and also at the present time, this way of performing this business, with very few exceptions, throughout the whole range of our denomination, has been pursued. It is a laborious, and generally, an unequal method of raising funds, and very often it is difficult to find suitable men for the service, and they retire from it as soon as possible. In my early day, in some parts of the northern States, mostly, however, in New England, the assessment plan was adopted in a voluntary manner, according to the acknowledged or reputed ability of the members. In some cases, churches had funds or farms which were devoted to the support of their ministers, wholly or in part, and the rest was made up by subscription. As to pew rents, I found nothing of the kind among the Baptists in my early researches into their history, except in the few churches then in Boston. The idea of paying any thing for seats in their meeting houses had not then entered the minds of our people, or of scarcely any other, much less did they think it practicable to support, not only the minister, but to pay all the expenses of a church establishment in this way.

But to return to the subscription system. The evils and embarrassments attending it, among unwilling members, were often by no means small. Those who had the business in charge would often meet with a decided veto from brethren of the hyper-careful class. Their language was, "I believe in a free gospel, and do not want to make a show of my name on the pa-

per, nor to bind myself beforehand. If I feel like
handing out any thing to the elder, I will do it and
done with it, and not let my right hand know what
my left doeth. But it must be a free gift, and in my
own time and way. Hireling ministers I don't like
at all." In a few instances such impracticable members were dealt with for covetousness, but as a general
thing the churches let them slide.

There was another class of members in former times,
and possibly some of them are still to be found in
some of our churches, who were equally the slaves
of mammon; they were entirely outspoken in their
opposition to ministerial support, and on this subject
they each reasoned in the following manner: " I
want ministers to go by the Spirit, and deal out what
is handed down to them immediately from above. It
takes them no longer to go to meeting and preach,
than it does for me to go and hear them, so we will
balance the account and call it even."

To the discredit of some of our old churches, men
of ample means, who manifested such a penurious and
withholding disposition, and who employed such offensive language when called upon to perform a plain
and bounden duty, were too often retained in their
fellowship.

Many poor ministers in the times now under consideration, suffered greatly in their feelings, not only

from the parsimony of their people, but also from the reluctant manner in which their scanty livings were dealt out to them. I distinctly recollect an account given me by one of these men, of the lectures which were often given him by one of his deacons, on the great importance of economy among ministers and their families in their mode of living. This deacon was a model of a man in the saving line, as many Baptist deacons have been. He being treasurer of the church, the funds which were collected at irregular intervals all passed through his hands, and whenever he dealt them out to the elder, his complaints of the cost of supporting ministers, and of the hard and difficult times among the parishioners, were not altogether unlike those made at *tithing time*, as described by Cowper.

It is not improbable that portions of our ministers throughout the wide range of our denomination still experience some of the trials above referred to.

On Religious Revivals in former Times.

As far back as my recollection and researches extend, these seasons, for the most part, were like angel visits, few and far between. From Backus, and others, I learn that during the great religious movement, under the labors of Whitfield, Tennant, Finley, and others, usually denominated the *New*

Light Stir, a few old Baptist churches participated in that extraordinary work, which, however, prevailed mostly among the Pedobaptists.

In the early part of the present century, and up to the age of the excitements, which, as I have already stated, had a paralyzing influence on the better feelings of Christians, conversions and additions among our people, were in many cases of the most exhilarating and encouraging nature.

This golden age of our denomination lasted about a quarter of a century, and the increase of our communicants was often a matter of astonishment to our people at home, and our friends abroad. During all this time scarcely any of the new measures of more modern times were adopted. In some locations, where the Methodists were numerous, and their customs prevailed, *rising for prayers* began to be practiced to a limited extent. But, as a general thing, the old way of conducting meetings, whether in seasons of revivals or declensions, was pursued, and all attempts to produce a high state of feeling among the people were carefully avoided. Depth of feeling was the main thing desired by our most efficient men, whether in the pulpit or the conference room. They also made much dependence on the silent workings of the divine Spirit on the hearts of the people.

9*

On these agencies the Baptists made much more dependence than on multitudinous gatherings and bodily exercises.

At length *protracted meetings* began to be much talked of far and near, and so many reports were circulated concerning the wonderful effects of them, that by many they were thought to be the very thing for promoting religious revivals. For some time *four days* was the amount of time allotted them, but soon these meetings began to overrun this time, and the original term was exchanged for *meetings of days* without any limit as to their number.

In connection with these meetings came along a new sort of preachers, who went into the business of conducting them by new rules of their own. In process of time the Baptists became a good deal engaged in these peculiar gatherings, and many of them seemed much pleased with them. The *revival ministers*, as they were called, soon became very popular; they were sent for from far and near, and in many cases very large additions were made to our churches under their ministrations.

But, in some cases, the old ministers and churches demurred, and were unwilling to have these new men, with their new notions, introduced among them. They were jealous of these wonder-working ministers in this business, and of a new machinery in the work of conversion. It was always customary with our old pastors to have other ministers to assist them in times of unusual attention to religion, but they never gave up the helm of the ship to new pilots for the sake of more rapid speed. Wherever this experiment was made, with rare exceptions, it worked badly, and many a good and well-settled pastor was, by its operation, either crowded out of his place, or else made uncomfortable in it, in consequence of the introduction of the new measures above alluded to, and the indiscretions of revival preachers.

To see converts coming into a church by wholesale was a pleasing idea to many members; and although they had been well satisfied with their pastor heretofore, yet now, they began to think that the new man who had been so active and successful in gathering in new members would do much more for them than they could expect from the one in office; that he would soon fill their ranks, repair their meeting house or build a new one, pay off their church debt, and place them in circumstances as flourishing as those of their neighbors.

But another class of members had fearful forebodings for the future, under the ministry of the new man. They had rather continue their old way of doing business than to place a mere revivalist in the pastoral office, and make the radical changes in their operations, which he and his ardent admirers considered of so much importance. Hence arose discussions at first; next, disputations; and in the end, not unfrequently, painful and injurious divisions.

FOURTH DECADE.

CHAPTER XVI.

A New Baptist Register, by I. M. Allin.—A List of Small Literary Institutions.—Manual Labor Schools.—American and Foreign Bible Society.

More than twenty years ago a compendium of Baptist history, under the title of an Annual Register, was presented to the Baptist public by the late Irah M. Allin, which work, I am inclined to think, has not been sufficiently appreciated by the denomination at large. Mr. Allin commenced the preparation of his Register about twenty years after the publication of my old History of the Baptists, and in it he has given a summary view of all that pertained to the progress of the society, its extension, the formation of its various institutions for missions, education, and other useful objects. The whole work was prepared with great care, and in a very intelligible manner, and from it we learn that there were then of Baptist members upward of five hundred thousand in all America, including the Freewill, the Seventh Day, and Six Principle Baptists.

Twenty years ago, according to Allin's Register, there was an abundance of young institutions in dif-

ferent parts of the country, which were designed by
their friends for the aid of young ministers, in connection with common education. Such institutions
were then found at Kennebunk, Maine; at Rocking-
ham, Hampton Falls, and Hancock, New Hampshire;
at Brandon, Ludlow, and Townsend, Vermont; at
South Reading, Massachusetts; at Brunson, Michi-
gan; at Brockport, New York; at Plainfield, Newton, and Burlington, New Jersey; at Haddington,
Pennsylvania; and in a number of the southern and
western States schools of this character had been established, and were in operation. But so few were
the theological students who attended them, that a
portion of them in a short time fell into disuse, others became wholly secular in their character, and in
a few cases, from these small beginnings, respectable
and permanent seminaries, both literary and theological, arose.

The foregoing list of seminaries, then newly started, exhibit pleasing evidence that our people, at the
time, were wide awake in the business of education,
and especially in that of their rising ministry.

Manual Labor Schools.

Under this head there was suddenly introduced,
and for a short time it went with a rush, a new
plan of assisting indigent students for the ministry,

to defray the expenses in their educational pursuits.
The practice of the ancient Hebrews in their schools
of learning all at once became a favorite idea with
the Baptists, and they tried the experiment on an
extensive scale at the North and the South, but
mostly in the southern regions.   Preparations for
working operations, either on the land or in shops,
were almost simultaneously made in a large number
of our young institutions, with great confidence in
the utility and the ultimate success of the new system.   Lands to a greater or less extent were set
apart for the use of the students, on which it was
expected they would work like farmers, and near by
the schools shops were erected, where they might employ a portion of their time in the trades at which
they chose to labor, or in which they had formerly
been employed.   In this way it was expected that
a considerable part of the expense of the students,
who would become working men, would be defrayed.
The theory was a very good one on the score of
health and economy, and for a few years very favorable reports were made of its success in different directions.

Three hours in a day for five days in the week
was the rule adopted in the seminary of this kind, in
Richmond, Virginia.

The Mercer Institute at Penfield, in Georgia, the

precursor of Mercer University, in its early operations made much dependence on its manual labor
department for the aid it might afford their theological students, who, as a general thing, were in need
of pecuniary assistance from some source or other.
This Baptist establishment was at first more amply
endowed than generally falls to the lot of similar
undertakings amongst our people. About a thousand acres of valuable land were set apart for its use,
where a large farming business was carried on for the
benefit of the concern. Ample grounds were devoted to the use of the students, and besides this facility
for those of the working class, there was a workshop
on the premises for such as were inclined to mechan-
ical pursuits. Here I suppose a good deal of work
was done at the commencement of the manual labor
system, in connection with literary training, but when
I looked into the place, a number of years since, I
saw no one at work, nor did it appear to be the seat
of much industry or skill.

Unhappily for the projectors of the system, now
under consideration, it did not succeed according to
the expectation of its promoters and friends, and it
soon fell into disuse to the detriment of the health
of the young men who were depended on to sustain
it, and to the disappointment of its patrons. It soon
appeared that *manual* labor was not much in vogue

with college youth, neither at the North nor the South.

A List of Baptist Institutions twenty years ago, which then, or soon after, were invested with a collegiate character; also the Names of the Presidents at that time :—

Brown University,........... F. Wayland.
Waterville College,........... A. Babcock.
Hamilton Seminary, now Madison University, ... Nathaniel Kendrick.
Columbian College, ... Stephen Chapin.
Georgetown College,.......... J. S. Bacon.
Virginia Baptist Seminary, now Richmond College,......... Robert Ryland.
Wake Forest Institute, now College, ... S. Wait.
Shurtliff College, ... Hubbell Loomis.
Mercer Institute, now University,..................... B. M. Sanders.
Granville Institute, now Denison University,............ John Pratt.
Franklin Institute, now College, ... ———
Furman Institute, now University, ... ———
Greenville Institute, now Howard College, ... D. P. Bestor.
Newton Theological Seminary, Irah Chase.

This seminary was the only one of the kind among us. Our people have done well in moulding a number of the infant seminaries above named into a collegiate form, but, as I shall hereafter attempt to show, it was not good policy to provide no substitutes for the schools thus superseded, in which multitudes of our young ministers, and some not very young, derived essential benefit in their struggles to prepare themselves for greater usefulness in the vocation without going through a college course, which their age and incumbrances in some cases, and their indigence in all cases, hindered them from doing. In the early efforts of our denomination to encourage ministerial education, neither those to be taught, nor the people whom they were to serve, were at all particular about the means of obtaining it. Diplomas were of but little account among our plain old-fashioned churches of that age. Where or how long studies had been pursued was then of but little importance. The scarcity of ministers for the increasing churches was almost everywhere felt, and the calls for such as would meet the moderate demands of the people were urgent and pressing. Men of but a moderate share of education, if their qualifications in other respects were promising, soon found places for labor in most parts of the country.

The Rise of the American and Foreign Bible Society.

Before I attempt an account of the origin of this institution, which now occupies a prominent place among the American Baptists, it may be proper to say a few things respecting their connection with the American Bible Society, which body for a long time was patronized to a considerable extent by a portion of our people, and, in one case, one of our members left it a legacy of ten thousand dollars. The Baptists often united with others in forming auxiliary societies of a mixed character, and in various ways they contributed to the funds of a general society, of a non-sectarian character, which was engaged in publishing the Scriptures without note or comment. On this ground, our people could cordially unite in helping forward such a needful and important enterprise—a society in aid of which was formed in my own place, with which I had considerable to do for about a quarter of a century. I generally attended the anniversaries of the mother body in New York, which to me were always welcome and interesting. Thus far all things went on smoothly, and, as far as I know, to the satisfaction of our community, who, by the way, had not much to do with management of the institution, nor in the regulation of its affairs; but still they seemed willing to go on in this way, and no efforts were made in favor of a separate organization

until an incident occurred which in the end led to
the formation of a new society. As a matter of equity
and friendship, in consequence of the confederacy and
coöperation above described, funds had been occasionally granted to our missionaries in the East, to aid in
their translating operations, in an unconditional manner; but at length, while a grant of this kind was
pending, of five thousand dollars, a clause, very offensive to many of our people, was added, namely,
that the versions thus made should conform to the
English standard. This new rule stimulated the Baptists to set about a new Bible enterprise, which was
organized in 1838.

Some of our strong men held back at first, and
doubted the expediency of a separate organization,
similar in its general character to the old body, for
the promotion of the Bible cause among American
Christians. Those men either did not feel the evil of
the restraint which had been imposed upon Baptist
translaters on missionary ground, and the dilemma
in which the old society had placed them, or else they
may have looked forward to the abrogation of the
rule, which by most of our people was considered
needless and unfair. But most of these men by degrees fell into the ranks of the new institution, and
are now its firm friends and supporters.

As about twenty years have elapsed since the society in question arose, and as but few of the present generation may be familiar with its origin, I have thought the brief details given above might not be amiss.

Although I am against multiplying benevolent institutions without urgent demands for them, yet in this case I approved of the formation of the American and Foreign Bible Society, for the following reasons :

Economy was my first argument, being persuaded that the Baptist denomination at large, throughout its wide extent, would do much more for the Bible cause with an institution of their own, and under the management of men of their own persuasion, whose names were familiar to them, than they had yet done or would be likely to do for the old society, however impartially its affairs might be managed. That society was then, in fact, a Pedobaptist concern, with a liberal provision for all parties united in it, to participate in its doings, none of which, by a general understanding, were to be of a sectarian character. And I know of no instance of the violation of this pacific principle, except in the case just referred to. But as the Pedobaptists of different names were overwhelming in their number, and but a very few Baptist names appeared in the list of its officers, the thing had but a feeble hold on a large portion of our community, who I

knew were much too remiss in their support of benevolent undertakings which were wholly managed
by their own men.

The unrestrained liberty of our missionaries in the
business of translations, and their freedom from all
dictation as to what terms they should employ in
making new versions of the Bible into oriental
tongues, had much to do in swaying my mind in
favor of independent action in our Bible operations.
I wished the men who were engaged in the arduous
and responsible work of preparing the Scriptures for
the use of the heathen among whom they labored, to
be under no control from abroad, and especially from
men of different creeds.

I saw but few of our people engaged in any of the
secular employments of the society. And this could
not be reasonably expected while nearly the whole
management of the concern was in other hands; and
I looked forward to an increasing business for all future time, of a secular and semi-secular character,
pertaining to the Bible cause in all its parts, at the
rooms, and in the whole country, in which our people as yet have hardly made a beginning.

CHAPTER XVII.

IN 1845 a new body was organized under the name of the Southern Baptist Convention. Thus the great body of the American Baptists, following the course of the Methodists and the Presbyterians in this country, drew the line of demarkation between the northern and the southern States, so far as their missionary and other benevolent operations, and their former free intercourse, were concerned. This separation was very quietly effected, and up to this time I have not heard of any collisions between the two wings of the denomination, which agree in all matters, except the lawfulness of southern slavery.

While I for myself regretted the cause of the rise of this new institution, yet I approved of its formation for various reasons, aside from the different views of the parties, which I may thus state:

1. That the people within the bounds of the new body would be likely to do much more for the support of all benevolent objects under the management

10

of their own men, whose names were familiar to them, than they had hitherto accomplished. Indeed, my arguments on this subject were akin to those which I employed in favor of a new Bible Society under Baptist rule.

2. There would be a great saving of cost and labor in attending the business meetings, and the delegates to them would be greatly increased, if they were held on their own ground. During the thirty-one years in which the North and the South coöperated together in the old Convention, but few delegates ever came from the South, and it never met but once south of the city of Washington, which was in Richmond, Virginia, in 1832. At this meeting, Drs. Cox and Hoby attended, as delegates from the Baptist Missionary Union of England.

3. There is considerable difference in the habits of the people in the two sections of country, and as each portion of them are well pleased with their own ways, they are more likely to enjoy themselves better in meeting by themselves.

4. I foresaw that the troubles between the North and the South were likely to increase, and by being in separate organizations the collisions would be avoided, which might occur if they continued to act together.

I attended the first anniversary of the Southern

Convention in Richmond, Virginia, where all things were managed with much harmony and decorum, and no reference was had in any of their doings to the difficulties which led them to form a separate body.

This Convention meets once in two years, and although it is confined to southern ground, in the broad sense of that term, still its field of operation is very extensive. A Western Convention will probably need to be formed at no distant day.

My general theory as to our institutions of all kinds is against multiplying them without plain and sufficient reasons, which in this case, as I have above stated, very obviously appeared.

And now as our denomination, like other great communities, has its grand divisions for the *North* and the *South*, I would disapprove of any new large organization, were it not that the great and growing *West*, where our people are gaining rapidly in numbers, in energy, enterprise and influence, may justly claim to have a general institution of their own.

A short time before the Southern Convention was formed I traversed the whole line of the Atlantic States, as far as Penfield in Georgia, the seat of Mercer University and of Baptist operations and influence in that State. Deacon H. Lincoln of Boston was my companion in travel. My objects were wholly historical, as I was then collecting materials for my late

edition of the History of the Baptists; while Deacon
L., then the treasurer of the foreign mission cause,
had two objects in view, namely, the augmentation
of the funds of his department, and the adjustment
of a difficulty which had arisen between some of the
southern members and the board of missions at Boston, in consequence of the non-appointment of one
of their men to a missionary station. There had been
a good deal of correspondence on the matter, but it
was thought best for the treasurer to use his personal
influence on the ground. For this purpose a meeting
was appointed at the house of the late Rev. B. M.
Sanders, a man of great influence at the time with the
southern Baptists. I and a few others, by the request
of the parties, were present. And here for eight long
hours we listened to the earnest but decorous discussions between the representatives of the North and
the South; the main topic of discourse being respecting the non-appointment of the man in question.
This discussion occupied two sessions, one of five
hours, the other of three. The question before these
two men at first view seemed of but little account;
yet it was plain to be seen that the union of the great
Baptist family was in jeopardy. The treasurer of the
body, which he represented, went to the extent of his
instructions and his own kind feelings in his conces-
sions, and I supposed at the time that that small apple

of discord would be laid aside for the future; but from the observations which I made in this journey, and from the uneasiness which was everywhere apparent at the South, with the opinions which were then strongly prevailing at the North respecting slavery in the abstract, and the holding of slaves under any circumstances, I became fully convinced that the wonted union and harmony of our people in the two sections of the country, in their benevolent efforts, as a general thing, could not long be maintained. And as a peaceable separation in such cases, like that which was made by Abraham and Lot, is always preferable to the one which is forced upon disagreeing parties, when our southern brethren soon after concluded quietly to withdraw from the old Convention, with which they had been identified from its beginning, and form one by themselves, I was prepared to approve of the measure, the wisdom of which soon became very apparent.

At the first anniversary of this Convention in Richmond, Virginia, to which I have already referred, Dr. R. Babcock appeared in behalf of the American and Foreign Bible Society, with a proposition for the southern brethren to still patronise the institution which he represented; but instead of this they preferred to have a Bible department in their general body.

On the Manner of Conducting Baptist Associations at this Time.—The Reading of the Letters.—Other Matters Press upon Them.—Their Interest is Diminished.

When I first began to attend these yearly meetings, they were conducted with great simplicity, and were very interesting to all who were identified with them, and to many who repaired to them as spectators of their doings. In that early age, and for a long time after, these institutions, which are peculiar to the Baptists, were wholly devoted to religious exercises and the care of the churches of which they were composed. A little before my early day, the few associations in New England had much to do in devising plans for the relief of their brethren in some sections of the country from the oppressive laws of the dominant party, in which plans the old Philadelphia Association sometimes united, and made contributions in aid of their brethren in this region.

The moderators and clerks in former times held their stations many years in succession. When the body had got good men for these stations, they would hold on to them, and find their benefit in so doing; but at length the rotation system was introduced, as more conformable to the Baptist notions of republican principles. This change, however, was not always for the better as to business operations, since the new men were often far inferior to their predecessors

in all that pertains to the duties of presiding officers.
How often have I been pained to witness the drag-
ging along of the plain business of an association,
under the leading of a man who was wholly unaccus-
tomed to such a position, and who had but little tact
or talent for the station in which the rule of rotation
had placed him. Some men have a natural aptness
for business of this kind, which experience greatly
improves. They learn when to let debates go on,
and when to check them and prepare them for a
close, and in a manner so skillful and unassuming,
that all is managed to the satisfaction of the debating
members, and to the relief of the whole company.
On the other hand, an inexperienced and unskillful
man, who himself needs a prompter at every step,
and who is wanting in the judgment and decision
needful for such a place, will suffer protraction and
delay on subjects of minor importance, and will lead
many to wish that a more energetic man was in the
moderator's seat.

According to the modern rules of some associations,
the moderator must be changed every year, and if all
the members were equally well qualified for the office, this system of rotation would not be liable to the
objections to which it is now most obviously exposed.

The custom of putting men of the lay brotherhood
into the moderator's chair by our associations, has

hitherto been practiced but to a very limited extent, and that in small bodies where there is a deficiency of ministers qualified for such a service. In our great conventional meetings, this class of our members are often preferred for these stations, and I see no reason why they should not be sometimes called upon to preside in our associations.

On the Letters from the Churches, and the Manner in which they are Read.

As Baptist associations are but annual gatherings for the benefit of the churches, without any power of discipline or legislation, on the character of the letters sent in, and the manner of reading them before the people, depends much of the interest and enjoyment of these interviews; and the great fault of the letters generally is, that they are either too long or too short; and the reading part is too often very imperfectly done. All compliments and courtesies in this business should be dismissed, and the best men for the service should be employed. This rule, I think, was more strictly adhered to in former times than at present. The old Warren Association, in my early day, while the churches in Boston and vicinity were connected with it, was a model body of this kind, so far as my experience was concerned, in the whole routine of associational doings.

In more modern times it is becoming somewhat common in some associations for the pastors to read the letters from their own churches. This does very well if these pastors are good readers, but if they are dull and monotonous, and are not distinctly heard, the people will wish that some more vivacious men had the letters in hand.

Other Matters often press upon Associations to the Hindrance of their appropriate Business.

Before the rise of modern benevolent institutions our associations were at full liberty to attend to their own proper work without any interference from any quarter, but as soon as agents began to visit them from different directions, and for different objects, a great change very soon took place. These new visitors, often in considerable numbers, came to these annual assemblies full of zeal in the speaking line, and sought to be heard in favor of their various objects. Mr. Rice was the pioneer in this business, and such was the native eloquence of the man, together with the novelty of his theme and the ardor of his pleadings, that his addresses for a while excited an unusual interest among the people. But in the course of a few years the visits of even this man became less welcome, and as new societies arose and new agents were sent abroad some associations were burdened

10*

with their number and importunity. As a remedy for this evil, in some cases, they would limit them to small portions of time, while in others they were excluded altogether. This latter course, however, was not often pursued. In process of time this numerous and ardent class of men adopted a different plan, in the older States at least, and made the applications to the churches individually with much less complaining and with much better results.

At an early period of our benevolent operations serious complaints began to be made of the undue cost of agents for the collection of funds to sustain them, and I have seen some rather alarming figuring in this business, which ought to have aroused the Baptist public to devise some remedy for this most palpable evil. But it has remained from year to year without much comment, only on the complaining side.

In view of this whole matter the two following statements, to my mind, are undeniably true : *First*, that the getting up of our benevolent institutions has been in advance of public opinion, which has had to be aroused in their favor after they were formed, and for the most part by the special pleadings of agents under pay and special instructions. This, for about forty years past, has been an up-hill, a laborious, and costly work. *Second*, if these institutions are kept alive and in motion this state of things must continue until the churches learn to *go alone*, or, in other words, until these churches, from which the funds must come, of their own free will do the work which hitherto, as a general thing, hired, and often unwelcome agents have performed. I propose to say more on this subject hereafter.

CHAPTER XVIII.

ONE year after the formation of the Southern Baptist Convention, or in 1846, the old Triennial Convention, after existing thirty-two years in its original
form, was transformed into a yearly meeting under
the appellation of the

Baptist Missionary Union.

This was a time of uncommon trial and difficulty
with the Baptists in some of the northern States, principally on account of the agitations among themselves
on the subject, which had formerly been the foundation of the main controversy between the North
and the South, and which, in the end, led the southern wing to go off by itself.

There were indeed other matters of dispute which
often came up in our great convocations, which were
not confined to any section of the country, among
which were some parts of the old constitution, which

had long been strongly opposed, and strong men on different sides made platform speeches at times not altogether agreeable, I might say extremely disagreeable in their bearings, to the mass of the members, who were not very zealous on either side, and whose great desire was to see the cause of missions go on with harmony and success. This cause, then, as formerly, lay near the heart of all our people who had imbibed the spirit of missions, and they were distressed to see the hindrances which were thrown into its way. They had not hitherto paid so much attention to the reading of the constitution, or the doings at the rooms, as to the interesting accounts which came to them often from the foreign fields. An unusually large assembly had convened, and in the then trying state of things, what shall be done so as to adjust existing difficulties, save the body from disruption, and enable it to go on with its wonted harmony and prosperity, were important questions on many minds. In this state of suspense the plan of the *Missionary Union* was presented to the embarrassed Convention, and without much discussion, as a matter of relief, the thing was very cordially adopted, and thus became the basis of future operations in the promotion of the work of foreign missions. As faulty as the document was, I hailed its adoption as an auspicious event at that time of danger and alarm. In-

stead of wishing for any delay I was glad the business moved on so rapidly; instead of desiring any
hazardous attempts at amendments at that perilous
period I felt more like having a *Te Deum* sung by the
great and agitated assembly for a providential deliv-
erance, for I felt then as I do now, that any parts of
the constitution, which, in their practical operations,
might be found to disagree with Baptist principles
and usages might be rectified at some future time.

*On the Differences between the Old and the New Con-
stitutions.*

Under the old dispensation it was required of all
members and delegates that one hundred dollars
per annum should be paid into the treasury of the
body, by themselves or friends, to entitle them to a
seat. In the new order of things no additional pay-
ments are required, but one hundred dollars makes a
person a member for life.

None but members in good standing in some Baptist church could belong to the *Convention*, but in the
Union there is no such requisition, but people of all
creeds and forms, of all nations and religions, are
equally eligible to membership.

The members of the old Convention could participate in all the transactions of the body at its public
meetings and vote on all subjects, but in the Union

none but managers can vote. This business, according to the eighth article of the new constitution, is thus arranged :

" All members of the Union may attend the meetings of the Board of Managers and deliberate on all questions, but members of the Board only shall vote."

Thus to the Board of Managers is entrusted all the legislation of the Missionary Union, consisting now of many thousand life members. The number of this Board is seventy-five, twenty-five of whom go out of office, and an equal number are appointed every year. The retiring members are eligible to re-appointment.

The life members have the right to vote in the choice of managers, but in no other case. These managers appoint all the officers of the Board, together with an Executive Committee of nine. This Committee has power " to designate by the advice of the Board the places where missions shall be attempted, and to establish and superintend the same, to appoint, instruct and direct all the missionaries of the Board," etc.

The power conferred on this Committee of nine, but more especially the stretch of this power, as their opponents have alleged, in certain cases, has been the occasion of a great amount of trouble for a number of years past, and now (1857) threatens greatly to

mar the harmony of the *Union*, if not to rend it asunder, if a remedy is not speedily applied.

As the anniversary of the Missionary Union is not
far ahead, when it is probable the causes of the troubles just alluded to will be investigated, I shall de-
fer any comments on this subject and on those peculiar traits of character in the constitution of the American Baptist Missionary Union, which many contend
are contrary to the primordial principles of the Baptists, and ought therefore to be amended or expunged.

The meeting here referred to was held in Boston.
Here it was that Dr. Peck and Mr. Kincaid had a
long public discussion as to the management of missionary affairs, at the close of which a conciliatory
resolution was adopted by the Union, with great unanimity, which took middle ground between the rooms
and the complaining missionaries. This measure, it
was expected by many, would lead to an adjustment
of existing difficulties. This expectation, however,
was but partially realized, as was too plainly shown
by the unpleasant state of things in the body at the
next anniversary in Philadelphia, in 1858.

*On some objectionable Things in the Construction of
the Old Missionary Convention, and in the Manner of
Conducting its Meetings.*

The whole business of foreign missions came somewhat suddenly upon the Baptist denomination; the ministers of any public spirit entered into the thing with a commendable zeal, but as the mass of the people were rather slow in coming into the measure, how to raise the needful funds was at first an embarrassing question. A direct appeal to them would most likely have been a failure; some other plan must therefore be devised, and this led on to the money qualification for membership, which worked very well at first, except with the poor churches and ministers; and in that direction there often appeared some very hard cases, where men who were much better qualified for a seat in the Convention than many who appeared there, were excluded by the money rule. Some of this class of men had friends in the more wealthy churches, who would think of them and have them returned as members on the strength of the contributions in their own churches, but many able men in counsel, and who would have been glad of a seat with their brethren with whom they had been accustomed to act in all other meetings, were not thus favored; and of course they either staid at home, or else were registered as *visitors* merely, all for the want of one hundred dollars per annum.

The close figuring to ascertain this point, between the committees on memberships and those who wished to secure seats for their friends, often partook too much of the nature of commercial transactions for religious assemblies.

Direct appointment of delegates by the churches, the seat of power, according to all Baptist rules and under a much modified tariff, was strongly urged for a long time by many of the warmest friends of the foreign mission cause.

There was often too little Time allotted for the Business of the Convention, even if no extra Matters had been allowed to enter into its Discussions.

This fault was more apparent after the rise of additional institutions for benevolent objects, and especially after, by mutual agreement, they all met at the same place. Then there was often a scramble amongst them for their due proportion of the time, and as the foreign cause was generally considered of primary importance, the minor institutions would sometimes complain of too much of a curtailment of their opportunities for doing their own business. As yet, the idea of separate meetings in different places was not entertained. When this plan was adopted, although the business of our societies for benevolent objects was more simplified, and each party was at liberty to protract its sessions at pleasure, yet even then, the hurry of business on the one hand, and the itch for speaking on the other, especially on the part of a class of young orators, often led to results which I most deeply deplored. I speak now particularly of the sessions of the old Convention while it embraced the whole country.

How often have I been pained and mortified with the want of any recognition or respect towards many modest and retiring members, who had made unusual efforts to attend the tri-yearly meetings of this great convocation. I have witnessed many cases where men of this description had traveled a thousand miles or more, not in the easy way in which journeys are now performed, on purpose to attend these meetings, of whom no notice whatever was taken by the body, except to enroll their names. At home they occupied important stations of influence and usefulness, and were distinguished for superior information concerning their own localities at least; but now they were entirely overlooked. They were placed on no committees, no services were assigned to them, nor was any door opened for them through whole sessions to make the most limited communications to the body, on any subjects whatever.

This neglect was not intentional on the part of the managers of these meetings, but it resulted from the imperfect arrangements of the business, the compound motion under which the body moved, but mostly from the pressure of hosts of speakers, all anxious

for their turns on the platform, some as agents for different concerns, but most of them to display their
logic and learning, which was not always particularly
edifying to the delegates in question. Often have I
feared that they would retire from the scene so much
disgusted and disheartened that they would relax
their efforts in their distant homes in favor of an institution in whose public celebrations they had so
little identity or enjoyment.

On one of these occasions I remember to have had
a conversation with a member of the great Presbyterian Assembly, which was then in session near by.
I learned from this man, that this people, with all
their formality, outdid the Baptists in their courtesy
towards their delegates of all grades, by setting apart
a time for *free conversations*, when all had liberty to
speak on matters of special interest in their own localities. But nothing of this nature ever appeared to
be thought of by our people ; but on they went, session after session, with the dry details of business,
which was often diversified with scrambles for their
turns among the different speakers, who for the most
part were of the *semper paratus*, always ready, class
of men. Mr. Speaker, I have the floor, Mr. Speaker,
I rise to a point of order, were sounds which in quick
succession came from the ardent debaters. Age and
experience often remained quiescent. while confident

inexperience held the platform, and sometimes to the
dissatisfaction of many of the assembly; but there was
no remedy, as the custom wàs, and we must sit it out
with as much patience as we could muster.   While
the fathers of my younger days watched over the doings of our important convocations, counsel was sometimes sought of the elder, retiring members.   This
thing, however, I have seldom witnessed in later
years, in any of our great meetings of any kind.

In the earlier operations of our old Missionary
Convention some distinguished men were selected to
preach on one or two evenings of the session.   This
custom, in the course of time, was superseded by the
appointment of four of the strongest men the committee of arrangements could select, to make addresses in succession. Intimations were given to these men
in advance, of the probability of their being called
upon, and they would come with huge preparations
for the occasion.   But unfortunately, the first speaker
would sometimes occupy half the time allotted for
all four; the second speaker must of necessity curtail his speech, and so of the next, and as for the
last man, what chance was there for him, while the
clock was striking ten and the people on the move?

Thus unequal in its operations was this quadruple
arrangement; and thus did the first speaker encroach
on the time of the others, when this custom was in

vogue ; out still, for any one to speak besides the favored four, would have been considered quite out of
order. I remember on one occasion, I think it was
in Baltimore, when all things were ready for the services of the evening to commence, and each speaker
was stationed at his corner of the platform, all at once
old Father Fry started up with a burst of impromptu
eloquence, as the spirit of speaking gave him utter-
ance, much to the satisfaction of all the people, who
had collected from all parts of the country, and were
anxious to listen to some animated discourse pertaining to the business of the meeting. This sudden movement was the occasion of no little embarrassment to
the men whose business it was to guard the rails of
the platform, and who were just ready to introduce
the first speaker. They suddenly interposed their decided veto. *Go on, go on,* sounded loudly from many
voices. "It will not do," said the guardians of the
well-arranged system; "the speakers for the evening
are all engaged, and are now ready to proceed; we
can not suffer any others to speak." *Go on, go on,*
again sounded through the house, and the good old
Christian Israelite, by standing firm to his post, although in an unconstitutional manner, soon got off
the most animated and edifying address of the evening.

This perfection of planning, as many supposed it

to be at the time, for stirring up the people in the foreign mission cause, did not always work to entire satisfaction; and it soon settled down into the quintessence of dullness, from the extra efforts of the speakers to exhibit a world of learning on one privileged occasion, and from their indulging in abstract reasonings which had no exhilarating influence on the minds of the people.

In none of our great meetings of any kind have I observed so much of the absence of the social principle and the want of recognition in an official manner of so large a portion of worthy members, as in the old triennial Convention, whose delegates, for a long time, were not remarkably numerous.

Some of the causes of the omission of the usual sociability of the Baptists, in all their intercourse with each other, have already been pointed out, and to these I may add the secular principles of doing the business of our great meetings, which were quite strictly adhered to. There was something new to our people in their whole operation; and, besides this, there was always a large company of new men among the delegates, mostly of the younger class, who were so confident of their superior powers in speaking and setting matters right in all difficult cases, that they could not wait for the slower movements of their elder, and less ardent, and less confident brethren.

The members of the Missionary Union, at an early period, became so numerous that it was impracticable for any special attention to be paid to them individually by the managers of its meetings; and as none of them have any privilege of voting, unless they occupy some official station, they have fewer inducements to participate in any of the debates which may arise in the body.

CHAPTER XIX.

THIS chapter and a few succeeding ones will contain brief sketches of the works which from time to time have been published with my name, as well as those which are now nearly ready for the press. And I prefer the plan of naming them all at once, to that of noticing them in connection with other matters; and as I became an author somewhat early in life, the narratives pertaining to my publications will run through all the decades of these reminiscences.

The History of the Baptists, now called my old work on this subject, has already been referred to, as has also some account of the circumstances under which, at an early age, my mind was led to engage in those historical pursuits which have been continued for more than half a century. This old history was brought out by Lincoln & Edmunds and Manning & Loring of Boston, in 1813. These two houses carried through the press one volume each, at the same time, and as but a small part of the work was fully prepared when the

printing was commenced, to supply two presses with
copy, and all the while maintain an extensive correspondence with men in all parts of the country, was
not a small undertaking, as those who are acquainted
with such labors well know. Rev. G. H. Hough, now
in India, copied my first draughts, and at the end of
two years the work came out. And all this time frequent visits to Boston, a distance of about forty miles,
must be made, in the slow, old-fashioned way. And
how often have I thought of these toilsome journeys,
while since passing over this same ground with rail-
road speed, which then occupied two days, going and
coming.

As this work was published on my own account, to
superintend the sales and settle all the bills required
a good deal of care for a new beginner in business of
the kind, which, unfortunately, was thrown on my
hands in the midst of the war with England, in 1812,
and onward. For a long time the usual communication by water, from one end of the country to the
other, was cut off, and whether the books were to be
sent down East or far South, all must go by land.
Public conveyances of this kind were generally employed, but much of the transportation was done by
men in my employ, whom I fitted out for the purpose.
The largest expedition of this kind was one through
the southern States to Georgia, to which regions no

books could then be sent by water; and it consisted
of one team of five horses, one of two, and a single
one for myself to superintend the whole concern. The
large team took a straight course for its final destination, while I and my companion circulated in different directions, but mostly through the lower regions
of Virginia and the Carolinas, often meeting on the
route; and soon after I arrived in Savannah, the ring-
ing of bells, and other joyful demonstrations, an-
nounced the news of *peace*. A little delay would
have been greatly to my advantage; but at the time
the expedition was fitted out, there were such strong
indications of a long continuance of the war, that the
measure was thought advisable by my friends at home,
and the distant subscribers to my work, who generously bore a part of the expense, by paying an extra
price for the books. In these times, denominational
publications were more eagerly sought for and more
readily purchased than at present. Most of the five
thousand copies of the work now under consideration
were subscribed for, and the main business of the undertaking above described was to carry parcels of various quantities to the men who had sent in the lists,
for them to distribute and collect the pay. The amount
collected by the late Dr. Mercer of Georgia, and his
associates in the business, was upwards of fifteen hundred dollars. But one man did a larger business in

this line—that was the late Deacon George Dods of Providence, whose sales alone amounted to over two thousand dollars. In this way, or something like it, Backus disposed of his books of Baptist History, and some of his old letters show how much trouble he had in effecting his sales, especially in remote regions, where his agents were not as successful in their efforts as he expected.

As stereotyping in that day was very little in use, the size of an edition must be determined in the outset, and as a prudential measure subscribers were obtained beforehand. In this way all my works of any considerable size were published up to my late History of the Baptists, which was stereotyped and worked off by the thousand at a time.

In 1817 the house of Lincoln & Edmunds of Boston published my abridged edition of Robinson's History of Baptism, in an octavo volume of between five and six hundred pages.

This work was first published in England in a quarto volume of six hundred and fifty pages, but it had become so scarce and dear that but few persons could obtain it. My volume, which I purchased of Dr. Wilson, a Presbyterian minister of Philadelphia, cost me ten dollars. In 1806 the Philadelphia Association, by a vote of that body, designated Dr. Samuel Jones to prepare an abridgment of this history in

a cheap volume for general circulation. This service
the Doctor did not live to accomplish. Others had
made preparations for the work, which, on the failure
of them all, I was induced to undertake. My edition
is the one, which, for the most part, is referred to by
modern writers on the baptismal controversy.

In 1820 Lincoln & Edmunds published an abridgment of my old Baptist History in a dollar volume,
which contained a complete list of our associations as
they then stood, and which brought down the statement seven years later than my first account.

My *All Religions* was published in Providence on
my own account, in 1824. This work came out in
two forms, one for one dollar, which was according to
my original plan, the other for double that sum. After the printing was begun I was inducced by a pub-
lisher in New York to purchase a set of plates, which
he had then lately imported from England, describing
the customs of All Religions, and a work to correspond, and thus I enlarged my first plan.

One of my principal objects in this publication was
to describe the different denominations of Christians
as they now actually exist, instead of making out an
extended list of varying sects, many of which were
rather nominal than real, and multitudes of these for
ages have been extinct.

In giving the outline of the history of the parties

whose names I placed on my list, I resolved to use
the precise language of each in exhibiting their peculiar dogmas and rites, and let them speak for themselves in all that pertains to their distinctive characters. *The Religious World Displayed*, in three volumes,
by Rev. Robert Adam, of Scotland, was my model in
this respect. Had I made my compilation from other
works on the same subject, according to the custom
of most authors on All Religions, my task would have
been comparatively light; but in addition to the examination of a large number of books pertaining to
the matter in hand, I encountered much conversation
with different men in a wide field of research. As
we have in this country the counterpart of nearly all
the churches and sects in Christendom, I took it upon
myself, as far as possible, to seek personal interviews
with some of the leaders, that thereby I might gain
from them, in their own language, a definition of their
primordial principles of belief, or else obtain from
them a reference to such documents as described these
matters to their satisfaction.   This was a laborious
work, but it was full of interest and information.
With scarcely one exception I found the men on
whom I called, whether Catholics or Protestants, affa-
ble and open, and ready to afford me all needful information respecting their faith and forms, and at the
same time they were often glad of an opportunity to

correct any erroneous opinions or misrepresentations
which common fame had ascribed to them. Having
attended as far as practicable the religious services of
the different parties, I of course became somewhat
familiar with their doings, both at their alters and
their firesides, and on the whole I found my charity
in some cases enlarged by this operation, and while
my attachment to my own people was not at all diminished, I became more and more convinced that
amidst the various forms which I observed, there was
not so much difference in the feelings and purposes
of good men of every name, as many suppose.

A brief Account of the Interviews above referred to.

In one of these visitations I spent a number of
days among the Shakers at New Lebanon, New
York. As I had corresponded beforehand with one
of their principal men, and had expressed a desire
to witness the interior of their system, my arrival on
the ground was not unexpected, and soon I found
myself at home, so far as the hospitality of the neat
and flourishing establishment was concerned; and in
my free conversations with its more intelligent members, I was not a little surprised to find how well
they were informed of all passing events in the world,
and how conversant they were with them all. In
my intercourse with this peculiar people the great-

est freedom was allowed me. I could go anywhere alone, if I chose to do so, into all the departments of this sacro-secular confraternity and make what observations or inquiries I pleased of any of its members. I found them good livers, very industrious, and apparently well contented with their singular mode of life. One of my sons, a mere lad, was with me in this visitation. I found the settlement of six hundred divided into families, as they called them, of different sizes, all of whom came to the same tables for their meals; the males and females associating by themselves. The quarters assigned us was in a family of about one hundred members; a young woman, who bore the title of deaconness, waited on us at the table, and was very attentive to all our wants while we were at our head-quarters. This woman, as I learned from her own account, was a niece of one of the sisters of my church at home, having been carried into the establishment while a child by her widowed mother.

The elder with whom I had the freest intercourse, and to whom I looked for general directions among this people, in my examinations as to their internal affairs, and with whom I had previously corresponded, informed me that there was nothing in their rules to hinder visitors from eating at their common tables, but that the policy was adopted for the purpose of

saving their own people from embarrassment, especially in their religious services at their meals, which
are somewhat different from others.

The public worship of the Shakers is of course
open to all; but as it was known what was the object
of my visit, I was permitted to witness some of the
more retired performances of this people, and among
them the marching exercise, which was practiced in
the night. I well remember being conducted into a
large hall, which appeared to have been fitted up for
the purpose, and at a given signal a large company,
in single file, of males only, began to march around
the hall, which performance, with some intervals, was
continued about an hour. As the procession went
round, the leader recited the peculiarities of the faith
of the community, which was often repeated in full
chorus by the whole company, with a shouting so
loud and long, as to startle those who were not accustomed to it. The company, however, seemed
much to enjoy this sonorous and exhilarating exercise. In the recitations above referred to, and, indeed, in the general conversation of the Shakers,
they dwelt much on the celibacy of their community, and uttered high commendations of their self-
denial in this respect.

The Millennial Church is the term the Shakers apply to their community; and while they repudiate

11*

baptism, the Lord's Supper and the rites generally of other communities, they still practice the auricular confession of the Catholics, or something that nearly resembles it, and to me recommended it as a very useful institution.

CHAPTER XX.

IN Boston I had long and free conversations with the Catholic priesthood on their own premises. A Mr. Taylor, who afterwards became a bishop in France, where he died long since, took the lead in the conversation with his accustomed affability. While on the points of grace and free will, such were his definitions that I said to him, "Then, if I rightly understand the position of your church, you approach the Arminian standard. Shall I say so in my book?" "That will not do," was his quick reply ; "we copy from no party." "Well, how shall I express the matter agreeably to the fact, and the true state of the case ?" "You may say, the Arminians *approach* us on the points of grace and free will. That will do. But to say that the Catholic church, the oldest of all churches, follows any other creed, would be an historical error."

Among the many topics which came under discussion during my visit to Catholic officials in Boston, was the pope's infallibility. " No such thing in our creed," said one. " Not at all," said another, " do we hold that doctrine, in the sense ascribed to us by our opponents." " The pope is not more infallible than you are," said Mr. Taylor. " It is true," continued he, " that Bossuet, and some other high churchmen, have flattered his holiness with this appellation, in the excess of their zeal for the apostolic prerogatives against the Protestants." At this point various definitions were given by the company of theologians by whom I was surrounded, the substance of which, as near as I can recollect was, that as the decisions of the church, in all matters of faith, were infallible, and as the pope is its head, this attribute is erroneously ascribed to him in his own private character.

The adoration of the cross also came under discussion at this time, with similar efforts on the part of the Catholics to correct the misrepresentations of the Protestants; when one of the company, touching the golden pendant on his breast, quaintly observed, "Too many of all parties worship the material of which this symbol is made."

At the time here referred to, the controversy between the Unitarians and the Orthodox was in full vigor, and it was plain to be seen, that the sympathies of these Catholic men were on the Unitarian side, notwithstanding they were bound to a very strong Trinitarian creed.

With other ministers of this order I at times had free conversations on various subjects, one of which was the power of priests to pardon sins, which they declared was a vulgar error to which no good Catholic subscribed. God alone can pardon sin, was their prompt decision; but when, said they, the priest at confession, gains evidence of sincere penitence for sins confessed, he grants absolution to the confessing party, and thus has arisen the error in question. As I was a mere inquirer after matters of fact, I gave no opinions of my own on whatever statements were made to me, but I received them and recorded them in this case, and in all others, as the sentiments of the men of whom I inquired, according to their own professions. And as to the Catholics, who, as a general thing, are intensely disliked, I have thought it best in all my intercourse with them to endeavor to treat them with more mildness than they generally exhibit towards their opponents, and show them by my language and spirit towards them that our religion is better than theirs. This idea was suggested to me a long time since by one of my correspondents, who was once a member of that church, but who, for many years, has been a very successful minister of our order.

In the city of New York I made an extensive survey of the different classes of Presbyterians, and especially the Scotch Seceders, most of whom have congregations in this great metropolis. When I returned to the house of one of these ministers who accompanied me in the round, I expressed my surprise to him at the similarity of all the parties of the Secession church, and I said to him, "How shall I describe these dissenting interests, and what difference in them shall I point out? Your parties all appear so much alike, that for any thing I can see, they all ought to be classed under the same head; and yet the lines between them are distinctly drawn and strictly maintained. You are all Presbyterians in your form of church government, you are all orthodox in your creeds, and you are all rigid Protestants and Pedobaptists. You all complain of the Baptists for their close communion, and yet you do not all commune with each other. Is not this an anomaly in church history?"

The comments of my friend I do not recollect, but this much I remember, namely, that throughout my whole interview with him he acted the part of a Christian gentleman, and displayed the sociability of a well-bred Scotchman.

I found the Lutheran ministers very tenacious of the term *evangelical*, as applied to their church, and that they viewed with much complaisancy the prosperity of their cause in this country. The clergy of this community, with whom I conversed, appeared sound in the faith, and lamented the defection of so many men of eminence in the Lutheran church, in the old country. In their public worship, I observed, they use a liturgy of a very limited extent. When I inquired of this people respecting Luther's famous doctrine of consubstantiation, instead of transubstantiation, as held by the church of Rome, they informed me that although it was in their creed, yet very little was said among them on the subject. Indeed, they did not hesitate to say that this mysterious and peculiar dogma of the great reformer had become a dead letter with many, if not most of their community.

With the Moravian ministers, on whom I called, I was very much pleased, especially their kind and unassuming manners. Their private dwellings and confraternity establishments I found remarkable for their neat and comfortable appearance, and their mode of living gave me to understand how this community can sustain their operations on so broad a scale, with so small an amount of funds.

The simple and moderate episcopacy of the United Brethren appeared to me a model of church government, of the Episcopal form, which I should be disposed to adopt, were I to relinquish the Baptist rule.

In one instance a singular result followed my call on a clergyman, who received me very kindly, and from whom I parted without any suspicion of rivalship. But it so happened that before my work came out, one on *All Religions*, about the same size, was issued, and put into the hands of book peddlers by a large publishing house in the city of ———. This book was hastily thrown together from other works, and I ascertained that the clergyman above referred to was the compiler of the production, which was without a name. I never saw the man afterwards. He died many years ago. The most singular part of the story is, that the agents who were sent out with the work in question, actually palmed it off on many of my subscribers. With this transaction, however, I did not suppose that either the compiler, or the publishers were concerned.

The Result of these Visitations.—I have already stated that my free and familiar intercourse with men so diversified in their religious opinions and pursuits, confirmed me in an opinion which I adopted long ago, namely, that the course I had pursued spoils a man for a bigot; and again, that a firm attachment to one's own church and creed, and a cordial Christian friendship for good men of every name, are entirely compatible with each other. In the visitations above described, where I discovered the vitality of religion, I often found my sympathies involuntarily enlisted on the side of the men with whom I was then associated, in all that pertained to their trials and embarrassments, and was really glad for them, when they could make out a good account of their affairs, and exhibit fair prospects for the future.

With almost all the parties I visited, I found them complaining, a good deal like the Baptists of the following things :

1. *Of misrepresentation and unfair treatment by other societies.* Something or other in their faith or forms was misunderstood or was erroneously stated. In some cases a slight modification of terms would make all right; and they were often grieved that their opponents would hold them accountable for language which they did not adopt, but which was put into their mouths by others, and for sentiments which were palmed upon them by analogy and construction. This complaint, according to all church history, I find has been common in all ages and countries, so much so, that in my judgment, *misrepresentation,* in some way or other, has been the bane of the world, especially in religious matters, and most of all, when dissenters from national churches have been made to feel its

power. This subject will be more fully discussed in
the next chapter.

2. *Of pecuniary embarrassments, and the want of lib-*
erality among the people. I soon found that the Baptists were not alone in these matters, but that many
other communities were groaning under embarrassing
debts on their houses of worship. They too had depended much on borrowed capital. This false principle, this most miserable rule of action in former years,
seemed to be a truly American idea, and many splendid sanctuaries have I seen, which had been dedicated
to the God of heaven, but which were owned in reality by men of the world, in part at least.

Many suppose, that as a whole, the Baptists are the
most backward of any denomination in the land, in
parting with their money for religious purposes ; but
I have heard grievous complaints on this score from
other quarters. I well remember the free remarks on
this subject, of an old Lutheran minister of Philadelphia, while he was showing me the spacious church
in which he officiated. The parsimony of his people
and the smallness of his stipend were freely comment-
ed on by the good old German divine.

" I thank the Lord for a free gospel," said a zealous
Methodist. "I have been a member of the society
twenty-five years, and it has never cost me twenty-

five cents." " The Lord have mercy on your stingy old soul," said the minister from the desk.

My late Edition of Baptist History.—After a lapse of about thirty years from the time my old history was published, I began to make preparations for a new edition, the principal object of which was to bring down the account of the denomination to the then present time. I also resolved to present to my readers all the new facts which I could obtain in favor of the main positions of the Baptists, relative to the antiquity of their sentiments, and the prevalence of the same in all ages and countries where any traces of them can be found. For this purpose a great amount of additional reading became necessary, and a considerable number of books, which I could not find in this country, had to be sent for from abroad ; but this labor was small compared with the long journeys which I found it necessary to perform, and the extensive correspondence which I found it absolutely needful to maintain.

A number of local Baptist histories had been published in different places since my old history was published, which supplied me with good materials to a limited extent; but still it was reduced to a certainty, after a full view of the field before me, that widespread and long-continued efforts must yet be made for the accomplishment of my new plan. The de-

nomination had increased many fold in the course of
thirty years; vast regions of country, which were in
a wilderness state at the time my old work was published, had been settled, and were filled with multitudes of our people among other settlers, all of which
regions must be explored anew, and historical facts
and documents collected from them, for the purpose
of carrying out my design to its full extent. This
amount of labor had a somewhat formidable appearance at first view; but by dint of perseverance, with
the aid of a long list of valuable correspondents, together with the post office facilities, which I shall
soon name, this greatest labor of my life, in the collection of historical documents, in the course of
about ten years, was effected, and the work was published by L. Colby & Co., New York, in 1848. One
of my sons was with me five years, constantly engaged in copying for the press, assisting in my correspondence, reading proofs, and other parts of my labor.

In the commencement of this laborious undertaking, I sent out a large number of printed circulars,
in which were stated the outlines of my plan, and the
kind of assistance I needed. These I often directed
at a venture to men whose names I found in the minutes of our associations and elsewhere, and in this way
I obtained many of my stated correspondents.

The Historical Correspondent and Enquirer was the name of a small paper which I published gratis for a number of years. This sheet was wholly devoted to my historical pursuits. It came out at different periods, as my wants required, and by being sent to Baptist papers of all kinds, on exchange, in this way they came to me free of cost. Large parcels of the papers thus received are now on hand.

During all this time I had no interfering vocation, except the care of the post office in this place, which I went into after I had resigned a pastoral station which I had occupied twenty-five years. This resignation was forced upon me by a severe pressure of one of the high excitements of those times. The post office, then the third in the State in size, I held ten years, so that I was literally "ten years among the mail-bags." Most of the labor, however, was performed by my sons. While thus occupying this official station, and at the same time pursuing my historical inquiries, I was often at head-quarters, where I became pretty well acquainted with the routine of Congressional affairs, with the interior arrangements, and the outside management of the General Post Office, and with many of the men in high official stations at the capital; and for a while I was a member of the board of the college there under Baptist rule.

My principal reason for going into a secular employment was the great assistance it would afford me in my historical pursuits by means of the *franking privilege,* which was then enjoyed by postmasters of all grades. This privilege was very useful to me in the extensive correspondence, which I was at that time obliged to maintain. But I found bigots among postmasters as well as elsewhere. Some of them challenged my little historical sheet as not being a *newspaper,* in the sense of the law, which defines their rights, because it did not contain general *news.* This construction, had it been admitted at head-quarters as correct, would have operated very much against me, especially in the business of exchanges. In that case neither my papers could go out, nor others would come to me free; and as newspaper postage was then very high my bill of expense in this department must have been much increased.

But my opponents failed at this point, and my little paper stood its ground, and brought me in papers and pamphlets to a large amount *free* of all cost.

The next and most serious complaint against me was for a too free use of the *franking privilege* in sending letters and circulars in such abundance all over the country in aid of a sectarian work. But as our government has nothing to do with sects and parties in its laws, which I had been careful not to violate, as I made it clearly to appear, the case was dismissed and my *franking* went on.

In vindication of my free use of the mails for the transmission of my documents far and wide, I stated to the men in charge of the General Post Office, that besides my right, by the laws of the Department, as a matter of equity I was entitled to a large share of mail facilities, since I claimed to be the historical representative of more than one fourth of the population of the United States, including Baptists of all classes, with their adherents; that I corresponded with them all of every name and nation, and was assisted by them in my historical pursuits.

The income of letters during the ten years in which I was engaged in collecting materials and publishing the work now under consideration, was very large. These epistolary documents are all preserved with care among my papers of this kind.

CHAPTER XXI.

AT an early day my thoughts were directed to a
work of this kind, and my argument for it was, that
so large and costly are our standard works on church
history that but few of our common readers feel able
to purchase them, nor can they find time to peruse
them. There was another consideration of some
weight with me in this undertaking, which was to
present to plain readers the naked facts of history,
free from false miracles, and to bring out more fully
and favorably the accounts of large parties of reputed
heretics of the early ages than had hitherto been done
by any author but Neander, and very briefly by him.
I soon found that my epitome would lead me into the
Fathers and others, in addition to all my former ac-
quisitions of historical knowledge from the works in
common use by English readers, for in order to make
summary statements with any degree of confidence
the whole ground must be surveyed.

As most of the authors of our standard works on church history have belonged to national churches, and have sympathized with the church of Rome in all her conflicts with dissenting parties, I, at an early period, began to suspect that as a general thing, these authors had not done full justice to these parties, but that they repeated the accounts of old Catholic writers whose prejudices were very strong against them without a thorough examination as to their correctness. High churchmen are apt to think that the affairs of non-conformists are of but little account. While thinking of this matter I read some candid expositions of Neander, respecting the real sentiments of a portion of these people in opposition to the unfavorable testimony of Augustine, and others, who copied from these authors. This first suggested to me the idea of going into a thorough examination from original sources of the genuine history of the Donatists and kindred parties of the early ages.

The Manichees also I found had been most grossly misrepresented, according to their own accounts, as given by Augustine. They frankly acknowledged the errors of their system, and wherein they differed from other professors of the Christian religion. The most prominent of these errors was a denial of the real humanity of Jesus Christ, as they held that he was born, lived, and died in appearance only. This

12

view of the character of Christ, they openly avowed
and zealously defended by Scripture passages and
other arguments. This theory came down from the
Gnostics; it was adopted by many other parties, and
some of the Fathers, it was supposed, were more or
less tinctured with it. But the doctrine of the government of the world by two beings, *good* and *bad*,
which was laid to the charge of this people, they ve-
hemently denied. The *unity* of God they unequivo-
cally maintained, as I have shown very clearly in my
account of them. The Manichees not only very often
and very loudly complained of being falsely accused
on many matters pertaining to their faith and manners by Augustine, their most bitter opponent, but
they made light of his story of having been one of
them, as he professed to have been, for about ten
years.

And as to the Donatists, all church historians close
their accounts of them by referring to an undefined
company of rude adherents, called *Circumcellians*, or
at least, they have always said something about this
rough appendage of the Donatist party. Mosheim
says these lawless men were the soldiery of the followers of Donatus, and fought their battles for them.
This old story I have sifted to the bottom and find it
a mere fabrication of the bishop of Hippo; and by
the many passages which I have quoted from his own

writings, in which he has given full accounts of his
controversies with this people, I make it plainly appear that they positively denied any connection with,
or even knowledge of, the men in question.

But the challenges and disclaimers above referred
to are entirely omitted by ecclesiastical writers, except Neander, and a few others; they have repeated
the impeachments of Augustine, as if they had never
been denied; and in some cases they have made them
worse than they are in their original form, or than a
true version of the original language will sustain,
with no intimations whatever of any adverse statements having been made by the adverse parties, and
recorded by the accuser himself, in his own works.
What he gave out as current rumors, they report as
sober certainties; and they assert as undisputed facts
what he did not pretend to have proved.

The history of the Donatists cost me a great
amount of labor, and the facts which I have collected from the writings of Optatus, Augustine, and the
numerous editors of their works, respecting the character, the publications, the sufferings, and the number of this people, and also their influence in the support of evangelical principles, have far exceeded my
most sanguine expectations. I had supposed that no
vestiges remained of the literary productions of that
large class of able men who are known to have ex-

isted among the Donatists; but on this point I was
agreeably disappointed, since I found in the works of
Augustine an abundance of quotations from Donatist
authors, in the veritable Latin in which they wrote,
in defense of their own principles and pursuits, and in
condemnation of the corruptions and persecutions of
their Catholic opponents. These passages are spread
out in detached portions by their adversary, for the
purpose of refuting them, in the same manner that
controversial writers manage at the present time.
And that these quotations are correctly made appears
highly probable from the fact, that from Augustine's
own showing, the Donatists cut up his corrupt system
of church building root and branch, and furthermore,
that they were bold assailants of his plan, and sturdy
defenders of their own. While the translations of the
passages above referred to are incorporated in my
narratives, a sufficient amount of the original matter
is placed in foot notes, that those who can read them
may see how clearly they reasoned, in support of
their own scriptural plan of church building, in opposition to the loose system of their adversaries.

The main scope of my Compendium is to give
my readers a summary view of the principal facts of
church history as they are recorded in our more elab-
orate works on this subject. For this purpose I have
labored to make myself about as well acquainted with

the affairs of the whole of Christendom, as I am with those of my own denomination; and to exhibit the most interesting facts in as brief a manner as possible, of whatever is recorded of all churches, sects and parties of all ages, and countries, and creeds, in an unsectarian manner.

Under proper heads I have described the state of things under the patriarchal and Jewish dispensations, during the first three centuries of the Christian economy, the ten great persecutions, the rapid progress of Christianity under them, the conversion of Constantine the Great, the first Christian emperor, the good and the bad effects of his policy and patronage, the increasing corruptions of the gospel in the following ages, the conflicts among the great leaders in church concerns for preëminence and control before the rise of the papacy, the great splits and divisions of the dominant church, caused by the Arians; the Nestorians, and others; the eastern and western, or the Greek and Roman churches; the history of the popes and patriarchs, general councils, and of those of Trent and Constance in particular; the Crusades, the Reformation in Germany, in Switzerland, in France, and England and elsewhere.

Interspersed with these narratives are the early apologies for the Christian religion, by Justin Martyr,

Minucius Felix, Tertullian and others, and copious details of Christian antiquities.

I have also given pretty full accounts of the dissenting parties in all ages and countries, which I claim as evangelical Christians, such as the Montanists, the Novatians, the Donatists, the Paulicians, the Paterines, the Waldenses, the Albigenses, the Petrobrussians, the Picards, the Hussites and others.

And finally my aim has been, in my condensed accounts of ecclesiastical affairs, to present to those who may peruse my narratives intelligent views of all that pertains to this department.

The term *Puritan* has been applied to many of the dissenting parties above named, but, as I have attempted to show in my accounts of them, it was in all cases used as a nick-name, by the way of reproach, by their adversaries, and was never originally adopted by themselves. This remark will be found correct as to the Novatians, the Donatists and other reformers of an early age. The same may be said of the Waldenses of different companies, and a large company of English reformers, many of whom never left the national church. All the parties now under consideration went for greater purity in their churches, at least as to their members, morals and worship, than they found in the worldly sanctuaries which they had abjured. A church "without *spot or wrinkle*" was a favorite passage with the Donatists.

"Stand by thyself, I am holier than thou," was sneeringly said by their opponents, for the purpose of exciting popular odium against them. Augustine dealt much in this contemptuous language, in his comments on the reforming efforts of the Puritans of his day. But when he reasoned soberly with them, his principal argument was, that the plan of the Puritans was utterly impracticable; that a thorough sifting of the bad members from the good, would do more hurt than good, by the disturbance and ill-will it would occasion; and he zealously maintained that, to let them both grow together until the harvest, was a Bible doctrine. The condition of his own church, we must remember, was held in view, in his reasonings of this kind, which, he said, "the rough discipline of the Donatists would rend into a thousand schisms."

In reply to all this kind of reasoning, the Donatists stood firm to their favorite principles of church purity, both in their preaching and writings, and in defense of them they quoted from the prophets all those beautiful passages which foretold the highway of holiness which the unclean should not pass over, and all the descriptions of the genuine character of the church of Christ which the New Testament contains.

And while the character of the Old Testament rulers was highly extolled by their adversaries, " God
commissioned prophets, not kings, to preach his
word," said the Donatists; and again, "Jesus Christ
sent fishermen, not soldiers and executioners," said
they, "to propagate his gospel."

On a review of the whole ground I have gone over
in my researches for materials for the work now under
consideration, I have formed a less favorable opinion
of some men of great renown than I formerly entertained of them, and particularly of the famous Bishop
of Hippo; and I advise those who wish to believe
him an honorable opponent, a fair debater, and a
friend of justice, not to examine very closely into his
treatment of the Donatists and Manichees, and especially into their complaints of his misrepresentations and persecutions.

Among the chief causes and instruments of all
persecutions, I am inclined to mention the two following:

1. *Misrepresentation*, in its various forms, in religious concerns, has been the bane of the world, and
has been more successfully employed than almost any
other means, by designing and unprincipled men,
against those whom they sought to injure or to de-
stroy.

2. *The priesthoods*, of all ages and countries, as a

general thing, have set in motion all the religious persecutions which have been carried on in the name of secular men, whether under Pagan, Papal or Protestant rule, and the fear of loss, or the hope of gain, has been at the bottom of all those cruel and destructive measures, in the prosecution of which it may be truly said,

"Man's inhumanity to man
Makes countless thousands mourn."

Civil rulers are so much occupied with worldly concerns of various kinds, their pleasures and ambitious schemes, that they would not meddle with religious matters, about which they generally know or care but little, were they not stimulated to it by the men who fear their craft is in danger.

Respecting a few subjects of ancient history, and *two* very eminent men, I have been somewhat disappointed as to the result of my inquiries.

The matters of history in question are,

1. The wide chasm or vacant space in the affairs of the Jews, from the latest of the prophets to the New Testament times. I well understood beforehand that this space was large, but I was disappointed in its unusual extent, and the impenetrable darkness that rests upon it. In making out my sketches of the earliest times, I went forward in a rapid man-

ner through the patriarchal ages, and in the same way I traced the history of the Jews till I came to the latest prophetic writings, and here I found a number of hundred years intervening before the New Testament history begins. I looked into Josephus and other Jewish writings, but darkness extended over the extended space. I have seen it intimated that some portion of this lost history has been found, but I have so little confidence in the account, that I have not looked after it.

2. In Christian history, I also found more darkness hanging over a few of the early centuries than I expected to find. Eusebius, Socrates, and a few others in the early part of the fourth century, have left some records in the form of church history. From the Apologies of Justin Martyr, Tertullian and others, and from Pliny and some other Pagan writers of early times, we learn something about the Christians during the ages now under review, as to their character and condition, but still only very scanty accounts have come down to us respecting them.

The Apostolical Constitutions, so called, are quite minute in their details as to the Christian practices of the times in which they were written, and so far, they are valuable guides; but instead of being the work of the apostles, they were evidently composed as late as the fourth or fifth century.

When we come to any thing like church history, it is mostly occupied in the controversies of great bishops, and their scrambles for places of emolument and power, and very little is said of the vital principles of the gospel, except among the reputed heretics. I am inclined, however, to believe, and have so stated in my work, that these principles lived and flourished among the common people, outside of the great cities, long after they had sadly declined in them.

The two eminent men to whom I lately alluded, were the wise king of Israel, and the first Christian emperor.

Solomon, with all his glory and fame during his long life, became so unpopular at the close of it, with the great mass of his subjects, that there were but feeble lamentations at his death ; and this change of feeling towards this illustrious man, it is said, was the result of the people being overtaxed for the cost of the temple at Jerusalem, and other public works, and for his own private mansions and family expenses, which must have been immensely great.

Such an unfavorable account of the close of the life of this very eminent man, was unexpected to me, and I was equally disappointed, when I made search for the offspring of this uxorious king, to find but two are ascribed to him in all the history of the Jewish kings, namely, a daughter, and Rohoboam, who by one rash decision rent the nation asunder, and caused ten tribes to go off no one can tell where.

My disappointment in the history of Constantine was, as tradition affirms, that he went off to found Constantinople out of disaffection with Rome, where he was so unpopular that he was treated with much disrespect, and that his unpopularity arose principally from his severe measures towards some of his own family, which the best friends of the emperor have always regretted.

Once more, the dissenting parties of the better sort, from the early ages, and in the whole history of Christianity, I have found much more numerous than I had supposed, and the sentiments and influences which have been ascribed to these despised and persecuted people by their enemies, indicate an efficiency in the support of the pure principles of the gospel beyond my most sanguine expectations. Indeed, I have been led to think, that the number of real Christians was as great, if not greater, among the reputed heretics, than in the great national churches by which they have been despised and oppressed.

One thing is very plain, from all church history, the Catholic church has always had its hands full of business, in its efforts to suppress the numerous parties of reputed heretics.

FIFTH DECADE.

[This decade embraces all the remaining facts yet to be noticed, from about 1840 to the present time; and in discoursing
upon them, I shall occasionally find it necessary to pass rapidly
in different directions over the whole fifty years now under review.]

CHAPTER XXII.

CHANGES IN MEETING-HOUSE FIXINGS AND COMFORTS.—CHANGES IN CHURCH MUSIC.—ORGANS.—TITLES OF MINISTERS.—MY EFFORTS FOR MINISTERIAL EDUCATION.—WITH OTHERS.

IN my early travels among our people I never saw any thing like a stove or a furnace in their houses of worship. In a few instances, in small houses, there might be seen chimneys with fire-places in them, at one end, and sometimes both. Foot stoves, for the use of females, were a very common article.

When we consider what poor buildings were then in use by most of our churches; that many of them were placed in remote and bleak situations, far from the homes of many of the people; that they were often reached by rough and rugged ways, and when arrived at were so cheerless and uncomfortable, it seems a wonder now that so many attended them.

Thus far I have had respect to country regions, and to houses of an inferior class; but in the cities and larger towns, where church edifices were well finished, scarcely any thing was done to make their inside conveniences and accommodations to correspond with those which the worshipers enjoyed at their homes.

Carpets and cushions were then but little known; and
for a whole house to be fitted up in modern style, was
never thought of in our most costly churches. Here
and there you might see a few pews of the meeting-
going aristocracy done off in a different manner from
the rest, and as each one consulted his own taste, the
colors of the fittings were sometimes as various as
those of Joseph's coat, and presented a grotesque appearance for a Christian sanctuary.

In the construction of the pews in the best of our
houses, in my early day, the old high-back, square
system generally prevailed, and as standing in prayer
time was then the uniform custom, in some cases the
seats were so fitted that they might be lifted up to
accommodate the worshipers in this position; and
when they were let down with care, all went on very
well, but when this letting down was done in a
hurry, as it often was by children and others, there
was a clattering throughout the house which would
startle those who were not accustomed to the sound.

I can hardly realize that I have lived to witness
the great and beneficial changes to which I have thus
briefly referred, and that at this early day I should
see such strong indications of a still more rapid extension of this needful reform.

The Changes in Church Music, so called, among the Baptists, during the Period which these Reminiscences Embrace.

In my earliest intercourse among this people congregational singing generally prevailed among them. In a few churches in the northern regions, mostly, however, in New England, gallery choirs took the lead in this part of worship; but nowhere then was there what would now be called a scientific performance of this service, but the nearest approaches to it were found in a few Baptist congregations at the North, where it often happened that the leaders and many of the members of the choirs were not members of the churches for whose benefit they sang. This was sometimes a matter of grief to some of the old members, which, however, was generally borne without any open murmurs.

Through all the country parts of the South and West, in my earliest explorations of those regions, the old-fashioned way of lining out the psalm or hymn, as the singing went on, was very common, as it was also in many parts of the middle and northern States.

As this reading of the lines was often performed by the deacons of the churches, who stood under or in front of the pulpits, the term *deaconing* was sometimes applied to the service.

In many congregations the old pitch pipe was seen
in the hands of the leader of the singing, and by degrees small instruments of music were introduced into
the singing galleries, where extra efforts were made
among the performers, and finally the *bass viol*, then
the *ne plus ultra*, the perfection of instrumental music,
became a permanent fixture in a portion of our congregations.   Strong prejudices, however, for a time
existed in the minds of many of our old members
against the "big fiddle," as the bass viol was called,
and indeed against all kinds of musical instruments,
and church difficulties often arose on this account.
But by degrees these prejudices subsided as the people became more and more interested in the performances of their singing choirs, and as their congregations were augmented by the new attractions in their
religious worship.

The Introduction of the Organ among the Baptists.

This instrument, which from time immemorial has
been associated with cathedral pomp and prelatical
power, and has always been the peculiar favorite of
great national churches, at length found its way into
Baptist sanctuaries, and the first one ever employed
by the denomination in this country, and probably in
any other, might have been seen standing in the singing gallery of the old Baptist meeting house in Paw-

tucket, about forty years ago, where I then officiated as pastor; and in process of time, this *dernier resort* in church music was adopted by many of our societies which had formerly been distinguished for their primitive and conventicle plainness. The changes which have been experienced in the feelings of a ˙large portion of our people has often surprised me. Staunch old Baptists in former times would as soon have tolerated the Pope of Rome in their pulpits as an organ in their galleries, and yet the instrument has gradually found its way among them, and their successors in church management, with nothing like the jars and difficulties which arose of old concerning the bass viol and smaller instruments of music.

The circumstances attending the innovation in question among my people, which was rather pleasing than offensive to the whole concern, may be thus related : As yet there was no other house of worship in the place, and our choir of singers were making vigorous efforts in behalf of their department, in connection with the Mozart Society, which for many years occupied an important position in the singing line, and frequently had concerts of a very popular character, which were always held in our house of worship. In aid of these performances a small organ was obtained by a joint-stock company, which, in the end, became a permanent fixture of the house. This

clever little concern, still alive in another congregation, took the place of all the inferior cymbals
on which our singers hitherto depended for instrumental aid, and by degrees became a favorite with all
the people however much some of them had previously been biassed against any artificial aid in the
melody of the sanctuary, and indeed, to the attractions '
of the gallery, rather than the pulpit, some people slyly
ascribed the full houses which we generally enjoyed.

This change in Baptist policy happened in a subur-
ban branch of the old Roger Williams church, at a
distance of four miles from its center, a number of
years before any movement was made by the mother
body in the organ business.

I have already stated that at the time above referred to, the house in which I officiated was the only
one in Pawtucket, or its vicinity, where are at present
accommodations more or less splendid for church-
going people of many different creeds. And I would
furthermore state that for a number of years past,
there have existed within my old parish bounds, six
good houses of worship for Baptists, in all of which
the instruments so indispensable for modern singers
are found. One of this number is of the Freewill order, but this community a few years since, following in
the wake of their brethren of a more stringent creed,
placed an organ in their own singing gallery.

How far this modern organ fever will extend among our people, and whether it will on the whole work a *re*-formation or *de*-formation in their singing service, time will more fully develop. The original purpose of our small instrument was to assist the old-fashioned gallery choir, and to gather it in full strength around it, and so long as the musical concern in question is thus employed, we may reasonably expect it will be viewed with favor by spiritual worshipers, but whenever it shall assume an overwhelming influence, and only a few artistic performers be retained in the singers' seats, to be directed by men who take but little interest in any of the services of the sanctuary, except what pertains to their professional duty, then a machine, harmless in itself, will be looked upon with disfavor if not with disgust by the more pious portion of our assemblies.

Concerning the Titles applied to Baptist Ministers at different Times.

From my earliest recollections, and from the most ancient records of the denomination in this country, all ministers who had received ordination were termed *elders.* This title, with our people, has respect to office rather than age, and of course they feel no embarrassment in applying it to the youngest of their ministers. Men of twenty or fourscore, with them,

are equally entitled to be ranked among their elders.
This scriptural term, against which none of the usual
objections which many are disposed to make against
high-sounding titles can be urged, is still employed
by a large majority of the American Baptists through
the whole country, and I am often sorry to see such
a decline in the use of it among our people. The attachment of old staunch Baptists to this familiar and
favorite designation of their spiritual guides, especially
among the sisterhood, who often applied it, in their
free discourse, to ministers of other denominations, has
been referred to in chapter twelve of these reminiscences, and as *elder* and *presbyter* are synonymous
terms, and as, moreover, *presbyters* constitute one of
the three orders of episcopacy, our old-fashioned
members did not make a great mistake in this business, so far as Episcopalians are concerned.

The term *Reverend*, now in such common use
among our people and all other parties, was generally very offensive to Baptists of the old school,
and was seldom employed by them in common conversation, in letter inscriptions, or in any other way.
Holy and reverend is his name, as a designation of the
Divine Being, was a passage often quoted by object-
ors to giving reverence to men. To the Deity alone,
said they, reverence belongs. At the period now under review, so generally was this objectionable title

avoided by our people, that when they saw it affixed
to the names of ministers in the public prints, on letters, etc., they concluded that they of course must belong to some other denomination, besides their own.

The few Doctors amongst us in early times, whenever spoken of by the people at large, and especially
the plainer sort, were ranked with the eldership ; by
those who were more observant of the courtesies of
life, the titles of these men were applied to them on
proper occasions ; but even by the more courteous
class, there was not so much parade about diplomas
at all times, and in all records as at the present day ;
nor did we then hear so many censorious comments
on the titles now under consideration, as have been
published for a few years past. The cases were so
few as to attract but little attention, and as a general
thing, the title was conferred on men of a good deal
of notoriety in the Baptist ministry.

The term *bishop*, in preference to those I have
named, was strenuously recommended by some of our
ministers a few years since, and in some instances, the
minutes of associations and other documents were
made out on this plan. The men who proposed this
new ministerial nomenclature for our use, plead the
native signification of the word which is translated
bishop, and that we are justly entitled to it as a
proper designation for the *overseers* of our churches.

But the proposal did not meet with general accept-
ance, nor did the few who began the innovation long
continue it.

While this experiment was being made, ministers
of humble pretensions were sometimes not a little surprised to find themselves in the public prints, and on
letters addressed to them, suddenly translated to episcopal honors, without a previous election or consecration.

In these times, postmasters and their assistants
were often embarrassed in their vocation. " What
can this mean ?" a mail clerk would say, while preparing to make up a mail. " There must be some
mistake in this direction. I have heard of a Baptist
minister of such a name in that place, and have often
done up letters for him ; but I never knew before
that the man was a bishop." The clerk at the other
end was in a similar dilemma, and when the owner
took the letter from the office, all joined in a hearty
laugh at its singular superscription.

At the period above referred to, I was in the midst
of my preparations for the publication of my late
edition of Baptist history, and as the titles of our ministers are so few, I would have been glad if that of
bishop had been added to their number, for then I
should have found more ample scope for circumlocution in my narratives. Then I could have spoken of

the episcopal order, of the bench of bishops, of bish-oprics, etc., when alluding to the persons and func-tions of our preachers and pastors. But as I was fully satisfied that this new plan would prove a fail-ure, I never departed from our old rule in designating our ministers.

Although there is no question in my mind, that in primitive times bishops and presbyters, or even eld-ers, stood on a level in the gospel ministry as to pow-er and influence; yet as a distinction in these offices has been made from time immemorial, by the consent of the greatest part of Christendom, I do not think it advisable for our community, in this late age of the world, to interfere in this arrangement. As mankind in general have been so long accustomed to associate with the term bishop, the idea of a superior order of the ministry, it seems improper for the Baptists, who have hitherto been loud in condemning the application of all high-sounding titles to their spiritual guides, to attempt the change here had in view.

Informal and unconsecrated bishops are already found amongst us in sufficient numbers, for all prac-ticable purposes in the operation of our simple ma-chinery in church management, without augmenting the list by any conventional rules.

The term pastor has been recommended as a gen-eral title for all our ministers, which will do very well

13

at home for pastors, indeed ; but the old name of elder
is the preferable cognomen after all. It is the freest
from objections of any other ; it is good for all times
and places ; and I have a full belief that it will be
retained as long as possible by all our plain and scriptural people.

*My Efforts for the Promotion of Ministerial Education
in my early and more active Days.*

As I well knew from painful experience what it
was to struggle with pecuniary embarrassments in
preparing for, and in pursuing a course of collegiate
studies, with a view to the ministry, I naturally sympathized with those who had to encounter similar
trials and difficulties, and stood ready at all times to
afford them all the assistance in my power. In a few
cases I took young men of the class now under consideration into my study, tuition free, and I sought
for them pecuniary aid, after the beneficiary system
had obtained some efficiency among our people, which
system, in my early day, had hardly commenced operations to any considerable extent. Some of the
young men who were thus patronized by me, intended to pursue a college course, while others did not set
their aim so high. These engaged only in those English studies which would enable them, in a more acceptable manner, to perform ministerial labors, a thing

quite common at that time. A number of these men, in both departments, acted well their parts in after times.

In addition to my doings of this kind on my own premises, in aid of my junior brethren, as I was located on the then great thoroughfare through the country, and was, moreover, somewhat known as the friend and promoter of ministerial education, I was often applied to by those who were making their early efforts in this business for advice and direction how to proceed. In that day it was a lonesome look for young men without funds or able relatives who were disposed to aid them. "Where shall we find a place to study?" and "How shall we be supported?" were questions not easy to be answered by many poor young men of those times, who in the end surmounted all the difficulties in their way, and arose to usefulness or eminence.

As yet there was but little system among us in the business of ministerial education, and the beneficiary system was in its infancy. We had but one college, and as for theological schools, we had none, even for a partial course.

One of the young men above alluded to is now at the head of one of our most flourishing and distinguished literary institutions. Another, somewhat his senior, for many years occupied an important pastoral

station in a neighboring State.   They, with others
of less eminence in our ranks, have kindly informed
me of my efforts to aid them by proper directions, a
long time after all remembrance of the events had
passed from my mind.

A little more than forty years ago, an education society was formed in the old Warren Association, expressly for the purpose of meeting the wants of our
rising ministry.   This society was very small at first,
but it soon became quite useful as a center of operations within our associational bounds.   The movement towards it was made at the instance of Mr.
Winchell, then pastor of the first Baptist church in
Boston.   In the minutes of the ancient body just
named, for 1816, I find the following list of officers
of this then young educational concern, namely, D.
Benedict, secretary; S. S. Nelson, treasurer; J. Going, J. M. Winchell, W. Gammell, A. Fisher, D.
Curtis, B. Bates and S. Glover, executive committee.
This institution still lives within the bounds of the
association in which it originated, and Dr. Caswell
of Brown University, who for a long time has been
its secretary, is its chief manager.   Abiel Fisher, David Curtis and the writer are the only officers of this
society, as it was originally constituted, who are now
alive.

At the period above alluded to, the most active

promoters of ministerial education were our ministers
of the younger class. To them our fathers in the
ministry gave up the management of this business, so
far as its more active duties were concerned. At the
same time, they most heartily encouraged the very
needful undertaking, at an early stage of which our
committee met serious embarrassments, not only for
the want of funds, but also for the want of confidence
in some who applied to us for recognition and assistance. And after all our care and caution, we made a
few mistakes as to the men we received and patronized. Difficulties of a similar character, I believe,
were experienced by other societies in selecting subjects for this then new method of helping forward
candidates for the ministry.

CHAPTER XXIII.

A LIST of all our public establishments for literary
and theological training to a late date, has already
been given. I have also stated that I have lived to
see the rise of them all, save one, namely, that which
I call my *alma mater*. That institution, now called
ancient, was about forty years old when I entered it
as a student, in 1804. Six years of this time, however, were lost for the purposes of education, while
the premises were occupied for a hospital and bar-
racks by the French and American troops in the war
of the Revolution.

Now, instead of one solitary school of a collegiate
character, we have about thirty ; one third of them
are styled universities. But a few of those which are
thus distinguished, however, have any thing like a
university of teaching on their premises. This term,
university, seems a very favorite one with the Baptists in many places, while that of *college* is more ap-

propriate for small literary undertakings, in their incipient movements. Should they increase in their dimensions they may in time be justly entitled to the first distinction.

Rhode Island College was the humble designation, for about forty years after it was founded, of the institution which for a somewhat longer period has been known by the name of Brown University. At first there was but one college building, where now there are four.

When the buildings, the professors and the general facilities for educational purposes were about to be increased, and the dropping of the old cognomen began to be discussed, the managers of the growing concern specified a certain sum which should entitle the donor of it to the privilege of conferring a new name. This sum was forthwith advanced by one of the most munificent patrons of the institution, and to it his own name was immediately added, where for all coming time it will no doubt remain.

As scarcely any of our literary institutions have ever had any aid of a public nature, unusual efforts have in all cases been needful, on the part of their projectors and patrons, to found them and carry them forward to self-sustaining positions. This was the case even with Rhode Island College for a long course of years, during its early operations. Not the least

assistance did it ever receive from the State from
which it took its name. And little do our people of
the present day understand what an amount of calculation and labor were necessary in early times to
keep the wheels in motion on College Hill, where
they now move forward with so much steadiness and
strength. In those times, the old Philadelphia Association made annual contributions " for our college
in Rhode Island."

Accounts somewhat similar might be given of the
difficulties which have been encountered by most of
our young colleges in their early days. Tuition fees
were small; students, in most cases, have been few;
and as for liberal patrons, as a general thing they have
been, like angels' visits, few and far between.

As yet, the more modern practice of planting funds
for the support of college operations, was but little
known, and in addition to the scanty income from a
few students, mostly of the poorer class, current expenses had to be borne by the annual collections of
agents sent out for this purpose through a wide extent of country. The salaries of the officers were set
at a low figure, and often poorly paid at that. But
the worst of all was, that these feeble concerns would
generally set out with debts of embarrassing amounts,
which would accumulate from year to year, to the
great hinderance of their prosperity.

Fifty years ago the Baptists and Methodists were about alike on the subject of ministerial education. Among both parties their preachers were numerous and active, and performed a great amount of ministerial labor, while as yet but few of the most successful laborers in either society had acquired any thing more than a common school education on the limited scale which was then in vogue. This state of things continued with these increasing communities until they had attained to great numerical strength and were spreading rapidly through the country, and both the ministers and the people, as a general thing, seemed satisfied thus to remain. Indeed, it was no uncommon thing to hear passing remarks of a disparaging nature on *college learned* ministers, in the language of the times, as greatly deficient in the pathos and unction of their ministerial performances. Comments of this kind respecting a portion of the educated ministers of the old societies were too well founded, and as the people of the New Light class ascribed the dullness of ministers of what was called the standing order, to their kind of training, the whole collegiate system excited their suspicion and dislike. Such was the state of things, and such were the feelings of the new and rising parties in a wide extent of country, and especially of a large portion of the American Baptists towards all that pertained to colleges, when

I began to think of attempting a college course. And this unfriendly feeling was strengthened and kept alive by the severe comments of many of the old priesthood on the illiterate character of the new men, who, without any proper training, according to their rule, had suddenly emerged from their farms and shops, and other secular employments, to become the spiritual guides of the people. As the men, thus lightly esteemed by the old clerical dynasty, as a general thing, could preach much more acceptably to the great mass of our people than their opponents, these good old Baptists could not see the need of spending so much time and money to learn how to preach, and they held on to the skirts of the garments of the young brethren with great tenacity who showed any disposition college-ward. A kind of inspiration in the business of preaching was a favorite idea with these people. To have the sentiments they uttered, come right down from above, that was the kind of preaching for them. "If the Lord has called men to preach, they will and must preach;" "Open your mouth and I will fill it," were terms frequently heard in my early years. But as these old members passed off the stage, and a new race took their places, who required more cultivation in their preachers, and as these preachers themselves became more and more sensible of their deficiencies in mental culture, they began to cast around them for the best means of attaining it. Some of them engaged in a course of self-teaching, some obtained the aid of ministers and men of other callings near them, while others went to neighboring academies, and a few, by dint of effort, pursued a college course, even after they had become settled pastors, and had families growing up around them.

Under these circumstances, by degrees, without any formal action, or the adoption of any conventional rules, our people began more generally to favor a systematic course of ministerial education. The absolute necessity of a change in the policy of the denomination respecting the literary qualifications of its spiritual guides was becoming daily more apparent, so much so, that a good portion of our leading men, both among the ministers and the laity, readily concurred in promoting it, and soon a new dispensation in this business was introduced among us.

The first institutions which were commenced under this favorable impulse had respect wholly to the training of theological students; and a partial course, so called, was the principal thing aimed at in these new undertakings. Most of these seminaries, however, thus begun, were afterwards moulded into collegiate form, with theological departments on the same ground, and many young ministers, and some of maturer years, derived essential benefit from the aids thus placed within their reach, and were enabled to occupy more important stations than they could otherwise have done.

"Better late than never," "a little learning rather than none," were then prevalent maxims among our people, whose interests were suffering prodigiously for the want of ministerial help; and I see no better way now, for replenishing our ranks with preachers and pastors, in the wide-spread regions of destitution in some parts of the country. I speak now of those churches which do not make it a condition, that, before they will present a call to a minister he shall be able to present one or two literary diplomas. "Has the man been to college?" in former times was the only question that was asked respecting candidates for settlement, by our people, who began to make inquiries of this kind, but now they want to know if he has been to Newton, or some other theological seminary. This rule of action has been steadily gaining ground for many years past, in certain quarters. This may do very well for those who measure young ministers by their diplomas, but I apply to them all, and especially the mediocrity class, the rule of Young in another case,

> "Pigmies are pigmies still, though perched on Alps,
> And pyramids are pyramids in vales."

As our little colleges sprung up in quick succession in different places, and as one set of officers would suffice for the students in a number of them, the plan of consolidation has in some cases been suggested, with which, for the following reasons, I have not been well pleased. Small colleges seem to be an American idea, and although the training in them may be less thorough than in large institutions, yet it suffices for the great mass of American students, who, as a general thing, are destined to an active rather than a studious course of life, whether in the ministry or in secular pursuits. As our small colleges have grown up spontaneously, to meet the wants of our people, in the regions where they exist, and as their friends will continue to nourish them where they are, to greater maturity, but would fall off from their support of them in other locations, my judgment has been adverse to the removal policy.

In favor of small colleges it is said that the cost of carrying students through them is considerably less than in those of larger size. They are generally far enough from each other not to interfere in their operations, and great advantages are enjoyed by students in being so near their homes that they can visit them without much expense, and be cared for by their home friends.

From the small colleges of different names, after

all, have gone out many of the most eminent men of
the country.

*On the best Method for Theological Schools among the
Baptists.*

Until within a few years past I have fully believed
that seminaries by themselves, after the model of the
one at Newton, and others of less note, were the perfection of planning, for the promotion of ministerial
education for our people, as well as others among
whom they are in successful operation. But in the
language of one of our aged ministers, with whom I
lately conversed on this subject, "I am a good deal
disappointed. The plan does not prosper as I expected it would, and I am in doubt about its being the
best one for us."

My reply was, that I now go for *theological departments* in connection with our secular institutions, as
we find them at Hamilton, Rochester and elsewhere,
and I would be glad to see the Newton School transferred to Brown University, officers and all, as a distinct department; and I believed it might be carried
on with much less expense and equally as well. In
this conversation I pointed out some of the advantages
which would result from the changes just named, and
among those which I specified were the following:
The theological company would be surrounded by a

literary atmosphere ; they might have access to the
ample library of the university ; those who graduated
there would be pleased to pursue their professional
studies on the premises of their *alma mater ;* the cost
of two sets of buildings would be avoided ; a less
number of professors for the theological students
would be needed, as all knowledge purely literary
might be imparted by professors on the ground, at a
great saving of cost over the present plan.

Our colleges have always done well for us, without
the departments in question, and with them, in as
many cases as are needful, I am confident they will
still continue their good offices to the denomination.

In the business of our seminaries, I remarked, we
have copied after other communities, on the presump-
tion that, with our more strict requirements of our
students, and the very different state of feeling among
our people generally, we could fill up divinity schools
and support them as easily as they do. But this was
a mistaken calculation, as long experience has shown.
We must lower our standard. " That will not do,"
said my friend ; " it is low enough now." " Then,"
continued I, " my prediction is, that for a long time
to come, the number of our candidates for the ministry, who go through college, and then go through another course of study of the usual length, will be too
few to support separate institutions for them. And

as our colleges must go on, let the plan in question be adopted, and let the secular and theological tuition for Baptist use be performed on the same ground."

One master for a school was the custom in the most ancient times, but we will allow double that number for our theological schools ; and why is not that sufficient, since the main business of these masters is to teach men how to preach and perform pastoral duties ? If we must prepare men for presidents of colleges, professors, etc., let there be *finishing houses*, expressly for this purpose.

CHAPTER XXIV.

THE Religious Remembrancer was the first paper of this kind that fell into my hands. It was published in Philadelphia by a Mr. Scott, a deacon or elder among the Presbyterians. It was commenced on a moderate-sized sheet, in 1813, and was continued a few years. Complete files of the paper for four years, bound in two volumes, are among my documents of this kind.

For a long time after religious papers began to be issued, the secular journals not unfrequently spoke lightly of them and their patrons, and represented this new undertaking as a visionary project, which in their estimation could not succeed. On the one hand, these journals had nothing to fear on the score of rivalship, nor did the newspapers reply to them. At this time, I had just published my old Baptist History, and as the slow and costly methods of communication then in vogue had occasioned me much incon-

venience in collecting my historical information, a
religious press was to me a most inviting project.
This cheap and expeditious method of corresponding
appeared just the thing in this business, in this country, where so little has been done to collate historical
documents, and where so few ancestral records are to
be found.

The Boston Recorder, published by Nathaniel Wil-
lis, a deacon among the Congregationalists, was the
second religious newspaper to which I became a sub-
scriber. This work assumed neutral ground, which
it maintained for a time to my satisfaction ; but at
length, as some things in it appeared somewhat sectarian, I wrote Mr. Winchell on the subject, by way
of complaint, and he, in reply, informed me, that a
project was on foot for a paper of our own, and soon
the old Christian Watchman made its appearance, and
Deacon James Loring for a long time was its publish-
er and principal editor. This paper was commenced
in 1819. Now I found myself at home in the newspaper line, and I gave the undertaking a hearty encouragement, both by promoting its circulation, and
also by contributing to its columns. Of this favorite
sheet I have files from its commencement, although,
in some cases, they are incomplete.

As other papers of the kind were begun, as far as
practicable, I gave them countenance and support,

mostly, however, by contributions of matter, original
and selected; and when I engaged in earnest in collecting materials for my late work on Baptist history, I
made an effort with a good degree of success to obtain
the religious papers of all sorts of Baptists in the United States, and in the British Provinces; and, as I preserve all documents of this kind, I have a large stock
of them on hand, which I would be glad freely to
dispose of to those who may desire them for historical
purposes, but if they must go the way of all such
publications, with rare exceptions I will leave them
to their fate at home.

Miscellaneous Remarks on Religious Newspapers.

The secular character which these journals have
more and more assumed was quite disagreeable to me
for a long time, but I finally became reconciled to it
as a matter of necessity, as but a few of them could
live without some advertising pay. I concluded it
was better to have a compound motion of a sacro-
secular character rather than none at all. While religious papers have been increasing in their details of
worldly affairs, those on the secular side, as a general
thing, have paid an increasing attention to religious
concerns. In my early day but few managers of the
secular press ever referred to serious matters in re-
spectful terms, but now they have reporters of their

own at all ecclesiastical conventions and assemblies of
an important character, and in their reports may be
found early and full accounts of the doings of these
bodies.   The same may be said of the passing events
pertaining to all churches and parties in the whole of
Christendom.

A ministerial friend of mine having become the
owner and manager of an old temporal concern, I rallied him on the apparent incongruity of his course in
the business.   "O," said he, "the secular press has
become about as religious as the religious, and religious papers are about as secular as the secular."

This sentiment has been very fully verified in the
accounts which are found of the great revival now
(1858) in progress through the land.

After religious papers became somewhat common,
and their beneficial influence began to be widely experienced and acknowledged, in some cases they were
started prematurely and the management of them was
committed to incompetent hands.   The credit system
also, in a profuse manner, was the bane of these papers at an early day, so anxious were the publishers
of them to spread them far and wide.   But if they had
been well paid for their circulation was generally too
limited and their prices were too low for them to live
long, and in the end losses were incurred, often by
those who were ill able to bear them.   "We must

have a paper for our own region," was a prevalent
idea with many, and at the solicitation of friends I
labored hard for a number of years in conjunction
with others to establish a small religious journal for
our own little State, of a general character, the only
plan which we could expect would succeed. But in
the end I advised our people to go for the Christian
Watchman, which they would find a decidedly denominational paper, and considering its size and superior quality, much cheaper than we could make at
home.

As to the size of our religious papers, the form of
them and the method of publishing them, different
customs have prevailed, but generally they have begun small, and those that have lived have gained in
amplitude by degrees, till in a few cases they have
become much too large for the convenience of the
readers and the profit of the publishers. A Kentucky paper was the most remarkable for its size of
any of our denomination that has come into my
hands. This sheet approached the bed-blanket standard, but ere long it was cut down to a medium size.

The folded form for binding has been sometimes
adopted, but very few of them, I think, are ever
bound.

Companies, conventions, and individuals have, at
first, been the owners of our religious papers, but so

far as I have observed, they generally do the best under personal ownership and responsibility. On the
whole, I recommend for these journals the folio form,
the medium size, and as little disputation as possible.

My Experience in the Business of Sunday Schools.

Fifty-four years ago, when I began my ministry in
Pawtucket, being then a licensed preacher, and student in college, I found a quiet little company of poor
factory children, under the care of the village school
master, who had a moderate compensation for his
services from a few factory owners, for the children
all were *free.* The main object of this juvenile seminary was to impart the rudiments of common school-
education, but from the day on which it was kept, it
was called a *Sunday School.* This benevolent undertaking was set in motion seven years before this time
by the late Samuel Slater, of cotton mill notoriety,
for the benefit of the poor, ignorant, and neglected
children who had gathered round his mill, then the
only one in the place. Pawtucket at this time was a
small village, with but few meeting-going people in
it, without any church or settled minister on the
ground. The first Baptist church was formed in
1805. We had heard of Raikes' enterprise in England, in the Sunday School line, and his plan was
copied by this new American institution, which still

lives on an improved platform in a numerous pedigree in Pawtucket and vicinity. This sacro-secular concern was moulded into the shape of modern Sunday Schools about forty years ago. By this time the little one had become two bands, with two masters, one of whom is now an aged deacon in a neighboring Baptist church. By degrees Bible reading and a moderate share of religious instruction had been introduced into our unusual but very useful establishment, until by mutual agreement the old system was dispensed with and a new one was adopted. The main body of the school went to the first Baptist church, then under my care ; a large branch of it was taken up by the Episcopal church, then newly instituted ; and as the Congregational, the Methodist, and other churches arose, their Sunday Schools had in their composition relics of this old peculiar band, now under review, some of whom are yet to be found amongst the aged citizens of the place.

This old *first day* school, as it was called by its patrons of the Friendly order, who were among its liberal supporters in its most enlarged operations, required a good deal of attention from some quarter ; books were to be procured, stationery supplied, incidental expenses to be defrayed, and the masters to be secured and paid ; and as I was the only minister on the ground, most of this labor for many years came on

me at an early day, and so it continued until about
the time of the dissolution of the old confederacy.
As my labors increased I proposed to one of the firm-
est friends of the cause either to retire from my post
or to have one or more associated with me.

"Friend B.," said the good old Quaker, "thee does
the thing very well; no new hand could take a hold
of it as readily as thee does. We will supply the
money, and if thee does a good deal of work, we will
give thee a good deal of credit for it."

I ought to mention, that serious scruples were entertained by many of our citizens as to the propriety
of common school keeping on the Sabbath. These
scruples operated strongly on my own mind when I
first fell in with the school, and whether to favor or
oppose it, was a serious question. The condition of
the factory help was deplorable. They had been collected from the highways and hedges, and such were
the prejudices against the cotton mills, in early times,
that no others could be obtained for them. By the
means of this school, the minds and morals of these
children of misfortune were improved. They were
kept from roving and mischief on the Sabbath, and as
Sabbath services increased, they were induced by degrees to attend them.

I have thus given a brief account of my early connection with Sunday School operations, under circum-

stances of a very peculiar kind. After the transformation of this old concern into modern shape, it soon became very prosperous, and now, it is doubtful whether many places can be found, of equal size, which do more in the business of Sunday Schools notwithstanding the abundance of natives, and the superabundance of foreigners, in our various manufacturing establishments, who altogether neglect the ample supply of schools and churches and reforming institutions, on the ground, which was so uncommonly destitute of every thing of the kind when the peculiar school now under consideration was commenced. Indeed, at that period, the age of benevolent operations had scarcely dawned upon any portion of the world, and not at all on this region.

The claim of Pawtucket, of having started the first Sunday School in America, for a long time remained undisputed; but of late years, a number of rival claims of priority in the business have been set up. Most of these claims, however, are in favor of old catechising operations, which we do not admit can be fairly brought into competition with our school.

Pawtucket people are not very sensitive or ambitious in this matter, and if living witnesses can be produced, of a Sunday School more than sixty years ago, which still lives in a dozen or more branches, and the whole history of it is attested by such testi-

14

mony as they can show, they will relinquish their
claim.

*On the Rise and Management of our Benevolent In-
stitutions.*

It has so happened that the getting up of these institutions has always been in advance of public opinion, or in other words, a few. active and influential
men set them in motion, and then labor to arouse a
public sentiment in their favor. They do a good deal
of special pleading themselves, and soon a company
of agents is sent out, with special instructions to perform the same special service. These men traverse
the churches in search of funds to sustain the new enterprises, and annually this course must be pursued.
But to begin at the right end, the churches themselves ought to take the lead in all new undertakings
which must be sustained by them, and keep them immediately under their control. If this course had
been originally and strictly pursued, much of the difficulty which we have witnessed in the management
of our benevolent efforts might have been avoided.

In the commencement of our foreign mission cause,
which was taken hold of more earnestly and generally by the whole denomination than any which it has
since been engaged in, it was confidently believed that
the work would soon be carried on by voluntary con-

tributions of the churches, and that soliciting agents
would not long be needful. But how different has
been the result of this experiment, and how far short
has this most popular cause among our people, for upwards of forty years, been from being sustained without the aid of the more and more unpopular system
of special agents. A similar infelicity has attended
all our societies for benevolent objects.   And this
state of things, in all probability, must continue until
a radical change is effected in the manner of their
support or the amount of their expenses. The churches must more generally learn *to go alone* in their doings for benevolent objects, as well as for other matters. The number of such as follow this rule, though
small, is probably increasing, and when all of them
have learned how to bring it into practical operation,
then the costly and much complained of agency system will be superseded.   And my theory for a long
time has been, that the *going alone* policy should be
more assiduously and earnestly urged upon our
churches, than it has hitherto been.   At present,
the great mass of them wait for agents to come
around, and after their departure, they wait again
till another year. And it is most likely that the
loudest complaints of the bad policy of spending
so much on agents come from churches of the above
description, whose pastors very quietly throw all the

labor and responsibility in this business into the
agents' hands, and then wonder why the support of
our benevolent institutions should cost so much.

Among the American Baptists of the regular or
associated class, we find some six or eight societies
for different objects, of a general character, and in
none of them have I observed any very serious
troubles in the management of their internal concerns, except the one which is devoted to the foreign
mission cause; and the difficulties in this body, which
have been exceedingly disagreeable to the great mass
of our people, appear to have risen and existed principally between the managers at home and a portion
of the missionaries abroad. This institution, formerly called the Triennial Convention, now the Missionary Union, for many years at first had no missionary
rooms; the labors of its officers were gratuitously
performed; and the few men then in the foreign field,
with Judson at their head, regulated their own affairs
pretty much in their own way. The churches, which
gradually arose under their labors, were settled on our
denominational platform, and were regarded by us in
the same light as if they had been planted on our own
soil. The pastors of these churches also, whether of
home or heathen origin, stood on a level, in our estimation, as to their official powers, with Baptist ministers of every land. Both ministers and churches

might be advised, but not compelled, in the ordinary operations of their missions, about which it was presumed they were better able to judge than their distant patrons. Such was the state of things in our foreign mission concerns in its early stages. And in it, as I understand the matter, we have an exhibition of the primordial and genuine principles of the Baptists from time immemorial, relative to all that pertains to their churches and ministers, under all circumstances, and in all locations. This policy has always worked well with our people. Under its influence there has been but little trouble among us, in the management of our churches, associations, conventions and ecclesiastical and benevolent institutions, of whatever nature. From this policy, in my judgment, it is both unwise and unsafe for any of our managing boards and committees to swerve in any direction. And if by chance they find an excuse for doing so, in constitutional rules in their platforms, which have been borrowed from other parties, whose customs differ from ours, they should ignore them, as spurious interpolations, and stick to the good old Baptist doctrine.

The complaints against our men at our foreign mission rooms, of a departure from Baptist usages in some of their theories and enactments, are too well known to need repeating. Amidst all the painful

discussions which have followed, I have pondered
and mourned, and the more so, as I have never seen
the time, since our eastern mission commenced, when
there was so much encouragement for prosecuting it
with renewed vigor, especially among the Karens,
that numerous, peculiar, and, in some respects, anom-
alous race of orientals, among whom our missionaries
have had, and are still having, a success almost without a parallel in more modern times.

While many of my brethren have made a free use of
the pulpit, the press and the platform, in commenting
on the disagreements between some of our missionaries and their opponents, I have carefully avoided
them all. I have never fallen out with our disagreeing men on either side. If I have seen what I
regarded as mistakes among any of them, I have
attributed them more to errors in judgment than to
hurtful designs; and if I have noticed non-Baptistical
ideas in any official documents, I have traced them
to a too literal construction of rules lately alluded to.
And while the parties, who by their protracted discords have so essentially retarded the progress of our
oldest and largest institution for the support of missions, have often treated each other in a somewhat
unbrotherly manner, I have nourished a brotherly
feeling for them all. Some remarks, which in my re-

tirement I have recorded on this family difficulty for insertion here, I have concluded to omit.

And now if I could act for all who may have been implicated in the discussions and jars above referred to, whether at home or in the foreign field, they would at once cease; the hatchet would be buried in deep oblivion; the dispersed missionaries would return to their work; and thus a new impulse would be given to our foreign mission cause. And if our new Baptist interest in the far East, with its growing strength, its numerous churches, its increasing associations and other institutions peculiar to our denomination, should exhibit signs of verging from colonial dependence to independence of action, let us favor such a manly effort, is my decision; and so far as it is successful, our churches will be relieved at home by such an auspicious measure, and will be encouraged to engage in new enterprises in other regions. And I look forward to the time when the great and increasing body of American Baptists, with their abundant means, and with the capacity which they have shown that they possess for the work of evangelization among heathen nations, shall plant the gospel standard in the opening fields of China and Japan, in the newly-explored regions of Africa, and in many other distant and benighted realms.

On the Death of Correspondents and Familiar Friends.

As this list was considerably extensive, the solemn tidings of their departure have quite frequently arrived. As my historical pursuits were commenced at an early age, I became familiarly acquainted then with many who were in middle life, or else were far advanced in years. This class has long since been gone to their rest.

When I set out in the ministry, such men as Baldwin, Gano, J. Williams, Staughton, Rogers, Semple, Furman, Mercer, and men of their rank, were in the meridian of their strength and activity ; all of them have long since ceased from their labors. The same may be said, with a very few exceptions, of a large company, who were about my equals in age, and were my associates and coadjutors in the various plans, for general good and for the special benefit of the Baptists, which they were either newly devising, or to which they were beginning to pay more earnest attention. Among the men of this second class, I might name Bolles, Sharp, Winchell, Going, Gammell, Davis, Galusha, Brantley, Peck of the West, and a long list of others. And very many young men, of unusual promise, who commenced their course when mine was nearly run, have in succession, and often unexpectedly, been called from their various posts. On many of the men above named or referred to, some of 'whom were in remote regions, and were little known by the Baptist public at large, I had made much dependence in my historical pursuits, and how to supply their places with correspondents, has often occasioned me no little embarrassment and concern. Although they were, for the most part, men of humble pretensions, yet they could afford me great assistance for their own regions, so that I had a double reason to mourn their loss, and the report of their deaths, has often been a funeral knell in a twofold sense.

For a long time past there has been a strangeness in the appearance of the large gatherings of our people. A new set of men are on their platforms, and are in their councils ; and when I look around for the old leaders, very few of them are to be seen.

And now, 1859, on the octogenarian list, I seem almost alone, as to the brotherhood of my early days, and to belong to a bygone age.

Amidst the crowd of a younger race, I often say with Young.

" I've been so long remembered, I'm forgot."

But when these new men recognize the old man, and recount their recollections of former years, this feeling is in some measure dispelled.

APPENDIX.

MISCELLANEOUS ARTICLES.

CHAPTER XXV.

ON CHURCH ORGANIZATIONS.

ARGUMENTS IN FAVOR OF THE EARLY CHRISTIANS COPYING, IN SUBSTANCE, THE MODEL OF THE JEWISH SYNAGOGUES.

IN my long experience in our own church concerns I have paid considerable attention to what is generally called *church discipline* in the general, rather than in the corrective sense of this term.

My main object, in all my inquiries into these matters, has been to ascertain as near as possible, without note or comment, the doings of Christ and the apostles, and of those who lived nearest to the apostolic age, as I consider this kind of information of much more importance than all the creeds and commentaries of after times. But still, in my historical pursuits in church affairs, I have attentively perused a large number of the most approved works by our own men, and those of other communities, pertaining to church building and management, preachers, preaching and pulpits, ministerial and pastoral duties, clerical manners, and other things of this kind, with a view to give our younger ministers my own experience and advice upon them.

I have not expected to give any new ideas to our reading men, but my object has been to present to some of our younger and less favored ministers the substance of many works, old and rare, with which they may not be acquainted.

But as a portion of my manuscript has disappeared from the hands of the publishers, now, at a late period, and in a hasty manner, I must reproduce most of the following articles in a greatly abridged form.

After I began in earnest my inquiries into the manner of forming churches by the early Christians, the first questions that occurred to me were, Did the church builders copy after any model? did Jesus Christ and the apostles lay down any rules for the prosecution of this business? or did the disciples collect together, without much formality, in private houses, in the synagogues, or wherever they found favorable places for their meetings, and thus commence church operations?

In looking over the list of the primitive churches, according to the New Testament records, I find the first one arose in Jerusalem, and that soon it became very large, and the new churches out of Palestine, it is natural to suppose, in the language of Giesler, formed themselves after the pattern of the mother church. Their presidents were *the elders*, officially of equal rank, although in many churches, individuals among them had a personal authority over the others. Under the superintendence of these elders were *the deacons* and *deaconesses.* * * * The duty of teaching, as an office, was by no means incumbent on the elders, although the apostle wishes that they should be *apt to teach.**

I infer that the whole membership of the Jerusalem church, at first, and for some years after it arose, consisted wholly of converted Jews, for as yet no conversions had been made among the Gentiles.

At Antioch arose the first church among the Gentiles, and this body also, at an early period, became very large, and was a center of operations for the Christians in that quarter. During the apostolic age, a large number of churches arose in Palestine, and in the surrounding countries, whose names appear in the New Testament narratives. But relative to the manner of their formation, in no one case is the least information given. All at once the names of these churches appear; some incident, or the name of some person or persons connected with them is given, but nothing in particular is said as to the time, or the circumstances of their origin. Although the foundations of many of the first Christian communities, were no doubt, laid in Christian houses, yet but three household churches are mentioned in the New Testament

* Ecclesiastical History, volume i., pages 91, 92.

naratives, the most important of which I am inclined
to think was that in the house of Aquila and Priscilla,
whose praise was in all the churches of the Gentiles.
We also read of churches in the houses of Nymphas
and Philemon. But of no others, then in being.

In only one case do I find mention made of the
church in the wilderness, which evidently refers to
the Old Testament economy.

As my object in my researches into this matter was
to find out as nearly as possible just how the early
Christians managed in getting up their churches, I
laid aside all expositions and went for the plain matters of fact in their doings, and as I found them much
in the synagogues, and joining in the services of these
humble sanctuaries, and appeared, for the most part,
to be as much at home in them as if they had been
prepared for the use of Christians, this consideration
led me to inquire into the history of these Jewish
places of worship; their origin, the manner of conducting religious worship in them, their officers, their
principles of government, and of the number of them
in Judea and elsewhere. In pursuing these inquiries
I examined the old Latin work of Vitringa, the title
of which is *De Vetere Synagoga*, Concerning the Ancient Synagogue, Jahn's Archæology, Neander, and
other works on the subject. The result of my examinations was, that synagogues originated during the

Babylonish captivity as a substitute for the temple
worship, of which the captive nation was wholly de-
prived ; that in most cases these resorts of the pious
Israelites were plain and humble edifices; that the
reading of the law and the prophets, or the Old Testament Scriptures, with .free speaking upon them and
exhortations to the people, constituted the substance
of the religious services performed in them, with the
omission of the sacrifices of the tabernacle and the
temple; that their officers and internal operations
were in many respects like those of the early Christians ; and finally, that synagogues were found wherever there were Jews, in their own land, or in the
nations in which they were dispersed.*

The abundance of synagogues among the Jewish
people may be estimated from the fact that in the
Saviour's time there were thirteen in Tiberias, four
hundred in Jerusalem, including prosauchas,† or small
chapels for prayer.

The few following passages show how frequently
and freely the synagogues were used by Christ and
his apostles and followers. When the high priest

* The Jewish people were by no means confined to Palestine. They
were to be found in Babylon, in Arabia, in Egypt, and in almost all
parts of the Roman empire.

† These places of prayer were also built in mountains, fields and
deserts, and some think our Lord entered into one of them when he
continued all night in prayer to God.

asked Jesus of his disciples and of his doctrine, he
answered him, "I spake openly to the world, I *ever*
taught in the synagogues and in the temple, whither
the Jews always resort, and in secret have I said
nothing." Paul at first persecuted the Christians in all
the synagogues, in his way to Damascus, by the authority of the Jewish rulers, but after his conversion,
while at Thessalonica, where was a synagogue of the
Jews, "*as his manner was*, he went in unto them,
and three Sabbath days reasoned with them out of
the Scriptures, opening and alleging," etc.

This whole matter is well explained by Coleman in
his work on Primitive Christianity.

"The apostles and first disciples were Jews, who,
after their conversion, retained all the prejudices and
partialities of their nation. *   *   *

"With the temple service and the Mosaic ritual,
however, Christianity had no affinity. The sacra-
ficial offerings of the temple, and the Levitical priesthood it abolished. But in the synagogue worship,
the followers of Christ found a more congenial institution. It invited them to the reading of the Scriptures and to prayer.* It gave them liberty of speech
in exhortation, and in worshiping and praising God.

* The Old Testament, or the law and the prophets, was divided into
fifty-two parts, one for each Sabbath in the year. The reading of the
Scriptures constituted a large part of religious worship with the early
Christians, and so it should be now.

The rules and government of the synagogue, while they offered little, comparatively, to excite the pride of office and of power, commended themselves the more to the humble believer in Christ. The synagogue was endeared to the devout Jew by sacred associations and tender recollections. It was near at hand, and not, like the temple, afar off. He went but seldom up to Jerusalem, and only on great occasions joined in the rites of the temple service. But in the synagogue he paid his constant devotions to the God of his fathers It met his eye in every place. It was constantly before him, and from infancy to hoary age he was accustomed to repair to that hallowed place of worship to listen to the reading of his sacred books, to pray and sing praises unto the God of Israel. In accordance, therefore, with pious usage the apostles continued to frequent the synagogues of the Jews. Wherever they went they resorted to these places of worship, and strove to convert their brethren to faith in Christ, not as a new religion, but as a modification of their own.

"In their own religious assemblies they also conformed as far as was consistent with the spirit of the Christian religion, to the same rites, and gradually settled upon a church organization which harmonized in a remarkable manner with that of the Jewish synagogue. They even retained the same *name* as the appellation of their Christian assemblies. ' If there come into your *synagogue*, assembly, a man with a gold ring' etc. Their modes of worship were the same as those of the synagogue. The *titles of the officers* they also borrowed from the same source. The titles Bishop, Presbyter, or Elder, etc., were all familiar terms, denoting the same class of officers in the synagogue. Their duties and prerogatives remained, in substance, the same in the Christian church as in that of the Jews.

" So great was the similarity between the primitive Christian churches, and the Jewish synagogues, that by the Pagan nations they were mistaken for the same institutions. Pagan historians uniformly treated the primitive Christians as Jews.* As such they suffered under the persecutions of their idolatrous rulers. * * *

" In support of the foregoing statements authorities to any extent, and of the highest character, might be adduced."

Neander is here quoted on the subject:

" * * * The disciples had not yet attained a clear understanding of that call, which Christ had already given them by so many intimations, to form a church entirely separated from the existing Jewish economy ; to that economy they adhered as much as possible. * * * Hence the establishment of a dis-

* Vitringa De Synago. Vet., Prolegom, pages 3, 4.

tinct mode of worship was far from entering their thoughts. * * *

" As the believers, in opposition to the mass of the Jewish nation, who remained hardened in their unbelief, now formed a community internally bound together by the one faith in Jesus as the Messiah, and by the consciousness of the higher life received from him, it was necessary that this internal union should assume a certain external form.   And a model for such a smaller community within the great national theocracy, already existed among the Jews, along with the temple worship, namely, the *synagogues*.   The means of religious edification which they supplied took account of the religious welfare of all, and consisted of united prayers and the addresses of individuals, who applied themselves to the study of the Old Testament.   These means of edification closely corresponded to the nature of the new Christian worship.   This form of social worship, as it was copied in all the religious communities founded on Judaism, (such as the Essenes), was also adopted, to a certain extent, at the first formation of the Christian church."

Neander also shows that this organization of Christian churches was the most natural under existing circumstances, and the most acceptable, not only to the Jewish converts but to those who were gathered from the subjects of the Roman government.

Archbisnop Whately avows views similar to those of the great German author, which, with his usual independence and candor, are thus expressed:

" It is probable that one cause, humanly speaking, why we find in the Sacred Books less information concerning the Christian ministry, and the constitution of church governments than we otherwise might have found, is that these institutions had less of *novelty* than some would at first sight suppose, and that many portions of them did not wholly originate with the apostles.   It appears highly probable, I might say morally certain, that wherever a Jewish synagogue existed, that was brought—the whole, or the chief part of it—to embrace the gospel, the apostles did not, there, so much *form* a Christian church (or congregation,* ecclesia,) as to *make an existing congregation Christian*, by introducing the Christian sacraments and worship, and establishing whatever regulations were requisite for the newly adopted faith, leaving the machinery, if I may so speak, of government unchanged, the rulers of synagogues, elders, and other officers, whether spiritual or ecclesiastical, or

" * The word ' *congregation*,' as it stands in our version of the Old Testament, (and it is one of very frequent occurrence in the Books of Moses), is found to correspond in the Septuagint, which was familiar to the New Testament writers, to *ecclesia*, the word which in our version of these last, is always rendered, not 'congregation' but 'church.' This, or its equivalent, 'kirk,' is probably, no other than 'circle,' *i. e.*, assembly, *ecclesia*."

both, being already provided in the existing institutions. And it is likely that several of the earliest
Christian churches did originate in this way, that is,
that they were *converted synagogues*, which *became*
Christian churches as soon as the members, or the
main part of the members, acknowledged Jesus as
the Messiah.

" The attempt to effect the conversion of a Jewish
synagogue, into a Christian church seems always to
have been made in the first instance, in every place,
where there was an opening for it. Even after the
call of the idolatrous Gentiles, it appears plainly to
have been the practice of the apostles Paul and Bar-
nabas,* when they came to any city, in which there
was a synagogue, to go thither first and deliver their
sacred message to the Jews and devout Gentiles, and
when they founded a church in any of those cities, in
which there was no Jewish synagogue, that received

"* These seem to have been the first preachers who were employed in
converting the idolatrous Gentiles to Christianity, and their first considerable harvest among these, seems to have been at Antioch in Pisidia,
as may be seen by any one who attentively reads the thirteenth chapter
of Acts. Peter was sent to Cornelius, a devout Gentile, one of those
who had renounced idolatry and frequented the synagogues. And
these seem to have been regarded by him as in an especial manner his
particular charge. His epistles appear to have been addressed to them,
as may be seen, both by the general tenor of his expression, and especially, in the opening address, which is not, as would appear from our
version, to the dispersed *Jews*, but to the sojourners of the dispersion,
that is, the *devout Gentiles living among* the dispersion.

the gospel, it is likely they would still conform in a great measure to the same model.*

" It is, then, an admitted fact, as clearly settled as any thing can be by human authority, that the primitive Christians, in the organization of their assemblies, formed them after the mode of the Jewish synagogues.   They discarded the splendid ceremonials of the temple service, and retained the simple rites of the synagogue worship.   They disowned the hereditary aristocracy of the Levitical priesthood,† and adopted the popular government of the synagogue.‡

" We are here presented with an important fact in the organization of the primitive churches, strongly illustrative of the popular character of their constitution and government.   The synagogue was essentially a popular assembly, invested with the rights, and possessing the powers, which are essential to the enjoyment of religious liberty.   Their government was voluntary, elective, free ; and administered by rulers or elders elected by the people.   The ruler of the synagogue was the *moderator of the college of elders,*

---

* Kingdom of Christ, pages 83–86.

† The custom of comparing the Christian ministry to the Levitical priesthood has come down from Cyprian, who was a strenuous advocate for the doctrines of sacerdotal power and sacramental efficacy.

‡ Totum regimen ecclesiasticum conformatum fuit ad synagogarum exemplar.   The whole ecclesiastical government was made to conform to the model of the synagogues.

but only *primus inter pares,** holding no official rank above them. The people, as Vitringa has shown, appointed their own officers to rule over them. They exercised the natural right of freemen, to enact and execute their own laws, to admit proselytes, and to exclude, at pleasure, unworthy members from their communion. Theirs was ‘ *a democratical form of government,*’ and is so described by one of the most able expounders of the constitution of the primitive churches.† Like their prototype, therefore, the primitive churches also embodied the principle of a popular government, and of an enlightened religious liberty.”

From all the above statements, in the absence of any precept or example for the manner of constituting the New Testament churches, after mature deliberation I have settled down in the belief, that the ecclesiastical polity of the Jewish synagogues was very closely copied by the apostles and primitive Christians, in the organization of their assemblies.

On the Independence of the Primitive Churches.

“The churches which were established by the apostles and their disciples, exhibit a remarkable degree

---

* First among his equals.— *Vitringa.*

† Rothe Anfänge der Christ. Kirch, page 14, as quoted by Coleman, page 46.

15

338 FIFTY YEARS AMONG THE BAPTISTS.

of unanimity, one towards another. One in faith and the fellowship of love, they were united in spirit as different members of one body, or as brethren of the same family."*

The independence of the churches, one of another, is fully and clearly presented by Mosheim, as all who read his Church History will discover.

* Coleman's Church Without a Bishop. Primitive Church, pages 39–49.

CHAPTER XXVI.

ON THE BAPTIST DEACONSHIP.*

The Original by Howell and Others.—Something Wrong in Our
Deaconship.—The Scripture Qualifications.—Crowell on Limited Appointments.—My Four Years' Rule.—Deacon Jones in
the Sunny Side. — Arguments. — The Number 7.—Proofs from
Antiquity.—Dialogue Between a Pastor and Deacon.

My remarks on this subject will have respect only
to our denomination. In my comments on church organizations, I do not propose any changes or revolu-
tionary measures, but in the business of our deaconship, some modifications of our present practice, in my
judgment, would be an improvement. I would go, in
part, at least, for a younger, more active and efficient
class of men for this office, than is now generally found
in our churches. I would have them appointed for a
limited time, instead of for life, with an eligibility for
reappointment, and have *seven* the standard number
for a full-grown church.

Before I proceed to any discussions of these matters, I will give some definitions of the original terms

---

* I had prepared the largest chapter in this work, on the deaconship; in doing which I was assisted by able hands; but as it is among
the missing MS., a shorter notice only can I now prepare.

pertaining to the service of deacons, and show the various ways it is performed. Howell, on *The Deaconship*, will, at present, be my principal guide.

" A deacon (*diakonos**) is a minister or servant." The term, in its broadest sense, describes ministers or servants of all classes, whether their department be temporal or spiritual. It has in its sense a similar indefiniteness with the word *ecclesia*, church, assembly or congregation.

The civil magistrate is called the *diakonos, deacon* or *minister* of God, for good.

The apostles are frequently called *deacons* or *ministers.*

Paul, speaking of himself and Apollos, says they were *diakonoi, deacons* or *ministers,* by whom the Corinthians believed the gospel.

Tichicus is said to have been *pistos diakonos,* a faithful *deacon* or *minister.*

Jesus Christ himself is called *diakonos,* a *minister* of the circumcision.

" And the Son of man came not to be administered unto, but to minister, and to give his life a ransom for many."

---

* I shall give the English version only of all the terms on this subject. I find the three following in the original Greek: Diakonos, a servant, waiting-man or woman, minister; diakonia, service, ministration; diakòneo, to wait on, serve, do service. Two of these terms are in the original, in the history of the seven men in Acts.

In this case, the passage might be rendered, He came not to be deaconized unto, but to deaconize and give his life, etc.

A deacon, then, is a minister or servant, whether the service be sacred or secular.

Doulos, also, means a servant, but generally, if not always, of a lower grade, and of a more menial character. Accordingly, where it is said of Jesus Christ that he took upon him the form of a servant, the term *doulos,* instead of *diakonos,* is employed.

To these general statements I will add, in the language of Dr. Howell, there is, however, a strict application of the term deacon to a specified class of officers in the church, who, in distinction from all others, bear this name.*

Here I would observe, that when I set about my enquiries many years since, respecting this class of church officers, I was a little disappointed to find them named but in two places, in our version of the New Testament, namely, in Philippians and Timothy; but our Dr. Johnson, formerly of South Carolina, now of Florida, in his work on Church Discipline, has stated that the original term occurs about thirty times in the New Testament. In one case, this term is applied to Phebe, a servant or deaconess of the church.

* Howell on the Deaconship, page 15 and onward.

But my main object, in these brief sketches, is to show that our churches need some important modifications in this business. In my extensive travels among them, for *fifty years*, in all parts of our own country, I have been very fully led to this conclusion. Very often I have seen churches suffer greatly for the want of better officers of this kind; and very frequently have I heard the remark, "There is something wrong in our deaconship, both in the character of the men, and their doings." And while this point is so generally conceded, I have been not a little surprised, that our strong men, and those who have written on the regulation of our church concerns, and who, moreover, have shown so much anxiety to set in order the things that are wanting, have said so little on this subject. They give the churches the same good advice that was given them when they were constituted, respecting the kind of men they should put in the deacon's office, but in very few cases have I seen or heard of any suggestions, which would lead to any changes in the polity of our deaconship.

To be full of the Holy Ghost and wisdom was required of the first seven deacons; and Paul to Timothy says of these men, "They must be grave, not double-tongued; not given to much wine; not greedy of filthy lucre ; holding the mystery of the faith in a pure conscience."

A correspondent, whose comments I had sought on this subject, writes me thus :

" ' *Full of the Holy Ghost*'—men of eminent piety.

" ' *Of wisdom*'—sound, practical men, of acknowledged ability in counsel.

" ' *Grave, not double-tongued, not given to much wine, not greedy of filthy lucre*'—of exemplary behavior in all their relations at home and abroad ; not given to intrigue; simple-minded, sober, charitable; and able to speak for Christ, whenever occasion presents, as Stephen and Philip did.

"This, I think, is the New Testament view of this subject. Such are the men whom we should choose for deacons, and if those who were once such, have ceased to be such, a mode should be provided for their retirement, that their places may be filled by others."

In conversation, lately, with an ex-pastor of another community, whose deaconship is much like ours, I inquired of him if he ever knew of a deacon, of good moral character being dismissed from office on account of age or inefficiency. " No, never," was his quick reply. " I have known of a few resignations, but of no dismissions." The same statement, I presume, may be made relative to our denomination. As our deacons are all appointed for life, it is expected, as a mat-

ter of course, that they will remain in office as long
as they live, if they avoid church censures, however
aged and infirm, or useless, faulty or displeasing they
may become.

" A *mode* of retirement *should* be provided," says
my correspondent; but no such provision exists in
the church polity of the Baptists. Our churches
would shrink from the attempt to dismiss from office
a deacon of the above description. The man himself,
also, would feel injured by such a move, and his family and friends would consider it a dishonor to his
name. Indeed, I am inclined to think, that it would
be difficult to find members, in almost any of our
churches, who would be willing to approach a deacon
on the subject of his voluntary resignation, however
much they might wish for his retirement, and that a
different man was in his place.

In all my conversations with our people, on matters
of this kind, I have found very few who appear to
have thought much about them, or to suppose that
there can be any remedy for the evils, now under consideration.

In the beginning of this article I have suggested
the idea of a limited time in the appointment of deacons, which idea I have entertained for many years;
and I am pleased to see that Dr. Crowell, in his
Church Member's Manual, recommends this plan in

the following terms: " As the office of deacon is not
an exclusive calling, and as it can be changed without
a violation of duty or personal inconvenience, there
are some reasons for limiting the term of office to a
shorter period than during life. It is impossible to
foresee, how well a man may fill any office till he is
placed in it; then, his health, his mental faculties, and
even his piety may decline, or God may raise up better men in the church. If he becomes unfitted through
age, or mental feebleness, or spiritual deadness, he is
usually the last to find out the fact. If the church
undertake to dismiss him by vote, an unpleasant excitement may be raised; if his brethren endeavor,
privately, to persuade him to resign, jealousies may
be aroused; if he, with the best of motives, resign
voluntarily, false and injurious inferences may be
drawn; all of which would be avoided, if his term
of office expired by its own limitation. Besides, the
church would have frequent opportunities to place
her most active and pious men in this office."*

Dr. Crowell names five, six or seven years as the
term of office.

Four years is the term I recommend for the appointment, not only of deacons, but for all officers of
the churches, and all our benevolent institutions. Had

* Church Member's Manual, pages 202, 203.
15*

this rule been adopted in the commencement of these bodies, much of the trouble which has been experienced by their managers, relative to men who turn out not to be of the right stamp, might have been avoided.

As yet, I am not fully decided about the application of this rule to church pastors, although I am inclined to think, there would be a gain in the duration of our pastorships; since four years is probably more than an average of pastoral longevity among our people, in more modern times, as the following statement will show: "During the four years ending April, 1852, in Massachusetts, out of one hundred and ninety Baptist pastors, one hundred and seventy had changed their places, and six had died. In New Hampshire, during the same time, sixty-one out of seventy-one had changed their locations, and three h d died. In Connecticut, Rhode Island and Maine these pastoral changes had been equally great." This information was communicated by Rev. S. S. Leighton, a traveling agent.

This four years' rule I learned from the present policy of our national government, with the working of which the people seem well pleased.* Thus far the

* There is a tradition, which I believe is well founded, that while Jefferson was studying out the principles of our national Constitution, he was accustomed to attend the meetings of a small Baptist church near

teaching of the Baptists in constitutional principles ; and I see no impropriety in learning, in our turn, a useful lesson in official appointments, which is briefly explained in the note below. Appointment for life is an aristocratic idea ; a republican one, is of a limited duration, so that there may be rotation in offices among men qualified to fill them. In all cases I would have the old incumbents eligible for reappointment. This might have a beneficial effect on such as are prone to inactivity and negligence, and, as Crowell well observes, the new men who arise in the churches, by this method, might be brought into more active service. There is another idea of Crow-

him, which, according to their custom, sat with open doors. In witnessing the doings of this *free, self-operating body*, he caught some of the leading ideas of the important document which came from his pen. The government which thus arose, and which was unlike any other in the world, at any period, was an experiment in free principles, some of which have since been slightly modified. When I became connected with the Post Office Department, more than a quarter of a century ago, all the postmasters in our country, of all grades, were appointed without any limit of time, and so it was in all other departments. But by a law of 18—, the terms of all official appointments, except some judges, foreign ministers and consuls, were made to correspond with that of the President and his cabinet, namely, four years. In this way the complaints of proscription are avoided. All go out of office with the head of the nation. Their term of office expires by its own limitation. If they can get a reappointment, it is their good fortune ; if not, a new man is installed. In this way the wheels are kept in motion, and there is no cause of complaint of unfair dealing by the man who accepts an office on such terms—and whoever heard of any one's declining it ?

ell's worthy of very serious consideration, namely,
the uncertainty attending new appointments in the
deaconship. And should any one decline an appointment on the plan proposed, instead of having any
argument with him, the better way, in my judgment,
would be for the church to let him slide.

I have lately given a pleasing view of the character of deacons in Scripture language, and I am sometimes led to inquire, How large a proportion of the
great number of our men in this office are *full of the
Holy Ghost and wisdom, are grave, not double-tongued,
not given to much wine, not greedy of filthy lucre, holding
the mystery of the faith in a pure conscience, ruling their
children and their own houses well?*

I am led to suppose that in the more than fifteen
thousand churches of Baptists* in all North America,
there are at least twenty thousand deacons.†

What a vast amount of good could be accomplished
by such a host of official men, if all of them were of
the right stamp and copied after the gospel model!

In a little work called the *Sunny Side,* the scenes
of which are laid in another denomination, whose

---

* In this number I include all the associated Baptists, the Freewill,
Six Principle, and Seventh Day orders.

† Two is the rule in most cases; some churches have but one, and a
few none, while a few of the churches in the cities and large towns go
a good deal beyond the old orthodox duality rule. On the whole I
think my estimate is within bounds.

deaconship is much like our own, is the following description of a Deacon Jones, who was styled a *peculiar* man. " A good man he was generally believed to be, yet no one liked him. There seemed to be some curious twist in his make which nothing would fit. If the church started any movement, it was almost morally certain he would oppose it. He helped along no plan which did not originate with himself. Notwithstanding his goodness, he made so much trouble at ———, that in a fit of desperation they chose him to the deaconship, thinking this would enlist his energies on the side of good order. It was jumping out of the frying pan into the fire. He so " magnified his office," that the ——— pulpit went for sometime begging. Yet, after all, there was no one in the parish who was so kind to the poor, so attentive to the sick, lived so simply, and gave away so generously as Deacon Jones. It seemed as if the church could neither do without him or with him.

    *   *   *   " Ah me !" sighed Mr. ——— (a candidate for settlement) " I am afraid I shall find a thorn there." The last conversation the young minister had with one of his elderly friends occurred to him, which was to this effect : " If when you are settled, you find a crooked stick in your parish, in the shape of an unruly deacon, don't hope to get rid of the trouble by running away. You may find one everywhere."

It would not be altogether strange if there should be found some Deacon Joneses in our numerous churches; and it is to be feared that we have too many men in our extensive diaconate of whom not so much could be said in their favor, as of the ill-esteemed deacon inthe Sunny Side.

Discrepancies in our Treatment of Deacons and Ministers.

We treat deacons like real estate, but ministers like personal property, and precarious at that.

With us young men are eligible for the ministry, but not for the deaconship.

We dismiss ministers from their stations for almost any cause in the midst of usefulness, while we retain our deacons in office, when their usefulness is over.

In early times there was a set of men called *archdeacons*, who kept so close to the bishops that they were called their hands, their ears, their eyes, etc.; but the bishops, now, are generally the first men modern archdeacons fall out with, and seek to undermine.

We consider a good deal of special training needful for ministers and pastors, but where do we find any treatise or set discourse to guide our deacons in their employment? How meager are all our instructions on this subject?

On the Number Seven for the Deaconship.

On examining the early history of the diaconate among the Pilgrims, and Puritans, and Baptists, in this country, I find that the number *two* was the maximum in all churches, however large, until *ruling elders* went out of use, and for a long time after.

In my early day, in meeting-houses of the old class, there might be seen two grave-looking, gray-headed old men, in the deacons' seat, directly under the pulpit. This, as an old Puritan author observes, was accounted a seat of honor, or good degree. It was a little elevated so that the occupants might be more easily seen by all in the house. Here this venerable pair of church officers might be seen, not only at communion seasons, but it was their privileged location in the sanctuary at all times.

In process of time large city churches enlarged the number of church officers, but by no settled rule, some going beyond, but most of them falling short of the number mentioned in Acts.

The old church in Providence, which for more than fifty years that I have known it, and which has always contained from four to five hundred members, and sometimes a good deal more than the highest number named, has never had but four deacons at a time.

This church, and also many other churches in New

England, have standing committees, composed partly of deacons, and partly of other members, to perform the deacons' service, and under such a compound motion the principal part of church business is managed.

The plan of having seven good deacons, ready for every good work, would render this modern system of committees needless, and obviate the serious objections which now exist in the minds of many old-fashioned Baptists.

Among our writers, and those of other parties, with whom deacons are not regarded as a preaching order, it is rather a modern idea that we are to look to the sixth of Acts, for the origin of the Christian deaconship. The comments of old writers are rather vague on this subject; the general tenor of them, however, has been, that the men in question, had but a temporary appointment. But no one to my knowledge has ever named the time, or the place, when deacons were first set apart to the office.

It must be conceded in favor of our own writers, and some others, that they have taken more decided ground than formerly in this matter, but still they do not come up to seven as the standard. They generally concur with Crowell " that the Scriptures give no rule respecting the number of deacons. A church, therefore, may elect as many as it seems necessary."

In some cases, as one of our ministers informed me, churches go by the number of their aisles.

Other churches go by the amount of their deacon timber, to use a familiar phrase. But a great majority of our churches have but two.

If the deaconship was instituted by the direction of the apostles as reported in Acts, I see no reason why the number then fixed upon, out of the vast multitude in the great church, who might have been chosen, should not be standard at all times. *Seven* was a sacred number among the ancients, which often occurs in the Scripture narratives, and this might have had influence on the minds of the apostles in their order,—*Look ye out seven men*, etc. At any rate, as we find the number of deacons specified in the account of the origin of the order, in my opinion, we have a safe *rule*, or at least a good *model* in this business. No more, and no less, was the doctrine of some of the oldest and largest churches of antiquity, as we learn from antiquarian authors.

"In some churches," says Bingham, "they were very precise to the number *seven*, in imitation of the first church of Jerusalem. The council of Neocæsarea enacted it into a canon, that there should be but seven deacons in any city, though it was never so great, because this was according to the rule suggested in the Acts of the Apostles. And the church of

Rome, both before and after this Council, seems to have looked upon that as a binding rule also. For it is evident from the epistles of Cornelius, written in the middle of the third century, that there were then but seven deacons in the church of Rome, although there were forty-six presbyters at the same time."*

In Alexandria, in Egypt, at Milan and other places, this rule was strictly adhered to in early times, long before the rise of the papacy, and while Christianity maintained in a good degree its primitive principles.

When great churches needed more officers, instead of adding to the list of deacons, they instituted a new order called sub-deacons, and here, again, they strictly adhered to the number seven.

But as ages rolled on this early rule was disregarded by many, and the number of deacons was greatly augmented, so that about three centuries after the period lately under consideration, namely, in the time of Justinian, who built the church of St. Sophia in Constantinople, now a Mohammedan mosque, there were one hundred deacons for that great establishment.†

My views in this business apply to full grown churches; all must see that small and feeble bodies can not conform to this rule. They can live with but

---

* Christian Antiquities, vol. i.

† Three other churches were connected with the metropolitan church. Justinian died 565, aged 83.

one deacon, or none at all. So they can without pastors, or houses of worship, which they obtain as soon as they are able, and so they should manage in filling up their deaconships, which may be done much sooner than some would suppose by using due diligence with their members,* and by putting into the office a younger class of men than formerly

The first church in Pawtucket began with two deacons, then they had four, and now seven. The last ones were appointed for four years. Those who were appointed for life, under the old rule, remain as they were, to serve out their time.

The following discourse relates to the dealings of some deacons with ministers; the facts were gathered mostly from a report in a public print:

A Dialogue between a Pastor and one of his Deacons, who wished him to resign his post.

Deacon.—I am sorry to say it, Elder A., but I have come with rather a disagreeable message

Minister.—Well, what is it, Deacon B. ?

Deacon.—I have been talking with some of our folks, and *we* think it is about time for us to be looking out for another minister. You have been with us nearly three years, if I remember right.

Minister.—This is news to me, Deacon. Has there been any

---

* An eccentric minister once said to a member, " we want to make a deacon of you." " O, no," said the man, " I am not good enough." " Well, we want to make a better man of you."

meeting on the subject? What are the reasons you give, Brother B.?

Deacon.—There ha'n't been any church meeting; only I have spoken to two or three members, and they pretty much agree with me. The most I have to say about it, I am not edified with your preaching.

Minister.—That does not surprise me at all. I do not think much of my preaching myself, and I sincerely wish it was a good deal better·

Deacon.—No doubt you can easily find another good place. Ministers often do better by changing, and the people too. I am a little particular about preaching.

Minister.—Perhaps, Deacon B., you had better join some other church. You can no doubt have a letter by asking. You may then hear such preaching as you want.

Deacon.—O no—I have no idea of that. This is my home.

Minister.—This is my home, too, and why should I leave it?

Deacon.—But my property is here.

Minister.—And I can say the same, Deacon B.

Deacon.—But your property is small, compared with mine.

Minister.—That is true, but still it is my all.

Deacon.—But you know, Elder A., that deacons don't move about like ministers. It would make a public talk if I was to take your advice; besides, ministers are bound to go where they can do the most good.

Minister.—I admit that; but are not deacons bound to do the same? There ought not to be one law for ministers and another for deacons. There are many churches that need more members like you, who are able to help. It is no uncommon thing for deacons and other church members to remove their relation for that purpose. You could do a feeble church more good by going to it, than I could. You would be a help. I should be a burden. Besides, you are able to make sacrifices.

Deacon.—You don't view the matter right, Elder A. I didn't come to talk about my leaving the church. You don't understand me, Elder.

Minister.—Your meaning is very plain, Deacon B. A man with half an eye can see it.

Deacon.—But how is your salary coming out, if you stay? You know I have a good deal to do about it. I myself shall not—

Minister.—I fully understand this hint, Deacon B. This is an old argument in such cases. As to that matter, I shall trust to God and my friends.

Deacon.—As for friends, Elder A., you have not a better one in the place than I am. Friendship is not the question in this case. We have changed pastors a number of times since I have been a deacon; but I have always been friendly to them all, and so I am to you, Elder A. It is the good of the church that I look at; that is always uppermost in my mind, in all I do.

Minister.—I think we may as well draw this conversation to a close, and permit me, Deacon B., to say, that as I view the matter, the main question before us is, which of us shall ask for a dismission from the church.

Deacon.—I must say, Elder A., this is a new way for a minister to talk to a deacon, especially one who has done so much for the minister, the church, the poor and all around, and who is able still to keep on doing and giving, if I can have such preaching as I like.

Minister.—I mean to treat you with due respect, Deacon B., but you must consider that ministers have the right of judgment and of speech as well as deacons. Thus far, no one of my people has given me any hint about my leaving them, but you alone. I hope you will not press matters on your own account. When you show me an official document from the church, respecting my vacating my pastorship, I will take it under consideration, and, in the meantime, I will keep on performing my pastoral duties.

At this point, the deacon, in a thoughtful mood and with a disappointed look, began to make preparations to take his leave; and by the last account from the place the minister was still at his post.

If more ministers, in similar situations, would meet their deacons of this class on their own ground, and if more churches would take a stand independent of such men, well formed pastoral relations would not so often be broken up. But in most cases heretofore, if one, or at least a majority of deacons, turn against a pastor, the whole body gives up in despair, and these officious managers have the regulation of pastorships all their own way.

CHAPTER XXVII.

"THE history of the pulpit is curious and entertaining. It has spoken all languages, and in all sorts
of style. It has partaken of all the customs of the
schools, the theaters and the courts of all the countries where it has been erected. It has been a seat of
wisdom, and a sink of nonsense. It has been filled
by the best and the worst of men. It has proved in
some hands a trumpet of sedition, and in others a
source of peace and consolation. But on a fair balance, collected from authentic history, there would
appear no proportion between the benefits and the
mischiefs which mankind have derived from it, so
much do the advantages of it preponderate. In a
word, evangelical preaching has been, and yet con-
tinues to be, reputed foolishness: but real wisdom, a
wisdom and a power by which it pleases God to save
the souls of men.

"The first voice that imparted religious ideas by
discourse to fallen man, was the voice of the Creator,

called, by the inspired historian, *The voice of the Lord
God, walking in the garden in the cool of the day.*
Whether he, who afterwards appeared so often in human shape, and at last actually put on a human body,
descended into the garden, assumed a form and conversed with our first parents on this occasion, or
whether the air was so undulated by the power of
God, as to form articulate, audible sounds, certain it
is, Adam and Eve literally heard a voice, and had
the highest reason for accounting it the voice of God.
The promise to the woman of a son, who should
bruise the serpent's head, was emphatically and properly called *The word* of God. It was a promise which
they had no right to expect; but, when revealed, the
highest reason to embrace.

"It is natural to suppose, God having once spoken
to man, that mankind would retain, and repeat with
great punctuality, what had been said, and listen after
more. Accordingly, infallible records assure us, that
when men began to associate for the purpose of worshiping the Deity, Enoch prophesied. We have a
very short account of this prophet and his doctrine;
enough, however, to convince us that he taught the
principal truths of natural, and the then revealed religion, the unity of God and his natural and moral
perfections, the nature of virtue and its essential difference from vice, a day of future, impartial retribu-

tion. Conviction of sin was in his doctrine, and communion with God was exemplified in his conduct. He held communion with God by sacrifice, and St. Paul reasons from his *testimony that he* pleased God, that he had faith in the promise of the Mediator, for *without faith* it would have been impossible even for Enoch, *to have pleased God.*

"From the days of Enoch to the time of Moses, each patriarch worshiped God with his family; probably several assembled at new moons, and alternately instructed the whole company.

"Noah was a preacher of righteousness, and by him, as an instrument, Christ, by his Spirit, preached to the disobedient souls of men, imprisoned in ignorance and vice, and continued, with great long-suffering, to do so all the while the ark was preparing.

"Abraham *commanded his household after him to keep the way of the Lord, and to do justice and judgment;* and Jacob, when his house lapsed to idolatry, remonstrated against it, and exhorted them, and *all that were with him, to put away strange gods, and to go up with him to Bethel,* to that God who had answered him in the day of his distress. In all these records of matters of fact, we perceive, short as they are, the same great leading truths that were taught by Enoch, the general truths of natural religion, and along with them, the peculiar principles of revelation.

16

"How charming, upon a primitive mountain, beneath the shade of a venerable grove, must the voice of Melchisedeck have been, the father, the prince and the priest of his people, now *publishing* to his attentive audience, *good tidings of salvation, peace* between God and man, and the lifting up holy hands and *calling upon the name of the Lord, the everlasting God!* A few plain truths, proposed in simple style, addressed to the reason, and expounded by the feelings of mankind, enforced by nothing but fraternal argument and example, animated by the Holy Spirit, and productive of genuine moral excellence, accompanied with sacrifices, comprised the whole system of patriarchal religion. Such was the venerable simplicity of hoary antiquity, before statesmen stole the ordinances of religion, and hungry hirelings were paid to debase them.

"Moses, although slow of speech, is the next preacher I shall name. This great man had much at heart the promulgation of his doctrine. He directed it to be inscribed on pillars, to be transcribed in books, and to be taught both in public and in private by word of mouth. Himself set the example of each; and how he and Aaron sermonized, we may see by several parts of his writings. The first discourse was heard with profound reverence and attention; the last was both uttered and received in raptures.

"Public preaching does not appear, under this economy, to have been attached to the priesthood. Priests were not officially preachers, and we have innumerable instances of discourses delivered in religious assemblies by men of other tribes besides that of Levi. *The Lord gave the word, and great was the company of those that published it. Joshua was an Ephraimite, but being full of the spirit of wisdom,* he gathered the tribes to Shechem, and harangued the people of God. Solomon was a prince of the house of Judah; Amos a herdsman of Tekoa; yet both were preachers, and one, at least, was a prophet.

"Before Moses, revelation was short, and might safely be deposited in the memory. But when God saw fit to bless the church with the large and necessary additions of Moses, a book became necessary. This book was the standard, and they who *spoke not according to this word* were justly accounted to have *no light in them.* Hence the distinction between scriptural instructors, who taught according to the *law* and the *testimony,* and were called seers, and fanciful declaimers, who uttered visions out of their own hearts, and were deemed blind, and thought to be in a dream, that is, under deception.

"The sermons of the old prophets often produced

amazing effects, both in the principles and the morals of the people. Single discourses, at some times,
brought whole nations to repentance, although, at
other times, the greatest of them complained, *Who
hath believed our report ? All day long we have stretched
forth our hands unto a disobedient and gainsaying people.*
In the first case, they were in ecstacies, such was their
benevolence ; in the last, they retired in silence, and
wept in secret places. Some, in first transports of
passion, execrated the day of their birth, and, when
deliberation and calmness returned, committed themselves, their country and their cause to God.

"Ezekiel was a man extraordinarily appointed to
preach to the captives, and endowed with singular
abilities for the execution of his office. He received
his instructions in ecstacies, and he uttered them generally in rapturous vehemence. He had a pleasant
voice, and the entire management of it ; he could *play
on the instrument,* that is, he knew how to dispose his
organs of speech, so as to give energy, by giving
proper tone and accent to all he spoke. The people
were as much charmed with his discourses as if they
had been odes set to music. He was a *lovely song* in
their ears, and they used to say to *one another, Come,
and let us hear what is the word that cometh forth from
the Lord.* The elders and the people assembled at his
house, and sat before him, and there, sometimes in the

morning, and at other times in the evening, he delivered those sharp and pointed sermons which are contained in his prophecy.

" When the seventy years of the captivity were expired, the captives were divided in their opinions about returning. Some traded and flourished in Babylon, and, having no faith in the divine promise, and too much confidence in their sordid guides, chose to live where idolatry was the established religion, and despotism the soul of civil government. The good prophets and preachers, Zerubbabel, Joshua, Haggai and others, having confidence in the word of God, and aspiring after their natural, civil and religious rights, endeavored, by all means, to extricate themselves and their countrymen from that mortifying state into which the crimes of their ancestors had brought them. They wept, fasted, prayed, preached, prophesied, and at length prevailed. The chief instruments were Nehemiah and Ezra ; the first was governor, and reformed their civil state ; the last was a *scribe of the law of the God of heaven*, and addressed himself to ecclesiastical matters, in which he rendered the noblest service to his country and to all posterity.

" *The first Pulpit of which we have any account in the Scriptures.*

" We have a short, but beautiful description of the manner of Ezra's first preaching.   Upwards of fifty thousand people assembled in a street, or large square, near the watergate.   It was early in the morning of a Sabbath day.   A pulpit of wood, in the fashion of a small tower, was placed there on purpose for the preacher, and this turret was supported by a scaffold, a temporary gallery, where, in a wing on the right hand of the pulpit, sat six of the principal preachers, and in another on the left, seven.   Thirteen other principal teachers, and many Levites, were present also, on scaffolds erected for the purpose, alternately to officiate.   When Ezra ascended the pulpit, he produced and opened the book of the law, and the whole congregation instantly rose up from their seats, and stood.   Then he offered up prayer and praise to God, the people bowing their heads, and worshiping the Lord with their faces to the ground; and at the close of the prayer, with uplifted hands, they solemnly pronounced Amen, Amen.   Then, all standing, Ezra, assisted at times by the Levites, *read the law distinctly, gave the sense, and caused them to understand the reading.*   The sermons delivered, so affected the hearers, that they wept excessively, and about noon, the sorrow became so exuberant and immeasurable, that it was thought necessary by the governor, the preacher and the Levites to restrain it.

" Plato was alive at this time, teaching dull philosophy to cold academics. But what was he, and what was Xenophon, or Demosthenes, or any of the Pagan orators, in comparison with these men !"*

* Most of this chapter, and a part of the next, is taken from Robinson's Dissertation on Public Preaching. It is prefixed to the second volume of Claude's Essay on the Composition of a Sermon.

CHAPTER XXVIII.

PREACHERS, PREACHING, PULPITS AND CLERICAL MANNERS.

PREACHERS UNDER THE CHRISTIAN DISPENSATION.—JOHN THE BAP-
TIST. — JESUS CHRIST. — THE APOSTLES.—THE EARLY FATHERS.—
CHRYSOSTOM, AUGUSTINE, AND OTHERS.—CLAUDE, DODDRIDGE, ETC

"JOHN THE BAPTIST was extraordinarily commissioned from heaven to announce the advent of the
promised Messiah, and he adopted a plan formerly
used by Ezra, appealing by public preaching to the
common sense of mankind. He took Elijah for his
model, and, as the times were very much like those
in which that prophet lived, he chose a doctrine and
a method very much resembling those of that venerable man. His subjects were few, plain, and important; *repentance* was the chief. His style was vehement, his images were bold and well placed; his
deportment was solemn, his action eager, and his
morals severe. The people flocked after him in great
multitudes, and surrounded him with a popularity of
which his enemies were afraid. He fell, however, a
sacrifice to female revenge at a tyrant's drunken bout,
where despotism gave whatever prostitution required.

"Jesus Christ had been openly introduced by John to the knowledge and affection of the people, and at his death Jesus appeared in public as a preacher.

"*Jesus Christ and the Apostles Model Preachers.*

"The ministry of the long-expected Messiah may be characterized as the most beneficial that can be imagined. He took his doctrine immediately from the holy Scriptures, to which he constantly appealed. The truths of natural religion he explained and established; the doctrines of revelation he expounded, elucidated and enforced, and thus brought life and immortality to *light* by the gospel. These doctrines were all plain facts: as, God is a spirit; God sent his Son into the world that the world might be saved. Respecting himself and his gospel we find the following declarations: 'Moses wrote of me; he that believeth on him that sent me is passed from death unto life; the dead shall hear the voice of the Son of God; the wicked shall go away into everlasting punishment, but the righteous shall go into life eternal. My kingdom is not of this world; the merciful are happy; happy are the pure in heart; but few find the narrow way that leadeth unto life, while many go in at the wide gate that leadeth to destruction.' All these and many more of the same kind are facts plain

and true, and they were the simple truths which Jesus Christ chose to teach.

"The *tempers* in which he executed his ministry
were the noblest that can be conceived. He was
humble, compassionate, firm, disinterested and generous. He displayed in all the course of his ministry
such an assortment of properties as obliged some of
his auditors to burst into exclamatory admiration,
'*blessed are the paps* which *thou hast sucked !*' Others to
hang upon his lips, wondering at *the gracious words
that proceeded out of his mouth, and all to acknowledge,
'never man spake like this man !*' This was not a temporary tide of popularity, it was admiration founded
on reason, and all ages since have admired and ex-
claimed in like manner.

"Add to these the simplicity and majesty of his
style, the beauty of his images, the alternate softness
and severity of his address, the choice of his subjects,
the gracefulness of his deportment, the indefatigable-
ness of his zeal,   *   *   *   where shall we put the
period? His perfections are inexhaustible, and our
admiration is everlasting. The character of Jesus
Christ is the best book a preacher can study.

"Jesus Christ never paid any regard to the *place*
where he delivered his sermons; he taught in the
temple, the synagogues, public walks and private
houses; he preached on mountains, and in barges

and ships. His missionaries imitated him, and convenience for the time was consecration of the place. He was equally indifferent to the posture—he stood or sat, as his own ease and the popular edification required. The time also was accommodated to the same end. He preached early in the morning, late in the evening, on Sabbath days and festivals, and whenever else the people had leisure and inclination to hear.

"Jesus Christ used very little action, but that little was just, natural, grave and expressive.

"The success that accompanied the ministry of our Immanuel was truly astonishing. My soul overflows with joy, my eyes with tears of pleasure while I transcribe it. * * *

"Was he to pass a road, they climbed the trees to see him, yea, the blind sat by the wayside to hear him go by. Was he in a house, they unroofed the building to come at him. As if they could never get near enough to hear the soft accents of his voice, they pressed, they crowded, they trod upon one another to surround him. When he retired into the wilderness they thought him another Moses, and would have made him a king. It was the finest thing they could think of. He, greater than the greatest monarch, despised worldly grandeur, but to fulfill prophecy, sitting upon a borrowed ass' colt, rode

into Jerusalem *the Son of the Highest* and allowed
the transported multitude to strew the way with garments and branches, and to arouse the insensible metropolis by acclamations, the very children shouting
*Hosannah ! Hosannah in the highest ! Hosannah to the
son of David ! Blessed be he that cometh in the name of
the Lord !*

"The birth, life, doctrine, example, miracles, cru-
cifixion, resurrection, and ascension of Christ made a
large addition to the old subjects of preaching. The
old economy was a rude delineation, the new was a
finished piece. It was no new doctrine, it was an old
plan brought to perfection, and set in finished excellence to last for ever. It was the religion of love to
God and man made obvious and universal.

"The apostles exactly copied their divine Master.
They confined their attention to religion, and left the
schools to dispute, and politicions to intrigue. Their
doctrines were a set of facts of two sorts. The first
were within every man's observation, and they appealed for the truth of them to common sense and
experience. The others were facts, which from their
nature could be known only by testimony.

"Their gospel was a simple tale, that any honest
man might tell. As to all the circumstantials of public preaching, time, place, gesture, style, habits, and
so on, it was their glory to hold these indifferent, and

to be governed in their choice by a supreme attention to general edification. * * * Great was the success of these venerable men.

"The apostles being dead, every thing came to pass exactly as they had foretold. The whole Christian system underwent a miserable change; preaching shared the fate of other institutions, and this glory of the primitive church was turned into a lie. The degeneracy, however, was not immediate; it was slow and gradual, and brought on by degrees, just as a modest youth becomes a profligate man.

"It must be allowed, in general, that the simplicity of Christianity was maintained, though under gradual decay, during the first three centuries. Christians assembled on the first day of the week, for public worship. Prayer was offered to the Deity in the name of Jesus Christ. Psalms and hymns were sung in praise of God, the Creator, the Preserver and Redeemer of men. The sacred writings were read. The word of God was preached, its doctrines explained, and its duties enforced.

"The next five centuries produced many pious and excellent preachers, both in the Latin and Greek churches. The doctrine, however, continued to degenerate, and the pulpit, along with all other institutes, degenerated with it. It is impossible in this

sketch, to investigate particulars. We will just take
a cursory, general view.

"The Greek pulpit was adorned with some eloquent orators. Basil, Bishop of Cæsarea, John Chrysostom, preacher of Antioch, and afterwards patriarch
of Constantinople, and Gregory Nazianzen, who all
flourished in the fourth century, seem to have led the
fashion of preaching in the Greek church. Jerome
and Augustine did the same in the Latin church.
Had the excellences only of these great men been
imitated by their contemporaries and successors, the
imitators would have been competent orators—but
very far from able ministers of the New Testament—
but their very defects were adopted as pulpit endow-
ments.

"The Greeks called sermons *homilies*, that is, public
discourses, spoken to the *common people*.. The Latins
named them at first *tracts*, or treatises, that is, public
discourses, in which subjects were stated, argued and
thoroughly *discussed ;* afterward they called them sermons, or *speeches ;* perhaps some sermons were nothing more.

" *Peculiarities of the early Preachers.*

" When a bishop, or preacher, traveled, he claimed
no authority to exercise the duties of his functions,
unless he was invited by the churches where he at-

tended public worship. The primitive churches had
no idea of a bishop at Rome presuming to dictate to
a congregation in Africa. Nothing, however, was
more common than such friendly visits and sermons,
as were then in practice. The churches thought them
edifying. In case the bishop was sick or absent, one
of the deacons, or sometimes a short-hand writer,
used to read a homily, that had been preached, and,
perhaps, published by some good minister, and sometimes a homily that had been preached by the bishop
of the church.

" We have great obligations to primitive notaries,
for they very early addressed themselves to take
down the homilies of public preachers. Sometimes
the hearers employed them, sometimes the preachers,
and sometimes themselves. For this purpose they
carried writing tablets, waxed, and styles, that is,
pointed irons, or gravers, into the assembly and
stood round the preacher, to record what he said.

" The deacons placed themselves round the pulpit,
and before sermon, one of them cried, with a loud
voice, *Silence! Hearken!* or something similar. This
was repeated often, if necessary; I suppose at proper
pauses, when the preacher stopped. Their manners
were different from ours; but, really, our manners
want some of their customs. It might do some
drowsy folks good to be alarmed every five or ten

minutes with, *Mind what you are about. Let us listen. Attend to the word of God.*

"The fathers differed much in pulpit action; the greater part used very moderate and sober gesture. Paul, of Samoseta, used to stamp with his foot, and strike his thigh with his hand, and throw himself into violent agitations; but he was blamed for it by his contemporaries. They thought his action theatrical and improper in a church; and yet, in every church, the people were allowed, and even exhorted, to applaud the preacher, by shouting and clapping their hands at the close of a period, as at the theater, or in a forum. The first preachers delivered their sermons all extempore, and they studied, while they preached, the countenances of their auditors, to see whether the doctrine was understood.

"Sermons, in those days, were all in the vulgar tongue. The Greeks preached in Greek, the Latins in Latin, for the preachers meant to be understood. They did not preach by the clock, so to speak, but short or long as they saw occasion. Augustine used to leave off when the people's hearts seemed properly affected with the subject. He judged of this sometimes by their shouting, and at other times by their tears. Their sermons were usually about an hour long; but many of them may be deliberately pronounced in half an hour, and several in less time.

" Sermons were generally both preached and heard standing; but sometimes both speaker and auditor sat, especially the aged and infirm. Their methods were, on some occasions, what we call expounding from several verses, on others, preaching from a single passage. In many things they imitated the Jews, by adapting parts of Scripture to particular seasons, and hence, in time, came the appointment of select portions for Easter, Whitsuntide, and other festivals.

" Most of the sermons, in these days, are divisible into three general parts. The first is a short introduction; the second an exposition of the text; and the last a moral exhortation arising out of the discussion.

" In this period many noble places of worship were built. The old Jewish temple was the original, the rest were all taken from it; a cathedral was an imitation of the temple, and a village place of worship of a synagogue."

From the foregoing account of the manner of the fathers in very few cases did they write out their discourses, either before or after delivery, and to the notaries or reporters, as they would be called, we are indebted for the ponderous volumes of sermons which have come down to us,[*] very few of which would be

* The nature of *wax tables* and the manner of using them by notaries or reporters will be explained in my history of the Donatists in my *Ecclesiastical Compendium.*

read with interest if they were translated. Chrysostom was no doubt a truly eloquent preacher. Augustine was logical, but I could never see a great amount of eloquence in his writings. He has always been accounted intensely orthodox, but on church discipline he was extremely lax, and if his language is to be literally understood he was a decided advocate for sacramental efficacy.

Through the dark ages there was not much preaching of any kind among the Greeks or Romans, but their services consisted in repeating church liturgies, and in public processions. We have good reasons for believing many of the reputed heretics preached the gospel in truth and sincerity; very little, however, has come down to us except of their sufferings. The preaching monks had one text which they always employed in their declamations against the enemies of the Church, namely:

"Who will rise up for me against the evil doers? Who will stand up for me against the workers of iniquity?"*

With this passage always in their mouths, the zealous defenders of *the Church* would traverse the country, and stir up the rulers and the populace, against those who dissented from the dominant party.

* Psalm xciv. 16.

I will now give some brief sketches of preachers and preaching of modern times.

Claude's Essay on Sermonizing, with Robinson's Notes on the same.

Rev. John Claude was a French Protestant, of the Genevan school. He died in the latter part of the seventeenth century at the Hague, to which persecution had driven him, where he was pastor of the Walloon church. *Rev. Robert Robinson* was a Baptist minister of England. He died about sixty years since.

Claude wrote many works, and among them an *Essay on the Composition of a Sermon*, which was a standard work on this subject for a long time after his death. The essay is of a moderate size. The notes are superabundant. Both together make two large octavo volumes. In the notes are found specimens of sermons by court preachers, prelates, and others, in great variety.

My limits will admit of but a few selections from this store-house of examples in the preaching line.

From Claude's Essay.

On the Choice of Texts.—"Never choose such texts as have not a complete sense; for only impertinent and foolish people will attempt to preach from one or two words, which signify nothing. When too *little text* is taken, you must digress from the subject to find something to say." I call it roving all around the Bible country, in search of matter to bring home to the text, instead of finding it in it.

"When too *much text* is taken, either many important considerations which belong to the passage must be left out, or a tedious prolixity must follow.

" In strange churches do not choose a text of censure, for a stranger has no business to censure a congregation he does not inspect.

" *General Rules for a Sermon.*—Respect should be had to simple people who constitute the great part of most congregations, all of whom need plainness ; and learned hearers will prefer it to obscurity, however learned. There must not be too much *genius*. A sermon must not be overcharged with *doctrine*.

" *Figures must not be Overstrained.*—This is done by stretching metaphor into allegory, or by carrying a parallel too far. A parallel is run too far when a great number of conformities between the figure and, the thing represented by it are heaped together. Critical observations, different readings, different punctuations, etc., must be avoided. Make all the use you can of critical knowledge yourself, but spare the people the account, for it must be very disagreeable to them."

On the division of sermons, this author says, those most admired have only two or three parts.

The treatise under consideration abounds with similar sensible rules, which are well worthy the attention of preachers of all countries and times.

From Robinson's Notes.

"I would send," says a divine of the last century, " a *worldling* to read Ecclesiastes, a *devout* person to the Psalms, an *afflicted* person to Job, a *preacher* to Timothy and Titus, a *backslider* to the Hebrews, a *legalist* to Romans and Galatians, a *libertine* to James, Peter and Jude, a man who would study *providence* to Esther, and those who go about great undertakings to Nehemiah.

" Never refute errors, except when your text requires you to do so."

" *Express Yourself in a Familiar Manner.*—There is a soft, domestic style, such as a wise parent uses to his family, but this is nothing like the silly cant of an old nurse. Dear souls, precious souls, dearly beloved, and a hundred more such phrases, however proper in certain connections, have been hackneyed out of their senses in Christian pulpits. Ministers, who aim at this excellence, should remember there is such a thing as being too familiar.

" An immoderate love of money, is an extreme opposite to prodigality—the first saves all, the last spends all. A virtuous use of money, is a narrow path that lies between two extremes. Moralists affirm that of the two evils avarice is the greatest. Profuseness, say they, may be reformed by poverty, but avarice is incurable. An extravagant man benefits others, while he impoverishes himself, but a miser neither profits himself, nor any other person," etc., etc. * * *

"In this naked manner, as a boy strings birds' eggs, did this old divine connect the parts of a sermon."

> "For rhetoric he could not ope
> His mouth, but out there flew a trope."

"This method of extorting a sense, is what one of our old divines calls *bombarding* the Scriptures, *storming a text and taking it by force.*"

These quaint expressions are made by Robinson with reference to other authors, beside Claude.

Dr. Doddridge on Preaching and other Ministerial Duties.

This famous divine, among the English Dissenters, delivered a course of lectures to his students, from a few of which, namely, those on *composing sermons*, on *different strains of preaching*, on *the style and the delivery of sermons*, I will make a few selections.

"When we are about to compose a sermon we are

to consider what *subject* is to be chosen, in what *strain* it is to be handled, the *style* of the composition, what *thoughts* we are to introduce, and in what *order* we are to show them."

Dr. Doddridge names a number of subjects on which even orthodox preachers should not often deliver full discourses, but instead of that, refer to them in an incidental manner, and among those topics are the doctrines of natural religion, the evidences of Christianity, inexplicable mysteries of the gospel, the highest points of Calvinism, supposing them to be believed, subjects of great terror, etc. "The hungry soul," says Dr. D., "will go away from a full discourse on these points but little refreshed. It is feeding the people with roots, instead of fruit.

"A continued series of discourses from the same verse, or even chapter, ought to be avoided by young preachers. This method tends to weary an audience.

"Having shown what subjects you ought, generally, to decline, I will now point out what subjects are to be *preferred*, and most frequently insisted on, namely, those which relate immediately to Christ; the glories of his person, and the riches of his grace, the Spirit and his operations, the love of Christ and a devotional temper, the evil of sin and the misery of sinners in consequence of it, death, judgment and eternity, and examples of Scripture characters, and pieces of sacred history. These are very interesting and entertaining subjects, and will often afford you natural occasions of saying useful things in a very inoffensive manner. Sometimes a virtue is better represented by such an example, than by a topical discourse.

" *Strain*," says Doddridge, " differs from style ; the first has respect to the composition, the other to the aspect of a discourse.

" The strain should be pathetic, insinuating, spiritual, evangelical and scriptural.

" The style of sermons should be intelligible and clear, strong and nervous, calm and composed, grave and solemn, orthodox, and always plain and unaffected. The boyish affectation of crowding every thing with ornament is despicable. A discourse of this kind is like a mean dress bespangled with jewels.

" *On the Delivery of Sermons.*—This is evidently of great importance, and almost everybody pretends to be a judge of it. A good delivery is much in a man's favor, and the contrary, is much to his disadvantage. In some instances, hearers judge of a man's character by the *manner* of his speaking as much as, or more than they do by his *matter*. It should be *distinct, affectionate, various, natural*, and *free*, that is, above the *servile* use of notes. And to be able to preach without notes raises a man's character.

" Accustom yourselves to look about much on your auditory."

Doddridge, I conclude, was standard authority in his day on the manner of conducting the pulpit service, in his own country.

American preachers have all sorts of customs in the business of preaching, but of later years the theological schools do much to direct their pupils in the *modus operandi* of the pulpit, which is about as various as the institutions referred to.*

But in this whole concern without much impropriety we may say with Pope,

> " What's best administered is best."

I did intend to make a few selections from Dr. Miller's work on clerical manners, as it is well worth the serious attention of young ministers. But all I can now say is, to recommend to them the book itself.

---

* Porter's Homiletics, I am informed, is the principal work on this subject at Amherst, and also at Newton. It is a very able work, of more than four hundred pages; much too large, I should think, for a text book, in this department.

17

CHAPTER XXIX.

ON CHURCH DISCIPLINE.

THE DISCIPLINE OF THE DUTCH ANABAPTISTS, SO CALLED.—MY EARLY
ADVISERS.—MY OWN MS. ON CHURCH DISCIPLINE.—A. FULLER ON
THE DISCIPLINE OF THE PRIMITIVE CHURCHES.—FIVE WORKS COME
OUT NEAR THE SAME TIME BY BAKER, WALKER, JOHNSON, HOWELL,
AND CROWELL.—REMARKS ON THE EIGHTEENTH OF MATTHEW, ON
COUNCILS, THE DESPOTISM OF THE MAJORITY, AND ON BAPTIST
USAGE.

THIS is a subject to which I have paid no small
degree of attention for a long course of years. My
first object was to ascertain just what precepts or examples I could find in the Scriptures pertaining to
this business, and in the next place to examine the
principal works of our own writers upon it. While
this class of men, except Robinson, whose writings
have been so freely quoted in the last two chapters,
have published but little on preachers and preaching,
they have devoted no small amount of labor in discussing the proper management of our churches.

The oldest comments I have found on church
discipline, date back about three hundred years.
They are contained in the old *Dutch Martyrology or
Martyr's Mirror*. There I discovered that the people
called Anabaptists, were very strenuous on two points,

namely, against their members marrying out of the church, and having no intercourse with excommunicated members. The strictly non-intercourse system they called *avoidance,* by which they practiced to the literality, the apostles' doctrine, *with such a one no not to eat.* But as they were very faithful in their church discipline, and in the exclusion of unworthy members, in process of time complaints came from some quarters, that the rigid rule of separation interfered with the domestic relations of husbands and wives, parents and children, brothers and sisters, masters and servants, and other social connections. These representations led to a church action which afforded relief to those who wished to embrace it.

In my early day we had no theological schools and tutors for young ministers in the business of preaching and pastoral duties, but they picked np their information by conversing and corresponding with their elder brethren and following their examples. My principal advisers were Gano, Pitman, Cornel,* Baldwin, Grafton, Stanford, J. Williams, Rogers, Staughton, O. B. Brown, Furman, Mercer, Dudly, Noel, J. M. Peck, of the West, J. Peck, of New York, and others. These men were spread all over the country,

---

* From Elder C. I heard the story of *hush, hush, hush,* which will appear in the chapter on a model church and a model pastor.

but as I became a cosmopolite in early life, I was a neighbor to them all.

Our lay brotherhood, also, in the times now under consideration, more frequently probably than at present, took a deep interest in the rules and regulations of our churches. Of these I shall only name Deacons Loring and Lincoln of Boston, the last of whom, now an octogenarian, is the only one that survives of the above list of my familiar advisers, *fifty years ago*. He was in Dr. Baldwin's deaconship when I first knew him, and by the line of succession I have marked out he might retain the office to the utmost bound of human longevity.

My rules do not permit me to say much of able counselors among our living men.

At an early period I made diligent search among the writings of our British brethren, especially those in Wales, where Baptist sentiments, it is generally believed, have been nourished through all the dark ages, for information on the subject of church discipline. I examined the most ancient confessions of faith; but I found them almost wholly confined to what Morgan Edwards would term the *credenda* rather than the *agenda*, of the Baptists; that is, the things to be *believed*, more than the things to be *done*.

The oldest and most laborious article I have found on this subject was from the pen of Rev. Benjamin

Griffith, of Pennsylvania. It was prepared at the request of the Philadelphia Association. It is a treatise of forty pages of small size, and is bound up with the Philadelphia Confession of Faith, as it is usually called, which is a reprint of that published in London more than a century before. It was printed by Benjamin Franklin while he was a Philadelphia printer. The document agrees very nearly with similar ones published by the ancient Baptists in Bohemia, Poland and Holland.

" *Of Ruling Elders,*" is at the head of one of the sections of this treatise, the practice of having church officers of this kind then being common in that region.

Among my own papers, I find one " *On Church Discipline,*" dated 1826. It appears to be the rough draft of an essay which was read before a *Ministers' Meeting.* Among the greatest defects of our churches at that time, according to the document under consideration, were,

1. *The want* of more strictness in the duties of personal and family religion, and of pious instruction to children and domestics;

2. Of more faithfulness in following the directions of the 18th of Matthew, relative to private offenses, whereby an abundance of extra trouble came upon the churches;

3. Of plain dealing with erring church members ;

4. Of procrastination and hurtful delays in instituting church dealings with such members, under the false plea of patience and charity ;

5. Of more frequent, friendly, old-fashioned, Christian intercourse, and familiarity with each other, in consequence of which coldness and distance ensue ;

6. Of liberality in contributing to the support of the gospel at home and abroad ;

7. Of giving more explicit instructions to new members at first, and of enforcing obedience to them afterwards.

Such were my views of the state of church discipline among the Baptists one third of a century since ; and it is to be feared they have not made much improvement in the business since.

Fuller on Church Discipline.

A number of years prior to the date of my short essay, there came over from England, a small treatise on *The Discipline of the Primitive Churches*, by Andrew Fuller, which was well received by the American Baptists,. a few extracts from which I will here insert :

" When the apostles, by the preaching of the word, had gathered in many places, a sufficient number of individuals to the faith of Christ, it was their uniform practice, for the further promotion of his kingdom in that place, to form them into a religious society or Christian church. Being thus associated in the name of Christ, divine worship was carried on, Christian ordinances observed, holy discipline maintained, and the word of life, as the light by the golden candlesticks, exhibited. Among them, our Lord Jesus Christ, as the High Priest of our profession, is represented as walking; observing the good, and applauding it; pointing out the evil, and censuring it; and holding up life and immortality to those who should overcome the temptations of the present state.

"Let us suppose him to walk amongst our several churches, and to address us, as he addressed the seven churches in Asia. We trust he would find some things to approve; but we are also apprehensive that he would find many things to censure. Let us then look narrowly into the *discipline* of the primitive churches, and compare ours with it.

"By discipline, however, we do not mean to include the whole of the order of a Christian church; but shall, at this time, confine our attention to that part of the church government which consists in *a mutual watch over one another, and the conduct we are directed to pursue in cases of disorder.*

"There is often a party found in a community, who, under the name of tenderness, are for neglecting all wholesome discipline; or, if this can not be

accomplished, for delaying it to the utmost.   Such
persons are commonly called the advocates for disor-
derly walkers, especially if they be their particular
friends or relations.   Their language is, 'He that is
without sin, let him cast the first stone.'   'My brother
hath fallen to-day, and I may fall to-morrow.'

This spirit, though it exists only in individuals,
provided they be persons of any weight or influence, is frequently known to impede the due execution of the laws of Christ; and if it pervade the
community, will soon reduce it to the lowest state
of degeneracy.

"In opposing the extreme of false tenderness, others are in danger of falling into unfeeling severity.
This spirit will make the worst of every thing, and
lead men to convert the censures of the church into
weapons of private revenge.   Persons of this description know not of what manner of spirit they are.
They lose sight of the good of the offender.   It is not
love that operates in them; for love worketh no evil.
The true medium between these extremes, is a union
of *mercy* and *truth*.   Genuine mercy is combined with
faithfulness, and genuine faithfulness with mercy; and
this is the only spirit that is likely to *purge iniquity.**

"Connivance will produce indifference, and undue

* Proverbs, xvi. 6.

severity will arm the offender with prejudice, and so harden him in sin. But the love of God, and of our brother's soul, are adapted to answer every good end.

"And if we love the soul of our brother, we shall say, 'He is fallen to-day, and I will reprove him for his good. I may fall to-morrow, and then let him deal the same with me.' LOVE *is the grand secret* of church discipline, and will do more than all other things put together, towards ensuring success.

"Finally, a watchful eye upon the state of the church, and of particular members, with a seasonable interposition, may do more towards the preservation of good order, than all other things put together. Discourage whisperings, backbitings and jealousies. Frown on tale-bearers, and give no ear to their tales. Nip contentions in the bud. Adjust differences in civil matters among yourselves. Bring together, at an early period, those in whom misconception and distrust have begun to operate, ere an ill opinion ripen into settled dislike. By a frank and timely explanation, in the presence of a common friend, *that* may be healed in an hour, which, if permitted to proceed, a series of years can not eradicate.

"The free circulation of the blood, and the proper discharge of all the animal functions, are not more necessary to the health of the body, than good discipline is to the prosperity of a community. If it were duly considered how much the general interests of religion, and even the salvation of men, may be affected by the purity and harmony of Christian churches, we should tremble at the idea of their being interrupted by us."

In this country, in the course of five years, from 1842 to 1847, there came out as many works on the proper management of our church concerns. The authors of them are still alive. Their names are J. BAKER, W. WALKER, W. B. JOHNSON, R. B. C. HOWELL and W. CROWELL. All these men, except Mr. WALKER, have the title of D. D. affixed to their names. BAKER, then in Georgia, and JOHNSON, in South Carolina, are both now in Florida; WALKER, then in Homer, New York, is now in Elgin, Illinois; HOWELL was in Nashville, Tennessee; and CROWELL, then in Boston, is now in St. Louis, Missouri.*

All these works are now before me. HOWELL's book, to which reference has already been had, is wholly devoted to the deaconship. The others treat of the matters of church discipline, generally, in a more or less copious manner. Each one has suggested some new ideas, and given some new directions as to the best manner of performing this important business. There are some diversities in the rules and regulations

---

* I am not aware that any other of our men have written on this subject of late years, except in our papers, and other periodical works.

which they prescribe; but they all unite in repre-
senting a Baptist church as a very plain affair; that it
is a self-acting, independent, religious body, which
owes no allegiance to either prince or prelate; and
that it is very easily managed, when right principles
are adopted and proper measures are pursued. They
all agree with our famous English divine, lately quoted, that "the free circulation of the blood," etc., "is
not more necessary to the health of the body, than
a good discipline to the prosperity of a Christian
church."

Our men, above named, have pointed out very
clearly the importance of nipping difficulties in the
bud, and that, where this is done, corrective measures
will less frequently be needful. Also, that churches,
like armies and families, may be said to be well disci-
plined, not when punishments are often inflicted, but
when, by due care and faithfulness, they are seldom
required.

The rule laid down in the 18th of Matthew, for the
treatment of private offenses, has always been strongly insisted upon by all our writers on church discipline. To this rule my own attention was called at
an early period of my pastoral charge, which was
gathered under my youthful ministry, by seeing how
prone many of my people were to introduce their
troubles with each other, in an informal manner; and,

also, from witnessing the embarrassments which followed this unscriptural practice.

And now, late in life, my conviction is very strong, that by far the greatest portion of cases of discipline in our churches, grow out of the complaints of church members against each other, partly by offensive words, but mostly on account of disagreements in their secular concerns. And, furthermore, I am most fully persuaded that these churches, as a general thing, experience more embarrassment and perplexity in their discipline, and suffer more alienations and divisions, by permitting their members to introduce their complaints in an informal and unscriptural manner, than from all other causes put together.

"No personal offense," says Fuller, "ought to be admitted before a church, till the precept of Christ has been first complied with by the party or parties concerned."

In former times, if, by inattention or mismanagement, a case of this kind got into a church wrong-end foremost, instead of attempting to manage it in that position, our best disciplinarians among the ministers and laymen would enter a *nol. pros.*, as lawyers would say, that is, *a stay of proceedings*, and insist on the complaining party following the gospel rule. "Let him *come to me and confess*," is the common language of offended members. " Your Master has told you to *go to him,*" says CROWELL.

In some cases we are obliged to spell out our auty by inference and construction. Here, we have plain directions from the Head of the church himself. He could foresee, for all time, the liabilities of his people to trespass against each other, either by indiscretions of speech, or in their various worldly transactions. And he has left an explicit rule for them to go by. One of his chief apostles has recorded it in his own code of laws, and there it stands, for the guidance of his churches in all parts, and in all ages of the world.

On Councils generally, and among the Baptists.

Cart loads of books have been written on the history of these bodies, from the early ages up to the Council of Trent, which was held about three centuries since, and was the last great convocation of the kind. For many ages the popes were fond of great councils, and were pleased to have them convene, as they found them good auxiliaries to the support of the power of the papacy, especially in their persecuting measures against the Waldenses and other reputed heretics. The members of these bodies, of old, generally talked one language ; but at length, and especially in that of Trent, there was a good deal of sharp-shooting among the delegates from different quarters ;

and the reformation of THE *church*, in its head, and in its members, was too strongly insisted on to be pleasing to his Holiness. I think there is no probability of another general council ever being called.

I have examined as many ponderous volumes as a strong man would want to carry, on the history of all councils, but mostly those of Constance and Trent, of which I shall give some account in my ecclesiastical compendium.

For a few centuries after the apostolic age, they had councils twice a year, in the spring and in the fall ; but so contentious did they at length become, that one of the Fathers resolved that he would never attend another.

The main business attended to in these semi-annual gatherings, was to settle the difficulties of bishops and churches with each other.*

In my early experience among the Baptists, small councils, for the settlement of church difficulties, were much more common than at the present time. In

---

* When the first general council met at Nice, in Bythinia, 325, composed of more than three hundred bishops, bundles of documents of the kind above referred to, were handed in to Constantine, then newly converted to Christianity, and who acted a conspicuous part in this great convocation. But the emperor, instead of examining them, threw them all into the fire, and advised the complaining bishops to go about the main business of the meeting, which was to settle the Arian controversy, then a very troublesome thing.

some cases they were called to canvass very small affairs.

To call a council was then the first idea, when feeble churches found knotty questions, or impracticable members among them. I find from Backus' old papers that he was often called upon to take part, and commonly to preside in the small local councils which were convened on account of individual members, ministers, or churches.

I approve of councils for all the different purposes for which the Baptists have been accustomed to convene them, if they are not clothed with undue power, but are held to their *advisory* character, according to the old Baptist doctrine on this subject. But when these self-constituted tribunals assume a controlling influence, and, most of all, when they continue their sessions, by adjournment, at pleasure, they become ecclesiastical institutions, which are at variance with Baptist usage.

We have no regular custom of appealing from the decisions of our individual churches to any higher power, as the Presbyterians have; but the doctrine of absolute church independence has always been a favorite one with our people. Under it they have greatly flourished, and very few have complained of its operation. In some cases, however, in times of high excitement, there is danger of so far running this principle up to seed, as to go over to what some have termed, *the despotism of* the majority. And here an aggrieved member, to whom a *mutual* council is denied, has no remedy, but in an *ex parte* one. If he fails in this, he must remain without church fellowship, or else unite with some other party, where he will generally find a welcome home.

For our own churches to receive members who have been excommunicated from sister communities, while remaining as such, has been considered hitherto contrary to Baptist usage. But for some time past, my apprehensions have been very strong, that amidst the many excitements of the times, and the *post facto* laws of many of our churches, this custom will more and more prevail, unless our people show more favor to *ex parte* councils, for advice in hard cases of excommunication, than they have hitherto done.

There is one kind of councils, namely, for the dismission of pastors, which are seldom, if ever, held by the Baptists; while they are very precise to this practice, when they settle them. Amidst the great instability of our pastors of late years, I have sometimes thought whether, we had not better follow the practice of some of our neighbors in this business. We should, in this way, learn more of the *whys* and the *wherefores* of ministerial changes, if we could not prevent them.

Again, if a change of this kind is about to be made, on account of a very few members, it is a serious question with me, whether this few had not better change their church relation, and let the pastor remain.

Some more explicit views of church discipline will appear in the chapter *on a model* church and *a model* pastor.

CHAPTER XXX.

A LETTER TO A YOUNG MINISTER

On Various Matters Connected with the Business of Preaching
and Pastoral Duties.

BROTHER EVANGELLUS :—

Many years ago, while as yet your age in reality corresponded with the title of this letter, I conceived the plan of addressing you a series of letters
something in the form of the works of Orton, Miller
and others, on matters and things pertaining to the
ministerial employment. For this purpose I prepared
a sort of commonplace book, in which I made entries
from time to time from my own experience and from
my observations of the doings of the ministerial brotherhood, whose performances I frequently witnessed,
some of which, according to my judgment, in some
respects might have been altered for the better.

Since that time both of us have considerably
advanced in years. The same may be said of my
memorandum book, although it contains notices of
a very recent date, among the last of which I find
one against long prayers either in the pulpit, the con-

ference room, or elsewhere; and another against spinning out the religious services to a tedious length at communion seasons, so as to be merely ready to commence the sacramental office, when the whole assembly ought to be dismissed.

But since so much of the contents of my sketch book has been incorporated in my chapters which refer to ministerial labors, that the plan above named has been almost wholly superseded, I shall now, in this single letter, merely insert a few remarks of a miscellaneous character, in addition to those which I have already made.

On the Preaching Service.

The great end of speaking is to be heard, and the more natural the speaker is the more agreeable will be his performance to his hearers; and so far as he is inaudible his labor will be lost, and he will sink below par. Good speakers with good voices will always be heard with satisfaction, and men who are thus favored by nature have but little more to do but to let nature have its course, so far as their delivery is concerned. Such as are not gifted with native eloquence will need to make special efforts to overcome their defects. But whatever may be a preacher's grade as to his speaking talents, away with all flips, and twists and twirls, and twangs, and all guttural, sepulchral,

and even ministerial tones; and, finally, avoid a bois-
terous vehemence on the one hand, and a whispering
cadence on the other. The variations of a speaker's
voice are always proper, but to depress it to an almost
or altogether inaudible point, in not only against all
the dictates of reason and rhetoric, but it is besides,
extremely disagreeable to remote auditors and such
as are dull of hearing. Why, say they, mentally at
least, the man is talking to himself and to those near
him; if he has any choice thoughts and important
ideas, why don't he out with them boldly and save
us the need of *speaking* trumpets? Dr. Wayland, in
his late work on Baptist affairs, has intimated that the
poorest specimens of public speaking are generally
found in the pulpit.

This statement I suppose was intended for men of
all parties; as for the Baptists, the great mass of their
preachers make but small pretensions to being finished
pulpit orators, since their training has been very deficient in this line; but still, by John Leland's rule,
namely, " he is accounted the best fisherman who
catches the most fish," many of them stand high as efficient laborers in their Master's cause.

Among our educated preachers, especially in this
region, the number is much too large who are much
wanting in that earnestness and vivacity for which
good speakers are always distinguished. Many of

them are very logical and precise, but at the same time, in their best performances they exhibit the quintessence of dullness, and the fixedness of a statue.

I once said to a professor in one of our theological seminaries, your students ought to go West for a while to add to their solidity and precision, flexibility, sonorousness and animation, so as to bring out more fully their native powers of elocution.

A preacher of the monotonous class, as the story goes, once inquired of a leader in public amusements how it was that the speaking on the stage was so much more attractive than that from the pulpit. "That is very easily accounted for," said the earnest actor. "We treat fictions as if they were realities, while you treat realities as if they were fictions. Our main object," continued the player, "is to secure the earnest attention of our hearers, a thing which most of your pulpit actors seem to care but little about."

Hearers may have full confidence in the sincerity of this dull class of preachers, but this feeling is inspired more from their knowledge of their general characters, than from any thing they discover in their manner of addressing them.

Against pulpit speakers being *confined* to their written preparations, of whatever amount, I will take the liberty here, as I do in all cases, of expressing myself in very strong and explicit terms. I will go for *confining* them to reading and study at home, very closely, even with penitentiary strictness, if needful; but when they stand up before the people on the great business of salvation, to address them on the important themes of sin and redemption, let them be free as God made them, in the use of their eyes and arms, I mean both arms, like an orator, and all their bodily functions.

Men of this class, other things being equal, always were, and always will be, the most acceptable preachers with the great mass of mankind. Indeed, there is such a radical difference between preaching and reading, that the one can never be made a genuine substitute for the other, either in the pulpit or elsewhere.

" Suppose a lawyer at the bar should read his plea, or the speaker at a political meeting should read his speech, just as ministers read their sermons, would they be at all endured? Or, suppose that, in an ordinary meeting of friends, any one should attempt to converse in the precise tones of voice which men use in the pulpit, would not the whole company stand amazed? When men preach without notes, it is not commonly as bad, but here there is frequently some bad habit which detracts from the effectiveness of the discourse.   *   *   *

" The great defect of all our speaking, is the want of naturalness. When we become confined to written discourse, this is almost inevitable. Men can not read as they speak. The excitement of thought in extemporary speaking awakens the natural tones of emotion, and it is these natural tones which send the sentiment home to the heart of the hearer. Any one must be impressed with this fact who attends a meeting of clergymen during an interesting debate. There is no lack of speakers on such occasions, and no one complains that he can not speak without notes. It is also remarkable, that they all speak well, for they speak in earnest and they speak naturally. We have sometimes thought if these very brethren would speak in the same manner from the pulpit, how much more effective preachers they would become."*

Miscellaneous Remarks on the Pulpit Service.

Respecting the length of sermons, in early life I read, in Watts, or some old writer, that it is much better to leave off before the people *think* you have done, than to keep on a good while after they *wish* you had done.

Against long prayers how much has been said and written; and yet, how many a minister, in the pulpit, in the conference room, at funerals, and elsewhere, keeps on praying, till the people pray for nothing but for him to stop.

* Wayland's Notes, etc., pp. 324, 325.

Do not exhaust your spirits by engaging in exciting conversation just before you are to preach, was the advice of old writers, on the proper preparation for the pulpit. This advice I have always found very useful.

Again, do not commence preaching in too rapid a manner. I once knew a young minister who usually started, as one said, as if he *had run* a mile.

On special occasions make special preparations, and if you have any great ideas pertaining to the subject of your discourse, then bring them out in a prominent and intelligible manner.

At all times, in your stated performances, whether you write little or much, or none at all, endeavor to see the end from the beginning.

Always, on communion seasons, let your text and your discourse have a special reference to the death and the sacrifice of Jesus Christ. What can be more incongruous, in a minister of the cross of Christ, than, with the emblems of the agonies of that cross spread out before him and all the people, to so preach and so manage his whole preparatory service, that none of the assembly would be led to suspect it was communion day, were it not for what they see on the communion table.

Not a long time since, I attended a ministers' meeting, as a visitor. According to custom, each one gave the outlines of the last sermon he had preached. After all had spoken, the chairman called upon me for some remarks; when I observed, that I would only say that I had listened to the texts and to the plans of twenty sermons, delivered on a communion day, and but one of them had reference to the sufferings and the death of Jesus Christ! This laconic discourse made something of a stir among the score of preachers and pastors, and I would fain hope that they all remembered the main point of it the next communion season, and on all succeeding ones, to the end of their lives. In the Scriptures, both old and new, are found passages in abundance, which are appropriate for discourses on the theme here recommended, to an indefinite extent.

We hear too little of the doctrine of the cross at all times, and from preachers of all creeds; and how much have I lamented that our preachers, who glory in this doctrine, should ever fail to proclaim it in the manner above described.

On the use of the Bible, I would say, let it be your hand-book continually; use much of its language in the pulpit, in the conference room and in your religious conversation.

No language is equal to it for fitness, and for force.

It was said by the persecutors of the old Waldenses, by way of reproach, that they always had the

18

Bible on their lips. Let no minister or Christian ever
be ashamed of this distinction.

Always read a portion of the sacred volume, not
only at the commencement of all your pulpit services,
but also in the opening of all meetings of the church,
whether for devotion or business. Let no injurious
excitements, on the most vexed matters in church
dealings, hinder the regular exercise of reading, prayer and praise. There is nothing better to soothe the
irritated minds of men.

Scripture reading may sometimes suggest more
edifying thoughts in the people, than they afterwards
hear from those who speak, whether it be ministers or
laymen. And from the inspired word all are sure to
hear the truth, without any mixture of sentiments of
a doubtful or dangerous character.

"If you do not hear the gospel in the pulpit," I
once heard the late Bishop Griswold say, on an ordination occasion, "you will be sure *to hear it there*,"
pointing to the place where the church lessons are
read. These lessons, it is well known by those who
are familiar with them, are mostly in Scripture language.

Before the art of printing was discovered, which
was not till about the middle of the fifteenth century,
the cost of Bibles in MSS., placed them beyond the
reach of the common people. Then it was highly

important that there should be a great amount of Scripture reading before the people; and at an early period, each church had a man expressly appointed for this purpose, who was called *The Reader*. This important officer held rank among the clergy, and sometimes officiated in other departments. "I will let you have my reader," said one Father to another, for a special service of another kind.

In my early day, the ministers of the old order of Pedobaptists, in some cases, did not read the Bible at all, in the pulpit. Instead of that, the little black book, with the text, sermon and all, was laid on the desk, in the place of the sacred volume.

On Plainness in Preaching.

Luther said he wished to preach so that the Vandals could understand him. These people were the poor, illiterate peasants of the country.

"Ralph," said the uncle of the late Dr. Wardlaw, of Scotland, after hearing him preach one of his first sermons, "did you notice that poor woman in a duffel cloak that sat under the pulpit when you were preaching to-day?" "Yes, sir," answered the young preacher. "Well, my man," resumed his uncle, "remember that people like her have souls as well as their betters; and that a minister's business is to feed the poor and the illiterate as well as the rich and the educated. Your sermon to-day was a very ingenious and well composed discourse, and in that respect did you credit; but there wasn't one word in it for the poor old woman in the duffel cloak."*

After a sermon by the late President Young, a plain man expressed to a fellow-hearer his disappointment and surprise : "I thought," said he, "that Dr. Young was a learned man." On being asked what evidence to the contrary he found in the sermon just delivered, he replied, "I never heard a man in my life that I could understand so easily."†

This was akin to Dr. Miller's story of a pious old woman, who said of an eminent minister, " *He's not a bit of a gentleman*," because he made himself so much at home in her humble dwelling.‡

Against long Introductions.

"In preparing a sermon, we should beware of too long an introduction. A minister sometimes fears that he shall not be able to find material for a sermon of ordinary length, and hence he prolongs the first part by long discussions on the context, or any other

---

* An address before the American Baptist Historical Society, in Boston, in 1857, by Silas Bailey, D. D., President Franklin College, Franklin, Indiana, pp. 28, 29.

† Bailey's Historical Discourse, p. 29.

‡ Miller's Clerical Manners, p. 43.

miscellaneous matter which happens to occur to him. This is dry and uninteresting to his audience, and they become weary before he really begins his work. A preacher of this kind was once asked by Dr. Stillman to preach for him. The brother declined on account of his inability to meet the expectations of Dr. Stillman's congregation. 'O,' said the Doctor, 'you will do well enough if you are only willing to say your best things first.' He took the advice and succeeded."*

This talking against time, to fill up time, ought always to be avoided.

Against Apologies in the Pulpit.

Never deal in apologies before, or after preaching.†

Never decline reasonable calls to preach, although they may be unexpected. In season, and out of season, always ready, should be a minister's motto.

Never falter in your course, for any trips or slips, but go straight forward in your discourse to the end ; leave off when you have done, and don't talk about it, in the pulpit, or out of it. You have made your mark for that time, which no apologies can alter.

---

* Wayland's Principles and Practices, etc., p. 319.

† Never deal in rum, tobacco, nor apologies, was the advice of a Methodist bishop to his clergy.

On Doxologies.

According to my judgment and experience, it is always well to close the last Sabbath service with one of these earnest and appropriate supplications; and the same may be said of social meetings, especially when they have been protracted to an unusually late period. In such a case, a doxology is preferable to a prayer.

My own Experience in Preaching, and in Preparations for it.

In my early day, a great deal of preaching was expected of the ministers of our order. Much of it, however, was merely talking to the people, in a plain and familiar manner, and generally in the extempore mode. But, from the beginning, I resolved not to be tied to any form, and accordingly I used notes when I thought proper, and for a number of years I often practiced the *memoriter* plan, with a temporary committment, as recommended by Bishop Jewel.

I finally settled down on the skeleton system, more or less full, as a general custom, but writing out in full on special occasions.

I found great advantage in retirement and meditation, after my preparation was made, in whatever form, in ruminating over the whole matter of my discourse, and in getting my mind deeply imbued with all that pertained to it.

In collecting texts for future use, I, by degrees, slid into a method of my own—at least, I had not then seen it mentioned by any writer. The way was this: I had blank books of my own making, in succession, in which I put down whatever texts occurred to me, at any time, as suitable to preach from, and also any thoughts upon any part of them. In this way I always had a store of texts on hand, and some partly expounded, to select from.

On the subject of clerical manners, I need say nothing to *you;* but to all ministers who have not enjoyed your advantages, I would say, in the language of Dr. Miller, " In all your visits, as far as possible, avoid giving trouble." This is done, by making as few demands on the time and attention of your friends as may be ; and remember that those who find you a very troublesome guest, will be glad of your departure, and that they will not be very anxious for you to repeat your visits."

CHAPTER XXXI.

ON A MODEL CHURCH AND A MODEL PASTOR.

IN addition to my descriptions of the origin of the first Christian churches, and my sketches of history pertaining to preachers, preaching and pulpits, and my various comments on the different modes of sermonizing in different ages, I shall make a few remarks on the proper course which churches and pastors in their daily operations ought to pursue.

On a Model Church.

I take it for granted that such a church as I am about to describe receives none into its fellowship only on a profession of their faith, and are baptized in the Baptist mode. And a church thus formed of the right stamp will watch over its members with maternal solicitude, and not suffer them to be dispersed to unknown regions beyond their knowledge and control, or to become incurable backsliders in the sight of all their brethren, without using due diligence to ascertain the condition of all who are without their bounds, and to reclaim those who are within them.

By all our writers on this subject a church has been compared to a family or a household; and all the bonds of consanguinity which such a relationship implies, are often referred to also by the sacred writers, to represent the endearing ties of the household of faith.

In a well-regulated family, every member, however large the number may be, knows his place, and at stated periods is found in it. If any are absent without leave, or a reasonable cause, all are troubled and concerned, and the longer they are away the greater is the solicitude of those at home for their welfare. What fearful forebodings often occupy the minds of a whole household on such occasions. It may be that some one of feeble powers has wandered into the dark mountains at an alarming distance, to be exposed to dangers of various kinds, while others, in the thoughtlessness of childhood, or the indiscretion of early years, may have been beguiled by vicious companions to forbidden ground, or to hurtful pursuits. In all such cases the course pursued by a natural family need not be described, nor need we portray the alarm and anxiety which will pervade it until the absent loved ones are reclaimed. And so it will be with a spiritual household of the model class. But how many of our churches fall very far short of the above description with re-

gard to their wandering and absent members. While
all are busy here and there about other matters,
many members go off without the proper certificates
of their membership, or else they fail to report themselves in their new locations, and there is often too
little pains taken by the churches to ascertain whether
they confer honor or dishonor on their home connection, or themselves. Thus churches go on, year after
year, with the reputation of great numerical strength,
and stand in false positions in this respect. Their lists
of absentees at length become somewhat alarming; the
discrepancy between the nominal and actual members
who are identified with any of the doings of the body,
or even appear on the ground, is too great to be longer endured, and one church after another report to
their associations the members who have been strick-
en from their lists.*

A model church will avoid the necessity of such a
measure by keeping its list well regulated.

A church which is managed according to gospel
rule will not suffer sin upon its members. However
important the delinquents may be to their worldly
interests, or however painful may be the task of
dealing with them, such a body of faithful Christians

* Some churches in this region use the word *dropped* in these cases.
One of our authors recommends *separated*, while another prefers *erased*.
The first I think is the most objectionable, as no labor is indicated, only
that they let them slide.

will decide that a plain duty must be performed, an
imperative law must be obeyed, and their camp
cleared of Achans and foul transgressors.

In a model church there are places for all the members and all find something to do, and become more
or less useful in some way or other. "Yes," said a minister to a female member who complained that she
was of no use in the body, "you do a good deal by so
uniformly filling your place in the church, and you
help me preach every time I see you there." For a
few years past, in this region, there has been a gradual giving away of that small portion of our ministers
and churches who formerly followed the rigid construction of Paul's rule on female silence in the church,
which came down to us from the old Puritans; as they
found, that, literally understood, it would hinder any
women from relating their experiences while they
were candidates for church membership, from speaking in covenant meetings, or from being witnesses
in cases of discipline.

The great mass of the Baptists in America agree
with the Methodists with regard to the freedom of
females in their religious assemblies. And with both
parties, if now, and then, some of the sisterhood are
not so edifying in their performances as they might
be, the same may be said of a still larger number of
the brotherhood.

By putting together what Paul said to Timothy, namely, " I suffer not a woman to *teach*, or *usurp* authority over the man," and what he said to the Philippians, " Help those women who labored with me in the gospel, and also with Clement, and others of my fellow-laborers," etc., the advocates for female freedom dismiss all scruples relative to the ancient doings of the sisterhood. Nor do they feel disposed to lay any special restraints on them in social gatherings, which, by the way, are not *church meetings*, in the proper sense of the term.

Of the old Waldenses, it was said by their enemies, that in their daily avocations their constant practice was either to learn, or to teach. " Yes," said an old inquisitor, " they say, every layman among them, and even their women, ought to preach."*

This, however, we must understand as the language of reproach. The true version of the story would, no doubt, relieve these worthy females from the charge of any improprieties in their method of teaching among their own people, and rank them among the Phebes and Priscillas of primitive times.

A church of the model character needs no agents from abroad for the collection of funds for benevolent institutions. Such a body will no more depend on

* Dicunt quod omnis laicus, et etiam, femina debeat prædicare.

outside aid, in doing up business of this kind, than ·in its own financial concerns.

And finally, a model church will take care of its own poor, and will not permit them to suffer even the *fear of the want* of reasonable aid, which, as a good writer has said, is sometimes more distressing than the thing itself.

Many other traits of character, as pertaining to a community of the description now under consideration, might be enumerated; but any one in which those named, in the above list, is found in vigorous operation, may be referred to as a good model for the imitation of others.

On a Model Pastor.

In the first place he enters his field of labor from a full conviction of duty; he dedicates himself to his peculiar laborious vocation for life, and resolves that under his ministry there shall be no occasion for others to say,

"The hungry sheep look up, but are not fed."

While such a pastor, as I am now attempting briefly to describe, strives to make his pulpit services acceptable to his hearers, yet he soon discovers the great importance of faithful pastoral labors. Such being the persuasions of a pastor of the working class, into

the business of visitation he goes with all his might.
Out he sallies in every direction with the fervent zeal
of a worldly campaigner. He makes up his mind in
the beginning for hard labor, and of course is not disappointed. "The grace of God will live where I
can't," said Whitfield, while engaged in his evangelical explorations. And such are the conclusions of
the self-denying pastor. But no matter for that, he
can sojourn awhile amidst moral miasmas and the
most loathsome degradations of mankind, for their
benefit and moral reform. With every nook and
corner of his parochial charge he soon becomes familiar ; the forsaken and forlorn are comforted and
encouraged by his counsels and his prayers ; and, as
the result of the self-sacrificing missions of this ag-
gressive pioneer, he often brings subjects to his Sunday School, and ultimately to his congregation and
spiritual fold, from the haunts of vice, the styes of
intemperance, and, generally, the abodes of squalid
wretchedness and pollution.

Peace and harmony among the people of his charge,
and with all around him, will be the constant aim of
the Christian watchman, now had in view, so far as is
consistent with gospel truth and ministerial fidelity.
Such were many of our pastors of olden times, and
the savor of the spirit of these pious servants of the

Prince of Peace, pervaded their churches and vicinities long after they were called to their rest.

The secret of conducting the Christian pastorship on this peaceful model, was disclosed by a then aged minister, some fifty years ago. It consisted in one word, repeated at pleasure.

In the language of the venerable elder, the story may thus be related : " My church," said he, " which has long been distinguished for quietness and concord, was somewhat different when I became its pastor ; and their difficulties, generally, were about matters of little importance among themselves. Being green in the business, I was often much perplexed in my mind to know what to say to my disagreeing members, who all wished me to help their own sides. In this dilemma, I chanced to overhear two of my female members discuss the subject of family government. Both their households were large, but quite dissimilar in their characters, which led the less favored matron to inquire of her neighbor how it was that she succeeded so well in the management of her numerous charge. ' My rule,' said the respondent, ' is very plain and easily followed. It is this : when I discover any difficulties arising among my children, or any members of my household I go around the house, and at all needful points I say, Hush ! hush ! hush !'

" ' That is it,' said I to myself; and now, for forty

years, I have found hush! hush! hush! the best argument I could use with disagreeing members."

In favor of pastoral assiduity, when accompanied with piety and wisdom, I think we may safely maintain, that it often does more towards comforting Christians and building up churches, than eloquent preaching, without it. It is not a little singular they seldom go together, or, at least, not so often as they ought to.

I have known many cases, in my travels, of men of humble pretensions as pulpit orators, who yet, were very successful in gathering in members and building up churches.

CHAPTER XXXII.

THE plan of this work, in the form of *Decades*, or periods of ten years each, so far as their running narratives are concerned, has already been stated in the preface.

The first decade I begin with events which happened *fifty years ago;* the second with those of *forty;* the third with those of *thirty;* the fourth with those of *twenty;* the *fifth* embraces all the remaining time to the present period. But remembering the advice of an old English writer, "not to follow time too close on its heels, lest you get now and then a kick," I have said but little concerning very late events; particularly, respecting some of our more recently formed institutions, with the doings of which I have not been very closely identified.

In the *first decade* I give a general view of the Baptist cause in our whole country, *fifty years* ago, which was before the rise of any of our institutions for benevolent objects, except a few female mite societies; of my early efforts in the business of Baptist history; and of various matters peculiar to that age.

The *second decade* begins with the rise of the Foreign Mission cause among the American Baptists; with the account of the conversion of Rice and Judson to the Baptist faith; the formation of the Triennial Convention, and its early history; with the new phases in the Baptist creed, from the writings of Andrew Fuller; my investigations of the Unitarian system; and on changes of various kinds.

In the *third decade*, the age of excitements, and their effects, are described, as are, also, the unpleasant affairs in connection with the agency of Mr. Rice. The Home Mission Society is next noticed, and the late Dr. Going is favorably mentioned in connection with it.

In the *fourth decade* mention is made of the change of this name of the *Triennial Convention* to that of *Missionary Union ;* of the Southern Baptist Convention, and approving remarks of this measure.

The *fifth decade* is a good deal occupied with my experience in authorship, in Sunday Schools, and on miscellaneous matters pertaining to Baptist affairs in general, through all the *decades*, or the whole *fifty years* of my life, in connection with the denomination.

I close my narratives with some general remarks on the late troubles in the management of the Foreign Mission cause, which I have not meddled with at all. These remarks are intended to pacify, rather than to irritate, the minds of all who have been identified with them. And, finally, I mention the sadness which I have experienced in the news of the death of many of my old friends and associates and correspondents, in the whole range of our wide-spread country.

The second part of this work, under the name of an Appendix, contains the substance of my observations on, and researches into, all things that pertain to the organization of the primitive churches, their principles, officers and doings of all kinds ; on the deaconship; on preachers, preaching and pulpits; on church discipline, both formative, edifying and corrective; with a concise view of what may be termed *a model church and a model pastor.*

I advance no different ideas from our writers generally, on this whole subject, except that I mention the theory, that the first Christian churches copied, in substance, after the model of the

Jewish synagogues. And the more I have studied this matter, the more fully am I confirmed in this belief. But still I shall not contend with those who maintain a different opinion, as I formerly did; and who still, on this subject, prefer obscurity to light from a Jewish source.

Either view of the matter does not affect our own *modus operandi* in this business.

My main object is to give some probable account of the manner in which the first churches arose, in the absence of any information in the Scriptures on this subject.

It is true, as a correspondent has suggested, that the temple was often resorted to by those who were near it; but here they were outside worshipers, and could not join in the sacrificial and other services of the old economy, while they were much at home in the synagogues, where no sacrifices were offered, but where the services consisted principally in reading and hearing the law and the prophets, in exhortation and prayer, in all of which the Christians could join without violating the principles of the gospel, which they could not do in the temple service.

I have also advanced some new ideas on the deaconship, and have proposed a remedy for some of the evils of our present system, namely, limited appointments to this office instead of for life. I sustain the position of *seven* being the standard number for a full-grown church, from its being fixed upon by the apostles when the first deacons were appointed. And that this became a standing order among the early Christians may be inferred from the fact, that about thirty years later, Philip is called " one of the seven," in the same way as the apostles were called " the twelve," without naming their office.

I have said that I have heard and read of complaints from many quarters, against our deaconship, the substance of which may be thus expressed : Many of our officers of this class are incompetent and unfaithful; custom has given them too much power, and they are too independent of the churches.

Dr. Howell, in his work on the subject, to which reference has already been made, has given a most gloomy picture of the condition of the deaconship, as a whole, in his region, and indeed throughout the country; and at the close he repeats a common inquiry, "Is there no remedy? Can such officers never, by any scriptural process, be displaced, and succeeded by others ?"*

In my article I have said in the language of another, "I never knew of a deacon being dismissed from office," and Howell says, "he never knew of any one being deposed, or even impeached, for want of fidelity and efficiency in it." From time immemorial, we may presume, such has been the impunity of the Baptist diaconate. Immorality or heresy have been the only causes of the removal of our deacons, while our pastors are removed for almost any cause.

To the question, "Is there no remedy?" my ready answer is, none at all, under life appointments, and while the deaconship holds its present independent, and irresponsible position.

---

* "Look into the condition of the church," says Dr. H., "whose deacons are not faithful to their trust, and what do you see ? Every interest is languishing. Her financial affairs become deranged and ruined; the poor and miserable weep unpitied and unrelieved; the sick are unvisited, the pastor is discouraged; * * * the congregations fall off; * * * and the genius of desolation broods over the whole scene! Is this picture overdrawn ? Would to God it were. On the contrary, its reality may at this moment be found in a thousand places all over our broad land. * * *

" Delinquent lay members may be easily subjected to church rule, and be either reformed or excluded; unfaithful pastors may be readily removed; but deacons remain in office for life, however unfaithful they may be."—pp. 148, 150.

But some may say, let the deacons be more fully instructed in their duty. That would be well, but how little would it do towards so great a reform as we need in this business? Thousands of good homilies on this subject have already gone out from the pulpit and the press. They have been approved by everybody, but nobody minds them.

As to the propriety of limited appointments, that is a matter which rests with the church alone to settle. But as deacons are only *servants* as the name imports, it is hardly to be expected they will assume any dictation in the business. It is only for them to accept, or not, on the terms proposed. If they decline, that ends the matter for them. If they accept, they know when their time will be out.*

This is the best, if not the only remedy, I can discover for the present evils, of our deaconship.

In speaking of the many changes which, in the course of *fifty years*, I have witnessed among the American Baptists, I have given a passing notice of the variations which have occurred in the style and conveniences of their religious sanctuaries, which in my early day were generally uncostly and very plain. I have also referred to the disposition which has appeared of late years among this people, in some places, to go to the other extreme, in vying with their neighbors in costliness and splendor.

I am never well pleased to see high figures in accounts of new church edifices with us, as, I at once conclude, that many worthy members of the congregation will not be able to obtain good sittings in them, and will be obliged to go elsewhere.

---

* I never knew of any government appointments being declined on account of the four years' limit. Instead of that, multitudes scramble for all offices, for that period, with the certain knowledge that no courtesy is due them, when their time expires.

I agree with Dr. Wayland, in the main, in his Notes on Baptist
Affairs, and go with him against churches of aristocratic style and
cost for Baptist use, but still I have some doubts about insisting,
in all cases, and in all locations, on holding on to the Puritan plainness, too strictly.

My great concern for a long time past has been about comfortable and respectable sittings in costly houses for that numerous
and generally attentive class of church goers among us, who have
no estates, but whose chief dependence in pecuniary concerns is
on the result of their daily toil.   I am much afraid that the *high
tariff* of our costly churches* will induce them to seek accommodations with other communities, unless our costly church builders
are more active and liberal than they have hitherto been, in getting up what, of old, were called *Chapels of Ease.*

I have stated in my narratives, that I have seen the rise of
all benevolent institutions among the Baptists in this country, and
I have also been somewhat familiar with the doings of those
which arose in earlier years, and with the troubles which some
of them have encountered, but have carefully avoided participa-
ting in the discussion of the matter of these troubles, either in
the pulpit, on the platform, or in the public journals; but according to my information, the sentiments of the whole denomination

---

* I use the term *church* instead of *meeting house*, in conformity to custom with many of the present time, who are not Episcopalians. *Fifty
years ago*, the term church applied to a building, conveyed, in New England, almost exclusively, an Episcopal idea, which is not the case now.
The principal objection, I believe, to this term is, that it is applied both
to the people and their sanctuary; but so it was with the Jews of
old. A synagogue might mean either an *assembly* of worshipers, or the
building in which they worshiped. *Chapel* is a good term and in point
of euphony is preferable to *meeting house.* But the term is immaterial
when all understand its meaning.

respecting them may be summed up in the following brief sentences :

" Most of our troubles in our public doings have originated with a few men, as inside managers, or outside actors ; and that the body at large has suffered injurious agitations about minor things to go on too long. This matter is well handled in the note below.*

" Too many have meddled with these troubles, uncalled for, to the annoyance of the peaceably disposed.†

* " What! has it indeed come to this, that the whole Baptist denomination, for seven long years, stops on her march as the host of God to fulfill his bidding ?   Seven long years stooping and wilting over a question of policy !   Allowing herself to be pushed, swayed this way and that, when, with her own *heart*, at a single impulse, she should have brushed away the difficulty, as a cobweb.   Seven years over this business of mending this tinkling tin kettle, and the *whole army stopped to see it done !*   Where are we ?   What are we doing ?   Whose business are we engaged in ?   Oh, God ! how shall we answer to the responsibility of this miserable trifling !   Oh, will not the people of God return and take up the cross of Christ, forget their organizations, and feel and bleed for the cause of the Saviour ?   Has not the Baptist denomination power, by the help of God, to make for itself a constitution, by which it can carry on the work of missions ?   Is it indeed too weak and vacillating to have a voice of its own ?   The whole people of God should be on their feet.   The work is worthy of it.   He who has commanded it, is worthy of it.   If God should choose to utter his voice in thunder, rather than entreaty, the burning curse of Meroz might smite our guilty indolence, and make us feel that we had better be on our feet.

" It is quite unreasonable that the churches have waited so long without setting themselves right on the policy of foreign missions ; but is it less unreasonable that all, young and old, learned and unlearned, should feel it a good excuse for sitting still—the young to hear the elders talk, and the elders to hear themselves ?"—*Extract from a letter from a missionary in the East.*

† There was a very keen, good-natured hit on our debating men, at the late anniversary in New York, when, in the midst of conflicting

"There has been too much managing in some cases, and too much positivity in some managers.

"Discussion has gone far enough; now let it cease. Let by-gones be by-gones, and let all true Baptists come together, and work together, for Christ and his cause, at home and abroad, even if some of their favorite plans do not go on all fours.

"Union and harmony in public operations, is what the Baptist public intensely desires."

This is a specimen of the sentiments I have heard expressed by some of our strong men, who are not platform speakers, on matters of difficulty; and some of them even stay away from meetings where they are to be discussed, or else attend these meetings with reluctance.

Of the comparative merits of Baptist institutions, I shall not here give an opinion. Nor shall I say any thing on the plan of reducing their number, only, that with Baptists, it is sometimes difficult to make measures sit easy on their minds, which grow out of conventional rules.

I am inclined to think that it is a pretty general belief, among the supporters of these institutions, that too much of their money is spent at intermediate stations, and that too little of it arrives at the points of destination. But the *modus operandi* of remedying this evil, I shall not attempt to pescribe, as it is my province to tell of things that are past, rather than plan for the future. But thus much I will say, I can not tolerate the idea of the perpetuity of our present agency system. Instead of this, in my judgment, all our institutions had better curtail their appropriations within

arguments, a member pleasantly said, "I wish, when the speaker has done, the assembly would sing,

"'From whence doth this union arise?'"

the bounds of voluntary contributions, and take a new start on this plan. But a better way would be, for the churches to follow out, at all times, their doings on the dollar system, which went on with so much ease. If pastors were all of the right stamp, they would not need agents to act for them, *pro tem.*, among their people.

Relative to fields of labor for our people, in benevolent undertakings, *America*, in my sober judgment, is the best field in the whole world, and promises the most speedy and important results, not excepting Burmah and the Karens, which are now the most promising fields we have in other lands.

> " Westward the course of empire takes its way."
> Westward the gospel is destined to spread.

Here we are not met at every step with strong ancestral, and often insurmountable prejudices, in all classes of people, in favor of ruinous, antiquated errors.

Here no State vetoes stand in our way, as they do in all other lands.

Never since the introduction of Christianity, did Christians of our profession find such a free country for the propagation of the gospel, according to their views of its principles and ordinances.

For the first three centuries, Pagan rulers harassed and destroyed them; and ever since, they have everywhere been beset by State churches and prelatical power; and the best safeguard against these evils in this country for us, and all who agree with us, on the subject of freedom, civil and religious, is, as fast, and as far as possible to spread this salutary doctrine broad-cast all over the land. An ounce of prevention *now*, may be worth a pound of cure *hereafter*.

In broad America, of more than Roman amplitude,* there is

---

* The United States has about double the amount of territory of the Roman empire in its greatest enlargement..

19

ample room for the Home Mission, the Free Mission, the Bible, the Bible Union, the Publication, and even the Foreign Mission Institutions, East and West, North and South, with all the missionaries, and all the colporteurs they may employ, without interfering with any coadjutors in the business of American evangelization.

I see no impropriety in our foreign department lending a helping hand in American missions, as was done in early times.

Since I retired from the pastorship and became a minister in ordinary, I have heard a great variety of preaching, and among the principal deficiencies of it I would name the want, more or less, of *intellectuality*, *vivacity*, *distinctness* and *brevity*.

The old Romans required of public declaimers, in their language, that they should speak, *ore rotundo et ab imo pectore*, with a full voice, and from the bottom of the heart.

How often have I wondered that men who can converse naturally and fluently and with animation, should speak so poorly in the pulpit.

Long sermons, and dull at that, with a paucity of striking ideas, and long prayers * have caused me many a tiresome sitting on ordinary occasions. Thirty minutes was Wesley's rule for his preachers in their common discourses. Sermons of this length can be endured if they are not very engaging.

Many ministers are apt to be long, not only in the pulpit, but also in the lecture room, and at funerals.

On Ministerial Education.

In my few remarks on this subject I have spoken in favor of having our theological schools on the ground of our collegiate institutions, for graduates at least, instead of being in separate locations.

---

* How much is said against long prayers in the New Testament, yet how many of them do we hear both in the pulpit and elsewhere.

I have also commended, in some cases, such schools as we had in my early years, where students, and even preachers who wished to qualify themselves for greater usefulness in the ministry, were accustomed to resort and study as much as they were able. And I have regretted that these schools of the prophets, so useful to us then, are not still kept up in new and remoter regions within our wide-spread community.*

On Lecture Rooms,

Which are improperly called *Vestries*, and which, as a general thing, are very badly constructed. Most of those which I have seen are partly underground, and of course are gloomy and unhealthy.† The best way for these rooms, which are so much used among the Baptists, is to have them in separate buildings where there is ground enough for it.

On Congregational Singing.

Much has been said of late in some places in favor of restoring this good old custom, but it is an up-hill work, if artistic leaders are opposed to it, and give out tunes with which the congregation are not familiar.

On the Communion Question.

How often have I most heartily wished that much less was said on the question, on all sides; and, no doubt, there would be,

---

* In reply to Professor Turney, relative to a new theological seminary for the West, I have said, if he will get up one of the above description, which will be open for all classes of students, I will favor it with a good donation of books.

† "Don't you think," said John Leland, "brother G. put me in his collar kitchen, to preach for him at night."

were it not for that everlasting clamor which, evidently, for party effect, is kept up by other people, and which seems to call for replies. But men of candor avoid this clamor.

"I do not blame your people for their rule of communion," said the late Bishop Griswold; "they have a right to adopt it."

"And I do not blame your people for their pulpit rule," was my reply; "all societies have a right to their own rules."

"Our church would soon cease to exist in some places, if our church service was omitted," continued the bishop.

"We should not be consistent with ourselves to fellowship any other baptism," said I, on my side.*

Thus ended our conversation on this subject.

On Church Debts.

Ever since the Baptists went so deeply into the business of building their church houses on credit, this unwise policy has been the bane of many, and the ruin of some of our flourishing communities; and others, which have survived their disastrous effects, have long been sadly embarrassed in their operations by them. But I am glad to see a commendable zeal in many quarters to wipe them off, and I trust all our churches will be careful to avoid them for the future.

Closing Remarks.

I have lived to see a great increase of our people, and I see a bright prospect for them for the future, if they mind Joseph's advice to his brethren: *See that ye fall not out by the way.* Bap-

---

* Bishop Griswold often preached in my pulpit before a church of his own order was erected in the place.

Baptists also often preached in his pulpit in Bristol, Rhode Island, after the church service was performed, by himself, or others.

tists can not well disagree about their primordial principles which are so scriptural and plain ; nor will they be likely to fall out about any thing, while they nourish the mild principles of the gospel.

While they should not be in haste to leave the old paths of their fathers, yet they should not without due consideration eschew all progress, as Robinson, the father of the Pilgrims, said was done, by many in his day.*

* "The Lutherans could not be drawn a step beyond what Luther saw, and you see the Calvinists stick where he left them. If God shall reveal any thing to you by any other instrument, be ready to receive it, * * * for I am very confident there are more truths and light to break forth out of his holy word."—*Robinson's Letter to his Flock in Holland,* 1620.

THE END.

THE BAPTIST STANDARD BEARER, INC.

A non-profit, tax-exempt corporation
committed to the Publication & Preservation
of The Baptist Heritage.

SAMPLE TITLES FOR PUBLICATIONS AVAILABLE
IN OUR VARIOUS SERIES:

THE BAPTIST *COMMENTARY* SERIES

Sample of authors/works in or near republication:
John Gill - *Exposition of the Old & New Testaments (9 & 18 Vol. Sets)*
(Volumes from the 18 vol. set can be purchased individually)

THE BAPTIST *FAITH* SERIES:

Sample of authors/works in or near republication:
Abraham Booth - *The Reign of Grace*
Abraham Booth - *Paedobaptism Examined (3 Vols.)*
John Gill - *A Complete Body of Doctrinal Divinity*

THE BAPTIST *HISTORY* SERIES:

Sample of authors/works in or near republication:
Thomas Armitage - *A History of the Baptists (2 Vols.)*
Isaac Backus - *History of the New England Baptists (2 Vols.)*
William Cathcart - *The Baptist Encyclopaedia (3 Vols.)*
J. M. Cramp - *Baptist History*

THE BAPTIST *DISTINCTIVES* SERIES:

Sample of authors/works in or near republication:
Alexander Carson - *Ecclesiastical Polity of the New Testament Churches*
E.C. Dargan - *Ecclesiology: A Study of the Churches*
J. M. Frost - *Paedobaptism: Is It From Heaven?*
R. B. C. Howell - *The Evils of Infant Baptism*

THE *DISSENT & NONCONFORMITY* SERIES:

Sample of authors/works in or near republication:
Champlin Burrage - *The Early English Dissenters (2 Vols.)*
Franklin H. Littell - *The Anabaptist View of the Church*
Albert H. Newman - *History of Anti-Paedobaptism*
Walter Wilson - *History & Antiquities of the Dissenting Churches (4 Vols.)*

For a complete list of current authors/titles, visit our internet site at
www.standardbearer.com or write us at:

he Baptist Standard Bearer, Inc.

No. 1 Iron Oaks Drive • Paris, Arkansas 72855

Telephone: (501) 963-3831   Fax: (501) 963-8083
E-mail: baptist@arkansas.net
Internet: http://www.standardbearer.com

Specialists in Baptist Reprints and Rare Books

Thou hast given a *standard* to them that fear thee; that it may be displayed because of the truth. -- *Psalm 60:4*

www.ingramcontent.com/pod-product-compliance
Lightning Source LLC
Chambersburg PA
CBHW020407100426

42812CB00001B/232